IMAGES
of America

EARLY EDUCATION IN THE ARKANSAS DELTA

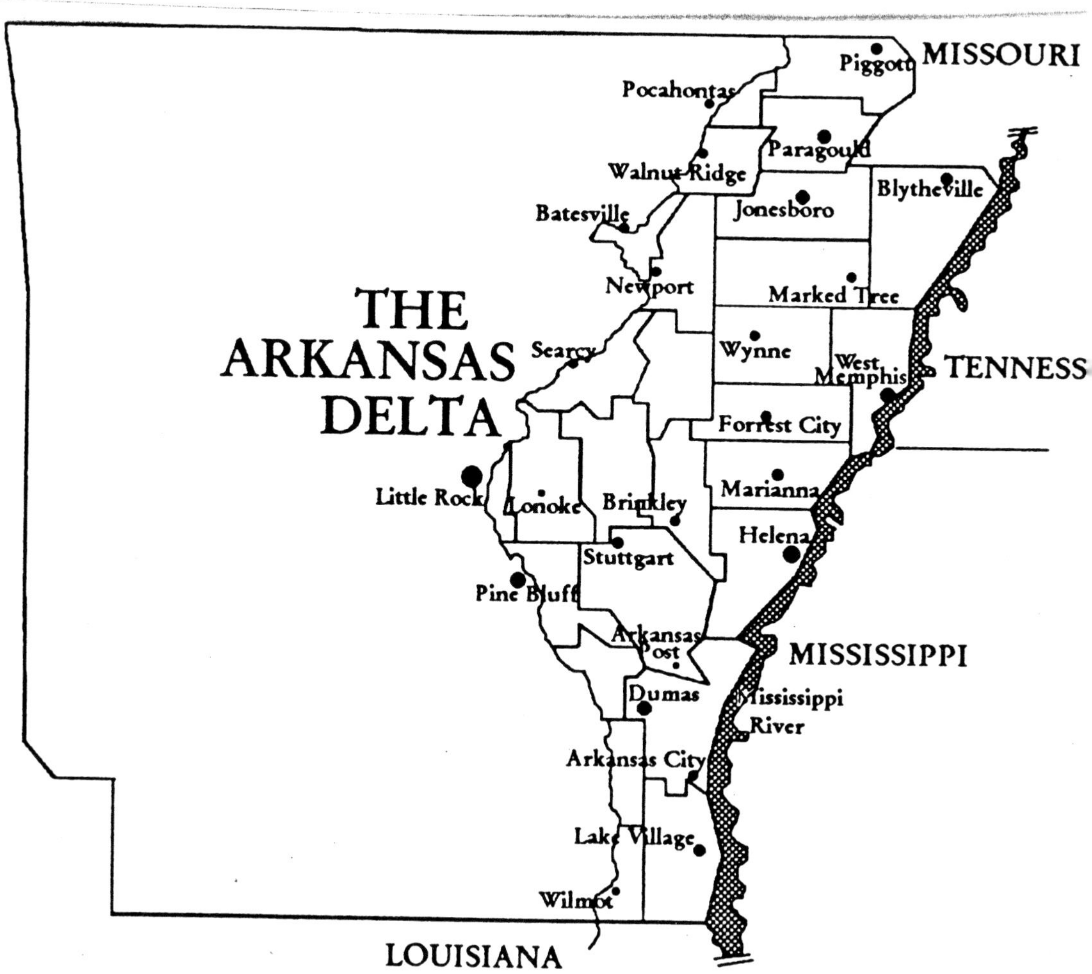

(Courtesy of Ken Hubbell and Janis Kearney Lunon, *The Arkansas Delta: A Historical Look at Our Land and People* [Little Rock: Department of Arkansas Heritage, 1990.])

IMAGES
of America

EARLY EDUCATION IN THE ARKANSAS DELTA

D. Antonio Cantu
Ball State University

C. Roger Lambert
Arkansas State University

ARCADIA
PUBLISHING

ISBN 978-0-7385-0818-4

Published by Arcadia Publishing
Charleston, South Carolina

Printed in the United States of America

Library of Congress Catalog Card Number: 00-111085

For all general information contact Arcadia Publishing at:
Telephone 843-853-2070
Fax 843-853-0044
E-Mail sales@arcadiapublishing.com
For customer service and orders:
Toll-Free 1-888-313-2665

Visit us on the Internet at www.arcadiapublishing.com

This book is dedicated to my wife and native Arkansan, Sandy, and to my three children, Derek, Dylan, and Deanna Cantu. Only through their love and support was I able to research and write this book. The stories of thousands of Arkansas Delta students who, when viewing their photographs, look no different than students of today, with the same ambitions, hopes, and dreams reflected in their faces, could only be told through the sacrifice of time spent with my family; I am forever in their debt.

-D. Antonio Cantu

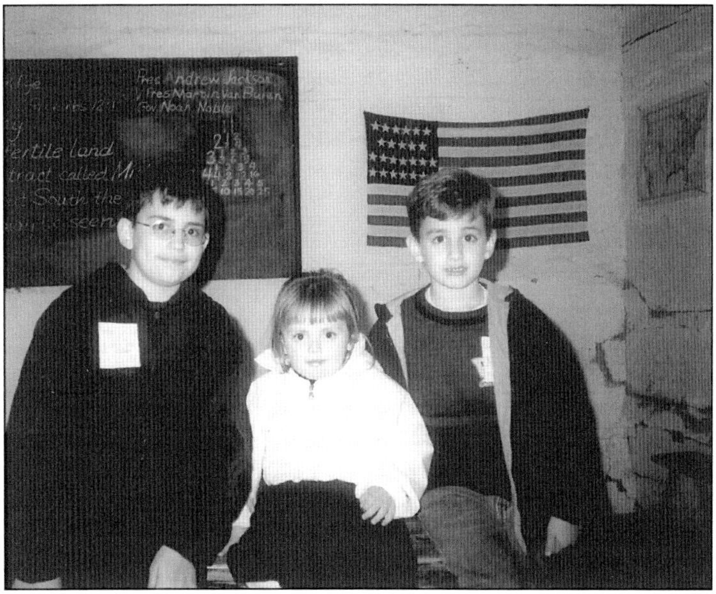

Derek, Deanna, and Dylan Cantu posed for this photograph on the interior of a nineteenth century schoolhouse, a classroom not unlike that in which countless Delta students of similar ages would spend their entire academic careers, if they were fortunate enough.

Contents

ACKNOWLEDGMENTS

A number of individuals played major roles in the completion of this book. Without their assistance, the history of education in the Arkansas Delta would have gone untold, and the photographs of these students, teachers, and schools of long ago would have remained locked away in attic trunks, family photo albums, and archival files. Instead, these items may now be shared by all who read this book of the history of education in this special place and time. Hopefully, the challenges and triumphs of these Arkansans may serve as inspiration for us all.

Special thanks goes to Kirk Overstreet of Ball State University, whose commitment and dedication to this project was absolutely critical. This book could not have been written without Kirk's technical knowledge, historical insight, and thoughtful input—as well as the support he received from his wife, Becky, and daughter, Ryann.

A number of other individuals also contributed to this project. Thanks to Jackie Stewart of White County Central High School in Judsonia, Arkansas; Larry Ball and Gina Hogue at Arkansas State University; Edgar Morrison of Bay, Arkansas; Elsie Dawson and Roselyn Horner of Jonesboro, Arkansas; the staff at Arkansas State University Museum Archives and Communications Office; as well as the archivists at the Arkansas History Commission in Little Rock.

Finally, I want to again give my most heartfelt thanks to my wife and fellow teacher, Sandy, and to our three children, Derek, Dylan, and Deanna Cantu. As I stare into the eyes of the Delta students of a century ago, I cannot help but see my own children sitting in those desks or posing for their class photo, beaming with that youthful sense of confidence and unlimited energy and excitement, dreaming of a world ready to be conquered just outside their classroom door. Despite the passage of time, that defining characteristic of students in the Arkansas Delta will hopefully never change.

-D. Antonio Cantu

INTRODUCTION

The Delta region, the area of deposited alluvium soil, extends into Arkansas many miles west of the Mississippi River. With some of the richest soils in the world, the region has always been predominantly agricultural. The Arkansas Delta developed its cotton system considerably later than other plantation regions in the South. The heavy forest, extensive swamps, and remote nature of the land meant that much of the region remained undeveloped until the nineteenth century. The arrival of the railroads permitted commercial transportation of lumber and provided valuable land ownership to railroad, lumber, and business interests from the developing towns. By the early twentieth century, these interests had initiated drainage districts to clear the swamps, brought in sharecroppers and tenant farmers, and founded a semblance of the plantation system.

However, the traditional plantation system, with its germane aristocratic families and grand, stylish plantation houses, never came into existence in the Arkansas Delta. It still included, though, the development of an economy and society with great disparity of wealth, along with widespread, chronic poverty. That economic situation continued throughout the first quarter of the twentieth century, despite significant fluctuations in the economy.

Beginning in the 1930s and continuing for decades thereafter, residents of the Arkansas Delta witnessed the transformation from intensive hand labor to mechanization, which resulted in a significant migration of both black and white sharecroppers out of the region. By the 1960s, landowners completed the economic transition to hired (wage) workers. A second change in the Arkansas Delta involved agricultural diversification. As cotton production became less profitable, owners began to grow rice, soybeans, and winter wheat. The basic agricultural system in the Delta, however, remained the same. Poverty unfortunately has proven to be the most persistent problem in the region, with the Delta representing the poorest region of the country—even poorer than Appalachia. At a recent meeting of the Arkansas Delta Development Initiative Work Group, Governor Mike Huckabee perhaps best summed up the history of the Delta: "The land in the Delta was once the most productive in the state. Most of the wealth and most of the political power in Arkansas was concentrated in this region at one time. But while the Delta reigned supreme during the agricultural age, the region largely missed out on the industrial age. We must work together to ensure it doesn't miss out on the information age. Delta residents have faced the hardships of poverty with a strong work ethic and eternal hope. No matter what part of Arkansas we call home, we should be committed to helping them gain the tools needed to improve education, health care, economic development, housing, and transportation."

The social and economic conditions of the Arkansas Delta exerted a clear influence on the development of education. The scattered nature of settlement, the disparity of wealth, which concentrated money in the hands of a few who educated their children as they desired, and the widespread lack of expectation by a number of the impoverished, many of whom held strong reservations concerning the value of formal education, all had a tremendous impact on shaping the face of education in the Arkansas Delta. As a result, the development of free public education was, for the most part, delayed until the mid-1880s. Even then, schools tended to concentrate in the larger communities. The more rural areas, therefore, were limited to one-room schoolhouses that seldom taught beyond the eighth grade and were placed in the charge of teachers with admirable intentions, yet limited education.

The focus of this book is to trace the history of education in the Arkansas Delta, from its root in the mid-nineteenth century to its current state in the dawn of the twenty-first century. Prior to an examination of education in the Arkansas Delta, Chapter One provides an overview of the social and economic conditions of the region. This is followed by an examination of nineteenth and early twentieth century education, in Chapters Two and Three in particular, the drafting of the educational blueprints for the Arkansas Delta, as well as the laying of the foundation of formal, public education in the region. The next three chapters trace the development of education in the Delta from its period of adolescence in the 1920s to full adulthood in the 1970s. It is during this period that residents of the Delta would face some of their most serious challenges, like the Great Depression, World War II, and 1960s social and political unrest. The immediate impact and enduring legacy of these events on shaping education in the region are both quite apparent and certainly inescapable.

Although this book is, for the most part, a chronological study, Chapters Seven and Eight adopt a more thematic approach. In Chapter Seven, the status and role of education for African-Americans in the Delta region is examined. While in Chapter Eight, the history and impact of higher education—in particular the largest institution in the region, Arkansas State University—is the subject of analysis. The final chapter traces those events that have shaped education in the Delta in the final decades of the twentieth century and perhaps provides some indication as to the direction it will take in the next millennium, a century in which Governor Huckabee reminds all Arkansans, ". . . whether you live in the Ozarks, the Ouachitas or the Arkansas River Valley, the problems of the Delta no longer can be ignored. . . . We can't alter the past. We can, however, set the stage for a prosperous future."

One

The Arkansas Delta: An Overview

Geographically, the Mississippi Delta runs from Cairo, Illinois, to New Orleans. It extends up to 100 miles in width and represents one of the most fertile regions in the world. Although parts of the Delta on the east side of the river produced many of the most expansive pre-Civil War plantations, to the west the Arkansas Delta remained heavily forested with much of the region covered by swamps. Not until railroads provided transportation, lumber interests cleared the land, and drainage districts converted the swamplands to farmlands, did extensive settlement begin.

Historically, Native Americans such as the Osage found the Delta to be an ideal location for the establishment of a "hunting-gathering-farming economy." The introduction of European explorers did little to change the geographical landscape. European exploration, however, did mark the beginning of tremendous economic and social change. Spanish explorer Hernando De Soto remarked, in a 1541 journal, on the abundance of wild game and fish indigenous to the region—in particular the bear, wildcats, and buffalo he encountered. Spanish explorers were followed a century later by the French. Among the first French explorers in the region were Marquette and Joliet, who explored the Delta region in 1673, coming in contact with Aksansa (Arkansea) Indians near present-day Helena. Nearly a decade later, LaSalle would claim the territory in the name of France. By the mid-eighteenth century, the French relied heavily upon the lucrative bear hunting posts that were scattered throughout the Delta. This represented a great source of income for those who sold the pelts, meat, tallow, and bear oil in New Orleans for a handsome profit. For this reason, Arkansas unofficially became known as the "Bear State" until the early twentieth century. It was not until 1803, with the Louisiana Purchase, that Arkansas came under the possession of the United States. It was organized in 1819 as a territory, and finally received statehood admission in 1836.

Today economic and social features remain characterized as "marked by extremes of wealth and poverty that more nearly resembles a third world country than post-industrial America." These factors of Delta society influenced educational development. While the twentieth century brought much needed development to the Delta, it still lagged behind other regions within the state and nation. This chapter introduces readers to the economic and social condition of the Arkansas Delta in the late nineteenth and early twentieth centuries.

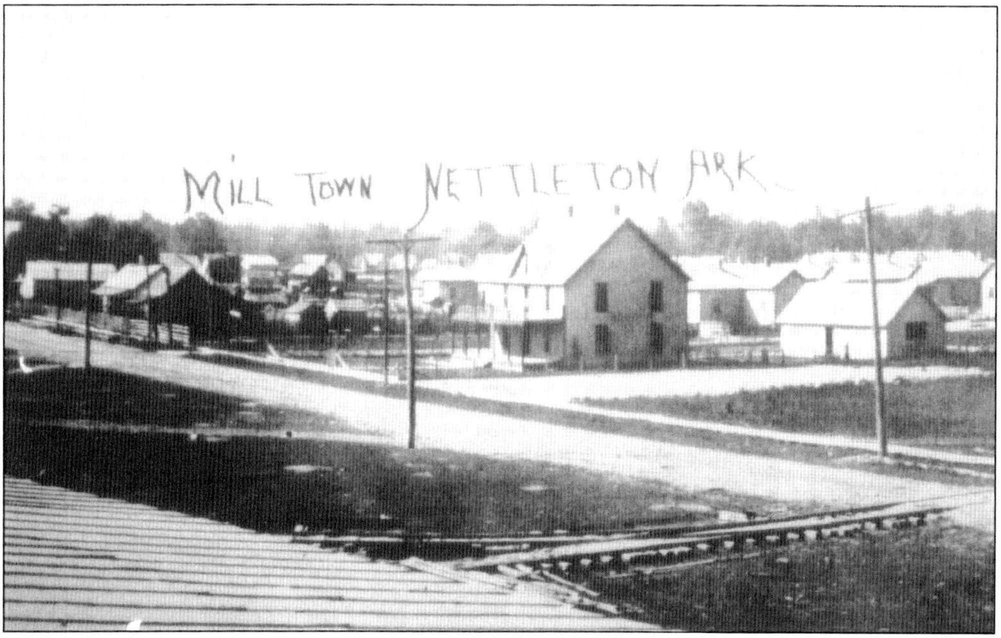

The lumber industry played a major role in opening the Delta area to settlement and agricultural development. This turn-of-the-century photograph of Nettleton, Craighead County, perhaps best illustrates the major extractive industry of the era and the opening of the Delta for agriculture. (Courtesy of Nettleton Public Schools.)

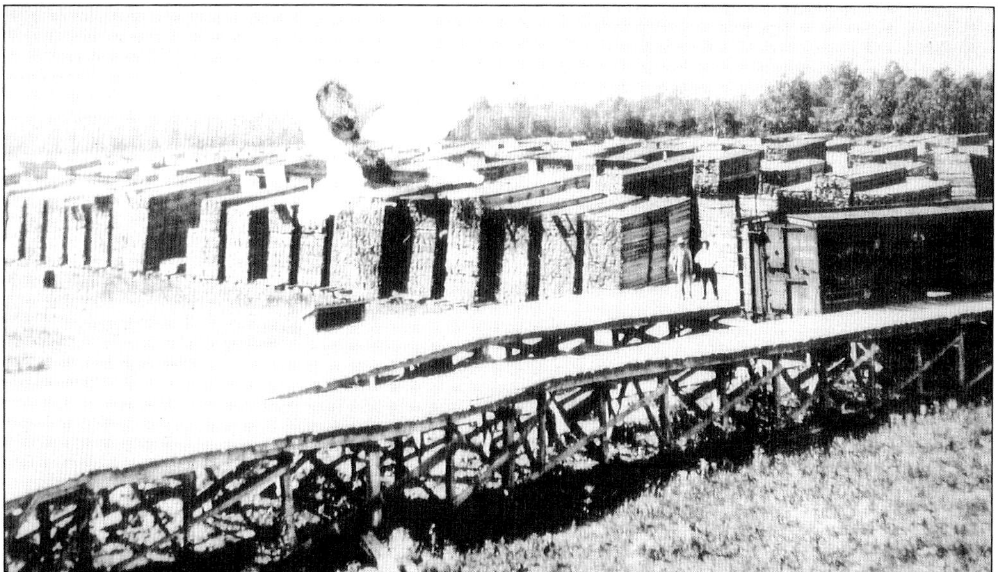

Although environmentalists would find great fault with this photograph today, to late nineteenth and early twentieth century Delta residents this scene represented both economic security and prosperity. Perhaps better than any other, this early twentieth century photograph of a Nettleton-Jonesboro lumber mill illustrates the massive physical and economic presence this industry had on many Delta communities. (Courtesy of Nettleton Public Schools.)

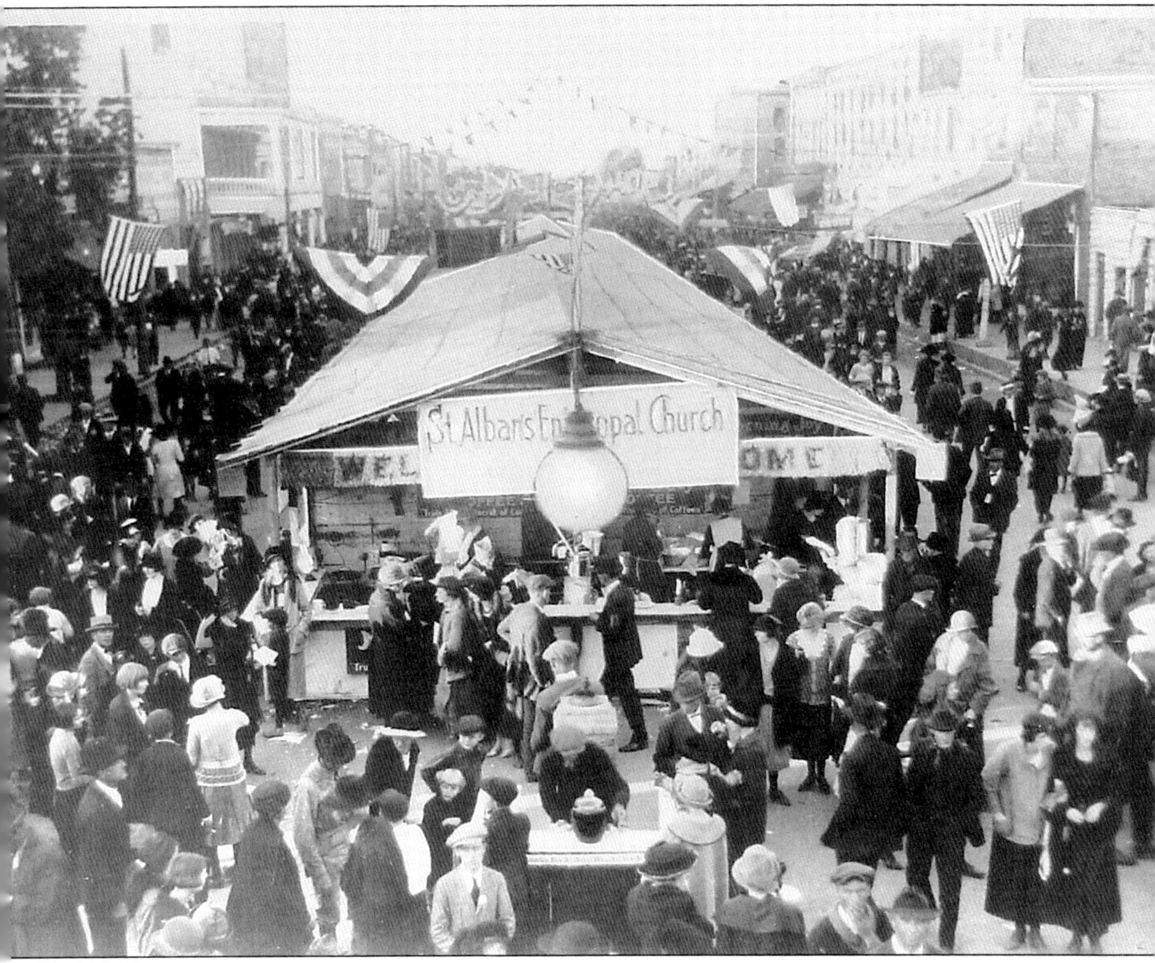

Stuttgart, Jefferson County, was an early agricultural center for the Delta. It also served as one of the first communities to recognize the economic potential the rice crop held for the region, particularly by reducing the previous dependence on cotton. By the early 1900s, many communities would honor the important role the rice industry played by holding annual rice festivals and celebrations, such as this 1920 Rice Carnival held in downtown Stuttgart. (Courtesy of Arkansas History Commission.)

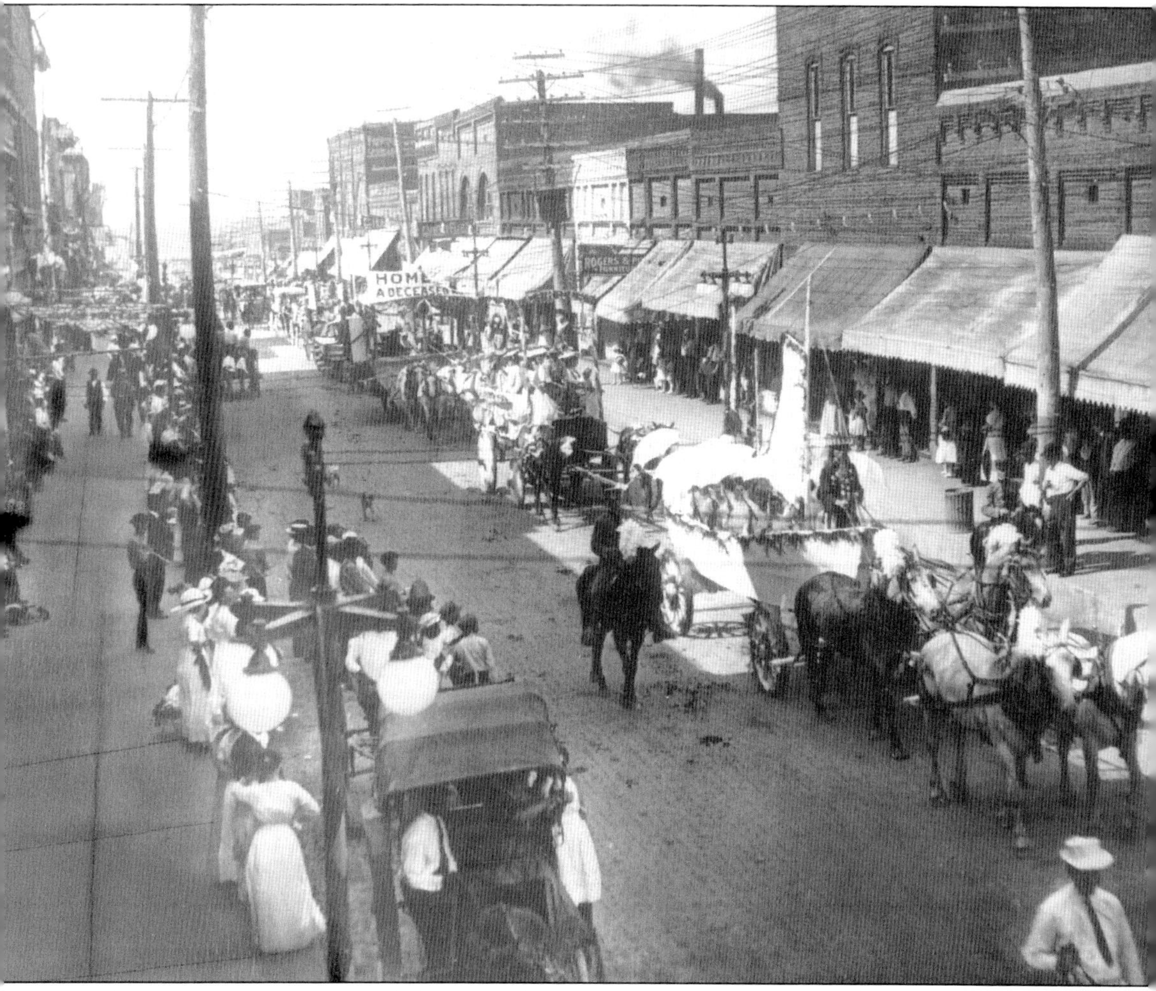

Yet another busy day, probably Saturday, is witnessed by many on this turn-of-the-century Delta main street—in this case Jonesboro, Craighead County, is the setting. Partly because of the frequent floods, people tended to settle and develop towns along Crowley Ridge, which was high enough to offer some protection against high water. (Courtesy of Arkansas State University Archives.)

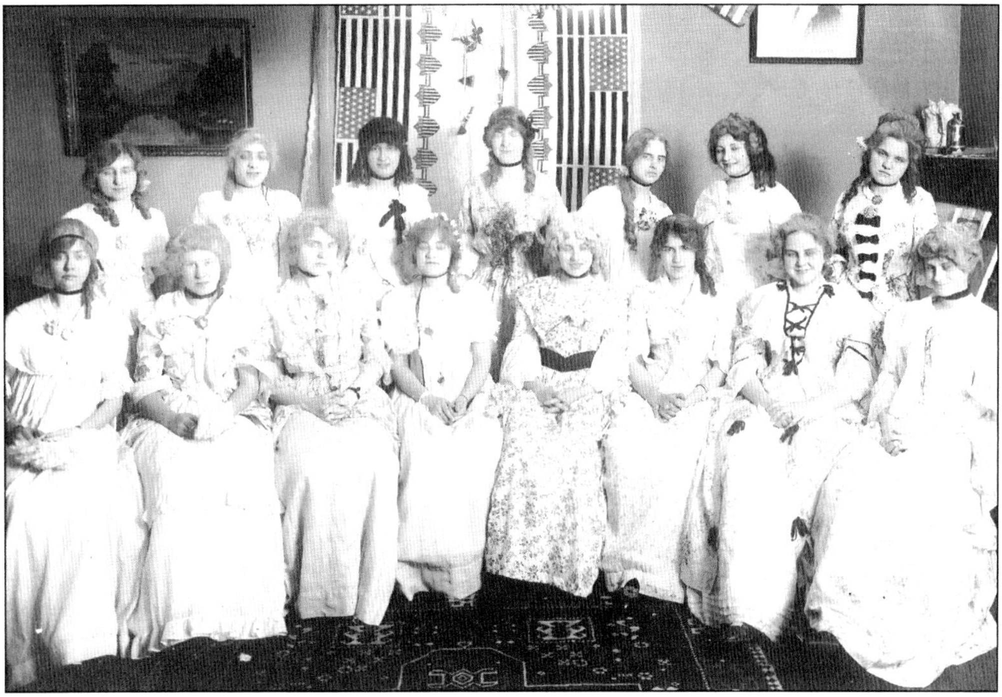

One can tell from the hairstyles and dresses that the Twentieth Century Club of Jonesboro appealed to both upper and middle-class women. Only the larger towns would have a sufficient population to form such social groups, which served to mark the clear class distinction found in numerous Delta communities. (Courtesy of Arkansas State University Museum.)

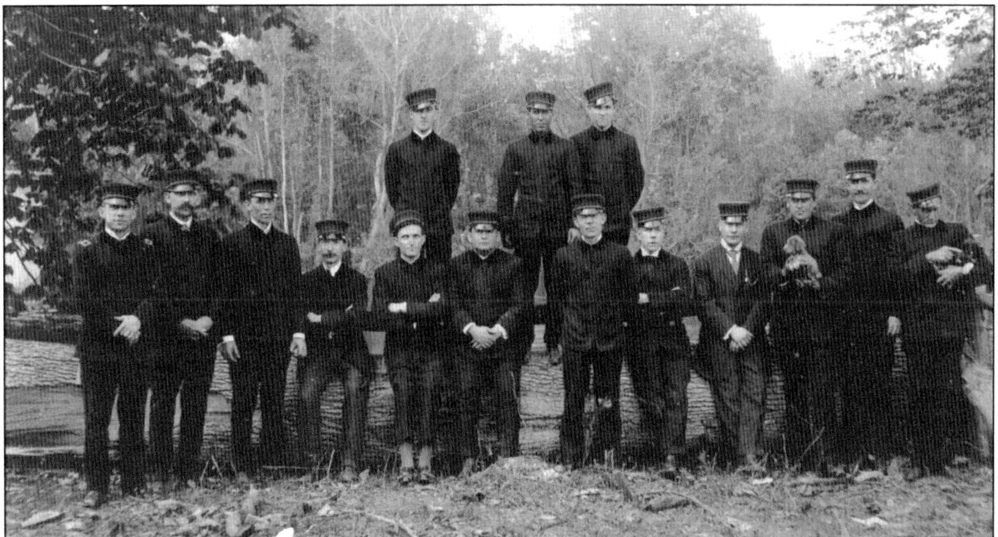

Many Arkansas Delta residents viewed larger communities in their region as cultural as well as economic centers. As these small cities grew, so did the number of opportunities they accorded to nearby communities. One of the most popular of these cultural undertakings was the formation of municipal bands, such as this turn-of-the-century group from Jonesboro. (Courtesy of Arkansas State University Museum.)

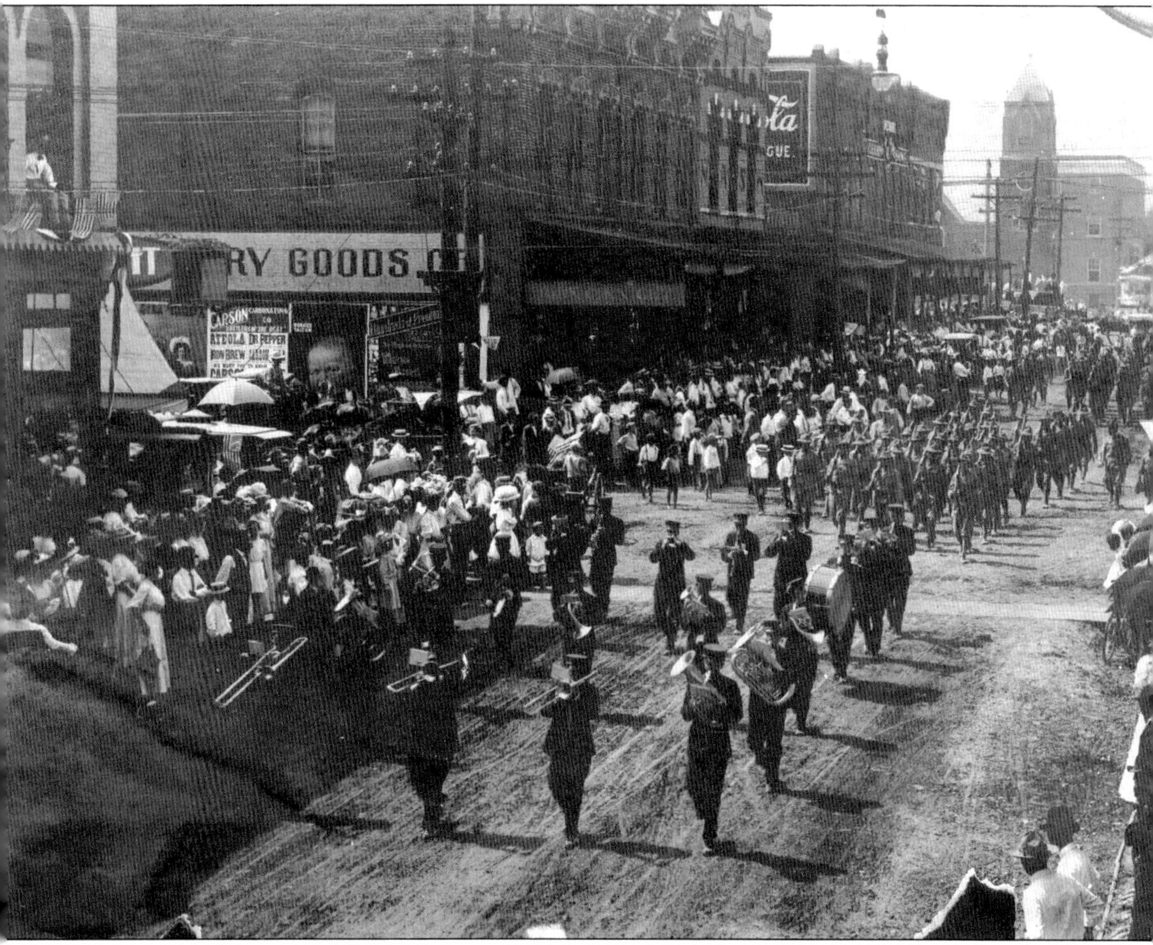

Everyone loves a parade, and Arkansas Delta residents are no exception, as evidenced in this July 4, 1910, celebration in downtown Jonesboro. In addition to illustrating the high degree of citizen involvement, such celebrations also indicate the tremendous level of patriotism indigenous to this region. (Courtesy of Arkansas State University Museum.)

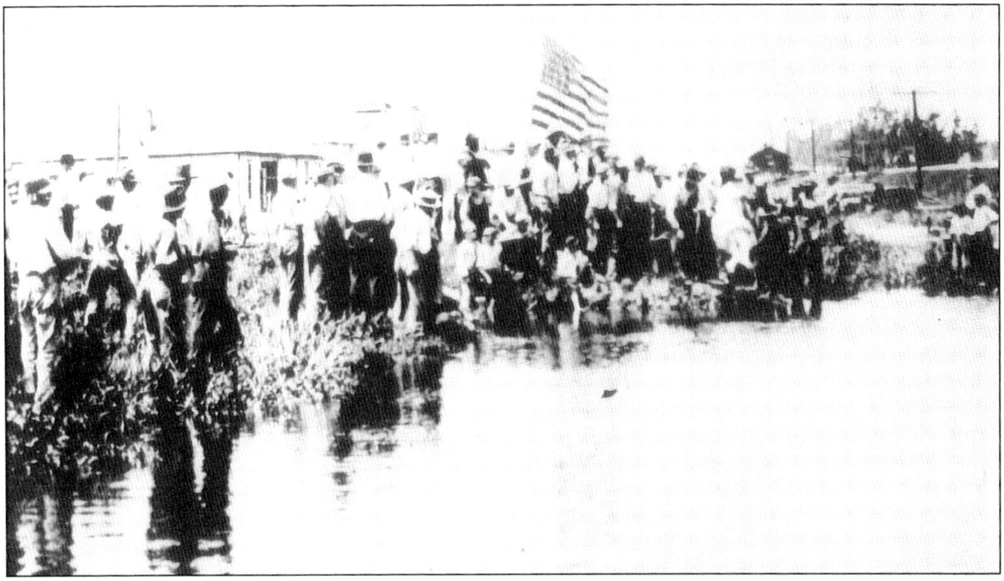

In turn-of-the-century Truman, Poinsett County, the punishment of the citizens for social, moral, or personal sin was common. Thus, the symbolic tossing of the town prostitutes into the overflow was a common occurrence. Red light districts were common in larger Delta communities such as Jonesboro, whose most infamous house of ill repute was the "Swamp Poodle." (Courtesy of Nettleton Public Schools.)

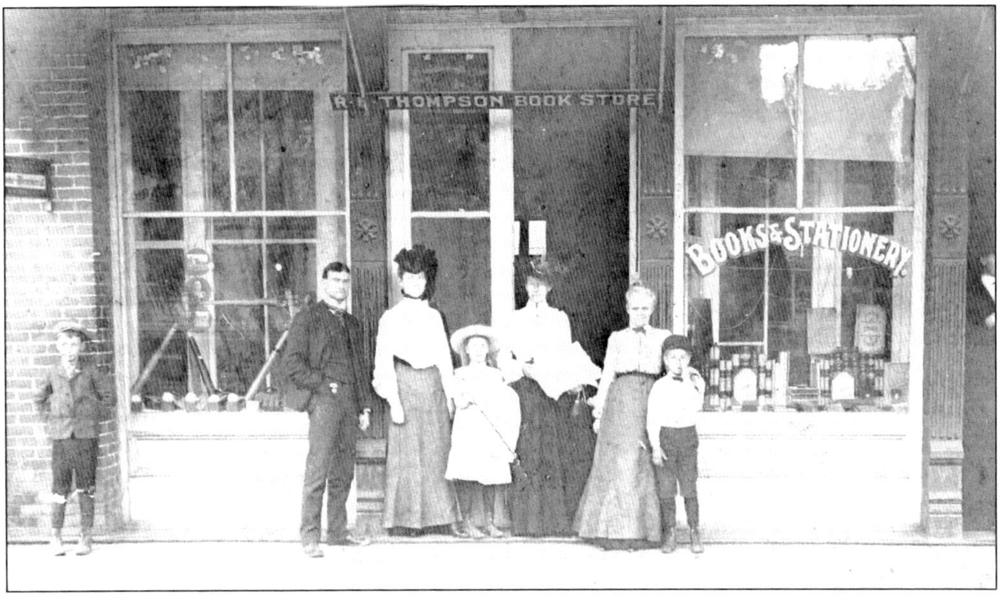

Although Arkansas, and especially the Delta region, would be the victim of stereotyping throughout the century, there was and still is a great emphasis on education—particularly on the three Rs. R.C. Thompson's Book Store, pictured above, would serve Jonesboro and surrounding community residents for years, providing them with the most current printed works. While all too common today, such establishments were still quite rare in the late nineteenth century, especially west of the Mississippi River, thus symbolizing the progressive nature of numerous Delta communities. (Courtesy of Arkansas State University Museum.)

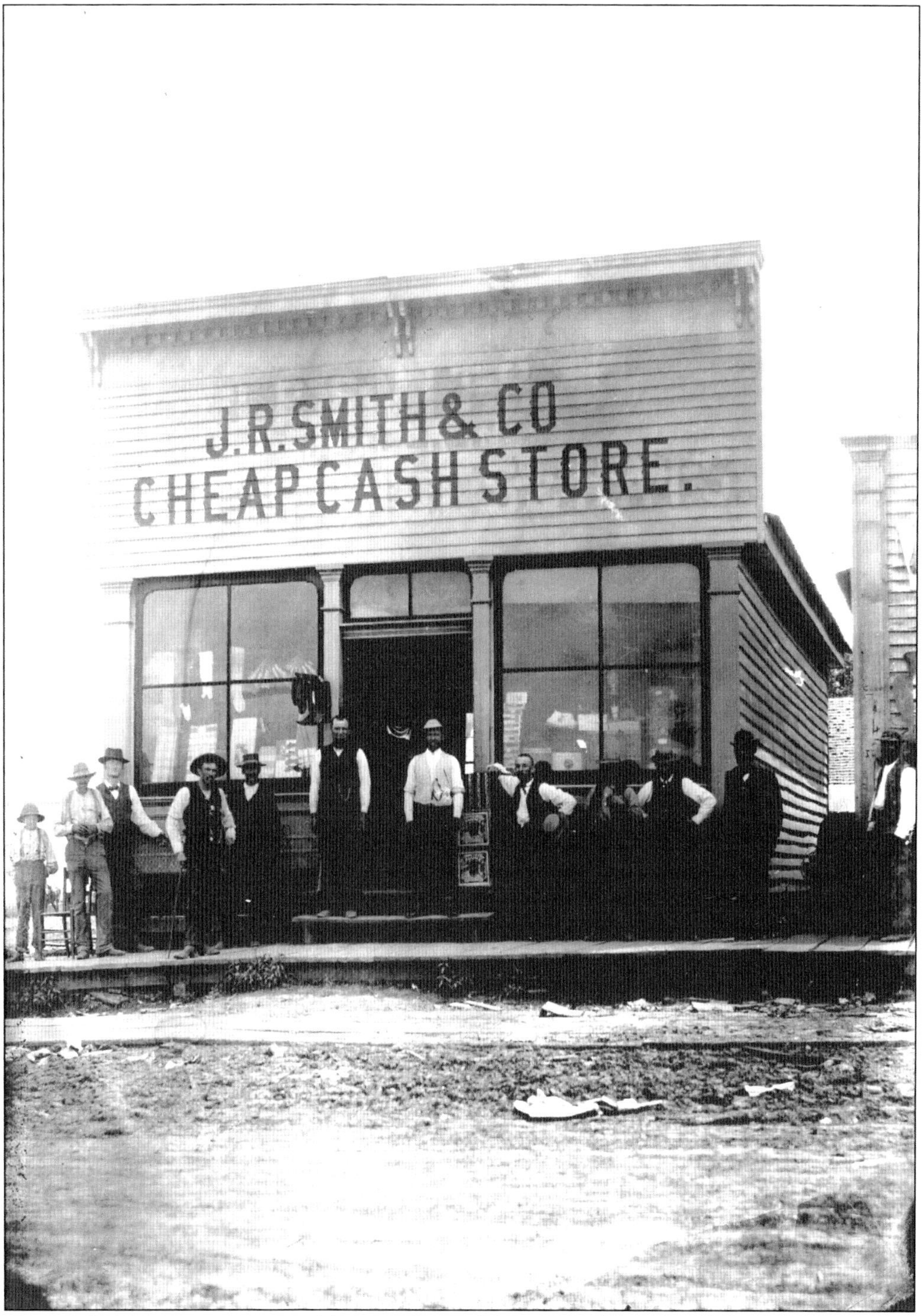

J.R. Smith & Company was one of the most successful nineteenth century merchants in Craighead County. The Jonesboro Cheap Cash Store was among the most popular sites for local residents, many of whom are posed outside. The name of the store perhaps suggests why this was such a popular destination for local consumers. (Courtesy of Arkansas State University Museum.)

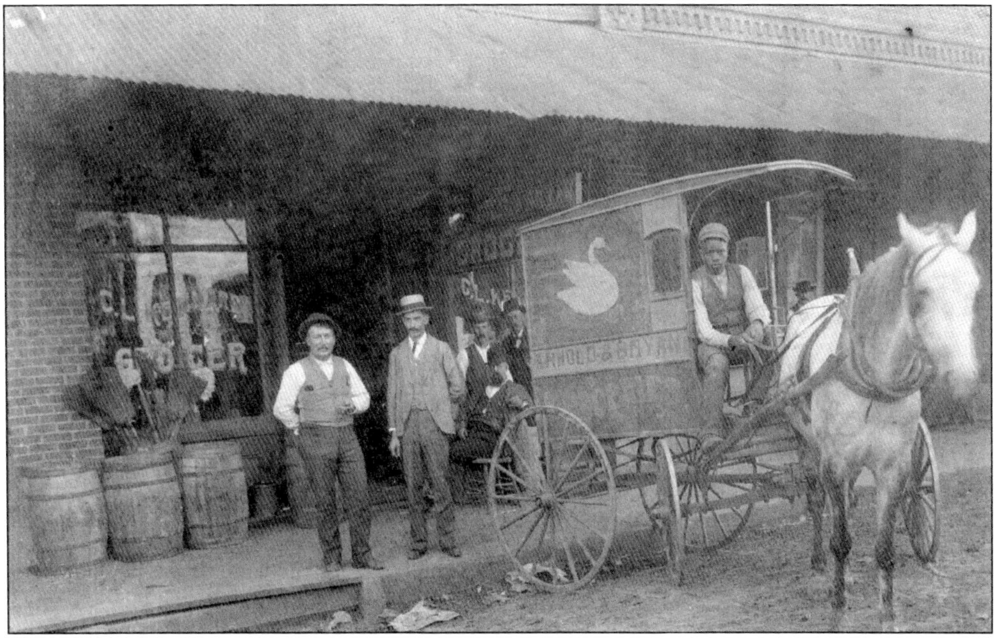

Due to the rural nature of the Arkansas Delta, a common nineteenth-century method for purchasing groceries was via a horse and delivery wagon. This decorative wagon, which reads Arnold & Bryan Grocery Delivery, is about to embark on such a trip in this 1893 photograph taken outside of Jonesboro grocer C.L. Kennard's store. (Courtesy of Arkansas State University Museum.)

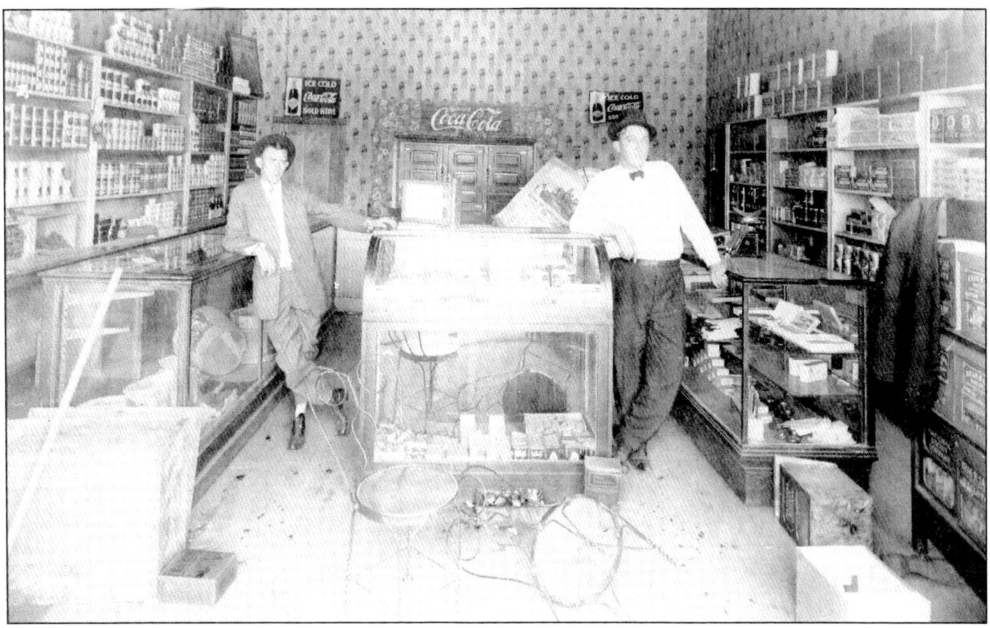

The interior of a small store in Jonesboro is the setting for this turn-of-the-century photograph. With two dapper men clearly posed looking on, the most visible evidence of content can be found in the three "Ice Cold Coca Cola" signs. Although well stocked, the aesthetics of this establishment (e.g., hideous wallpaper, fallen chair) leave something to be desired for twenty-first century onlookers. (Courtesy of Arkansas State University Museum.)

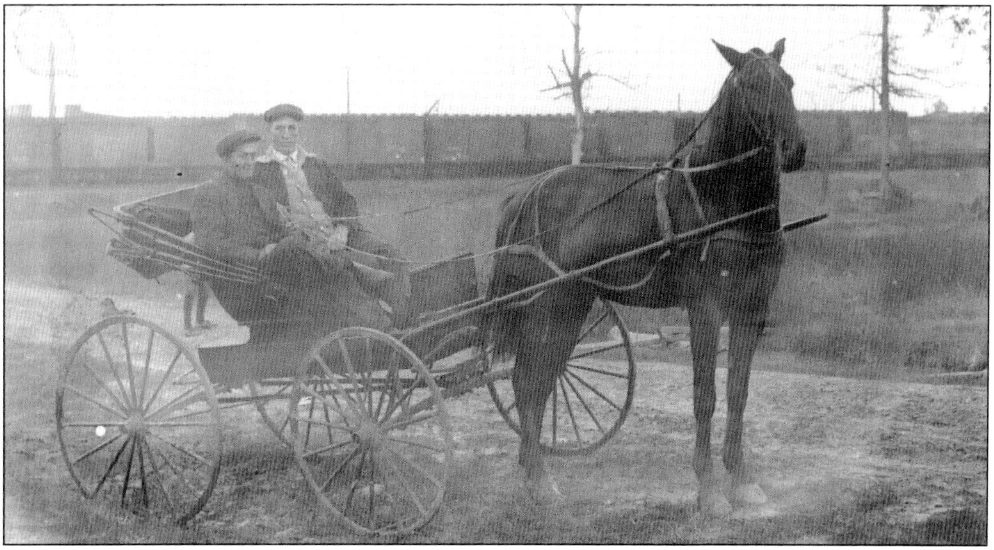

This late-nineteenth century photograph from Jonesboro was taken in front of a line of boxcars and barren trees, thus indicating that the time frame was late fall/early winter. The two individuals were identified simply as representatives of Berger Mercantile, suggesting that they were en route to the train station to check on the status of some newly arrived merchandise. (Courtesy of Arkansas State University Museum.)

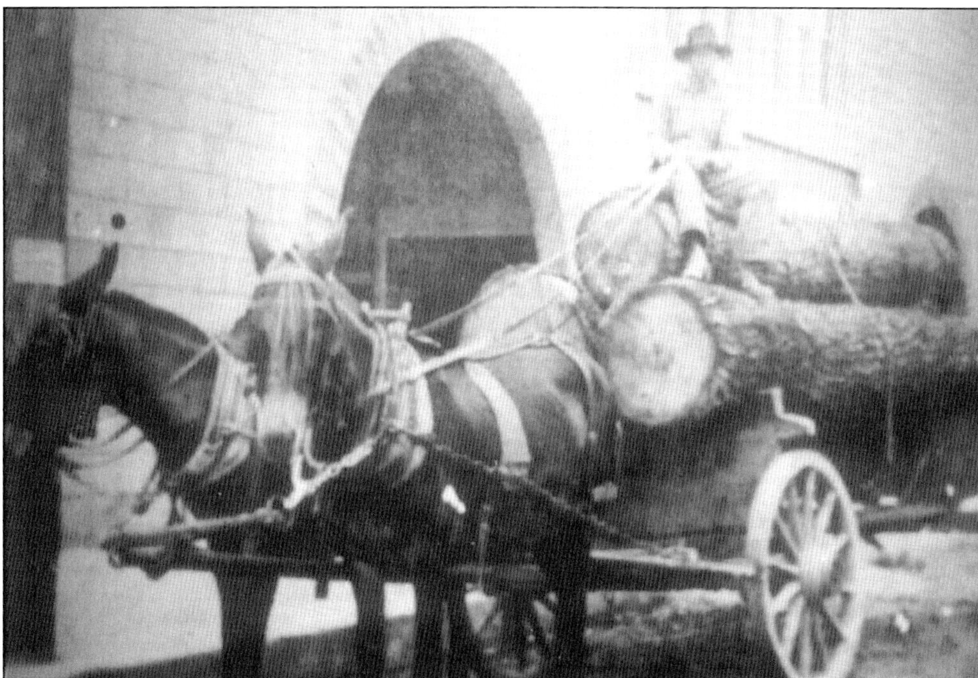

Certainly a common site in the Delta during the turn of the century, a lumber wagon is spotted bringing material to the lumber mill at Nettleton. Until well into the twentieth century, harvesting the natural forest of northeastern Arkansas was a major industry, providing the primary source of income for thousands of Delta residents. (Courtesy of Nettleton Public Schools.)

Two

The Nineteenth Century

Drafting the Blueprints

Some believe that formal education in Arkansas can trace its roots to the Delta. Reportedly, the first school in Arkansas was established in the tiny Delta community of Ravenden Springs in Randolph County. Those first classes presumably were taught not in a quaint, nostalgic, one-room schoolhouse, but inside of a cave under the direction of Professor Caleb Lindsay. If these predictions are accurate, the "cave school" was almost certainly a subscription school, where students were required to pay a small weekly or monthly fee. In some instances, students who could not afford such fees were still allowed to attend.

Public schooling as we define it today was still quite the exception in mid-nineteenth century Arkansas. The 1860 census, for example, showed that half of those individuals of school age did not attend any type of school whatsoever. Those who did receive some type of formal education were "equally divided" between private schools, often known as academies, and public schools, many of which were subscription schools.

The Reconstruction era ushered in certain changes in the Arkansas Delta educational landscape. First, certain initiatives brought about the establishment of the first schools for freed slaves in the region. Even before the close of the war in 1864, efforts were made to establish a school in Helena for children of slaves who, for various reasons, were orphaned. As was often the case, religious groups, a number of them from the North, established such institutions. In this instance, the Helena school initiative was led by, among others, Calvin and Alida Clark, members of the Religious Society of Friends, or Quakers, from Indiana.

Several legislative gestures were also made to bring about reform in public education for white students. Perhaps the two most significant events in the history of education in Arkansas were Reconstruction-era Governor Clayton Powell's call for the establishment of public schools in the state, and the provision in the Arkansas State Constitution of 1874 for the organization of school districts. The majority of new schools built in this period, however, remained private. The economic conditions of the period also prevented any real public school development until the 1880s, when, for the first time, many communities found themselves in a position to begin the process of building public schools. This chapter examines this critical period in the history of the Arkansas Delta.

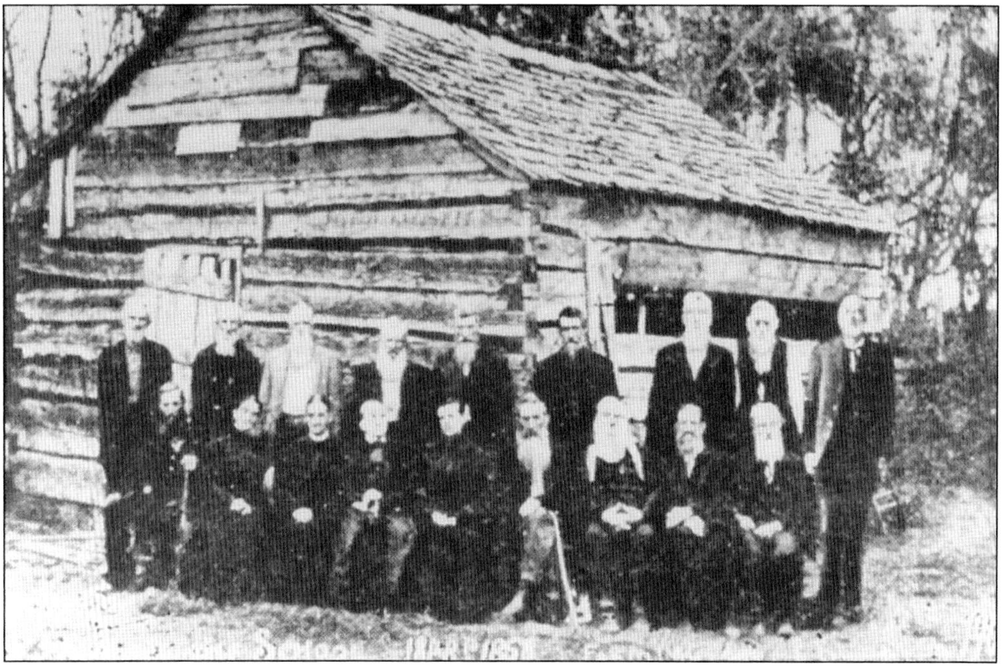

Among the first educational institutions in Arkansas, Pioneer schools were formed to teach the three Rs to community residents. The elders of the community often served as the teachers, as is the case in this 1858 photograph of a Northwest Arkansas Pioneer school located in Farmington. (Courtesy of Arkansas History Commission.)

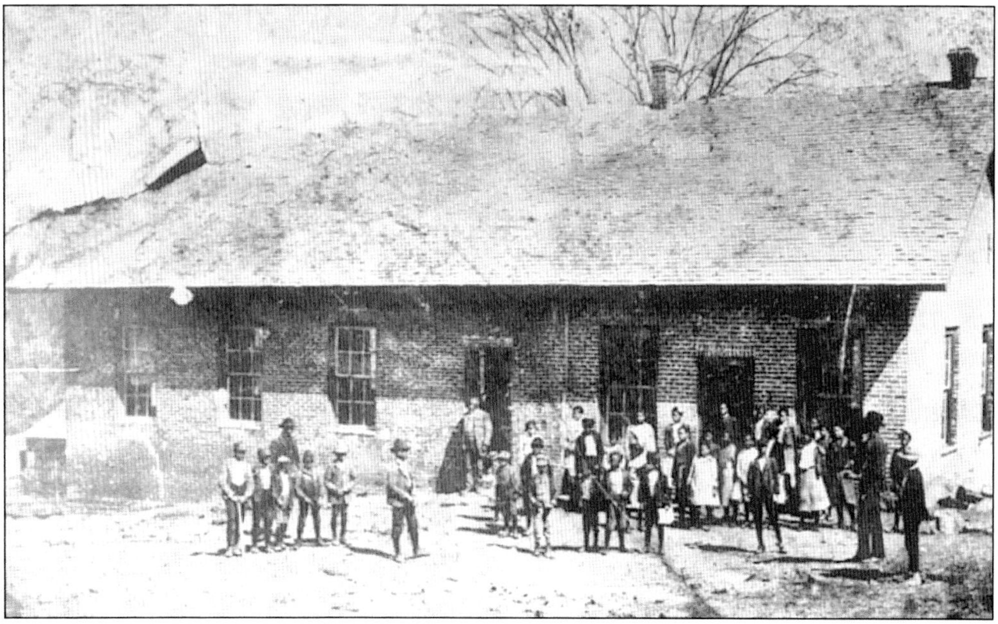

For the first time in its state's history, the Arkansas Constitution included a provision calling for the organization of public schools in 1874. Years prior to this edict, however, the first public school, known simply as Old Henderson School, was established in 1868. (Courtesy Arkansas History Commission.)

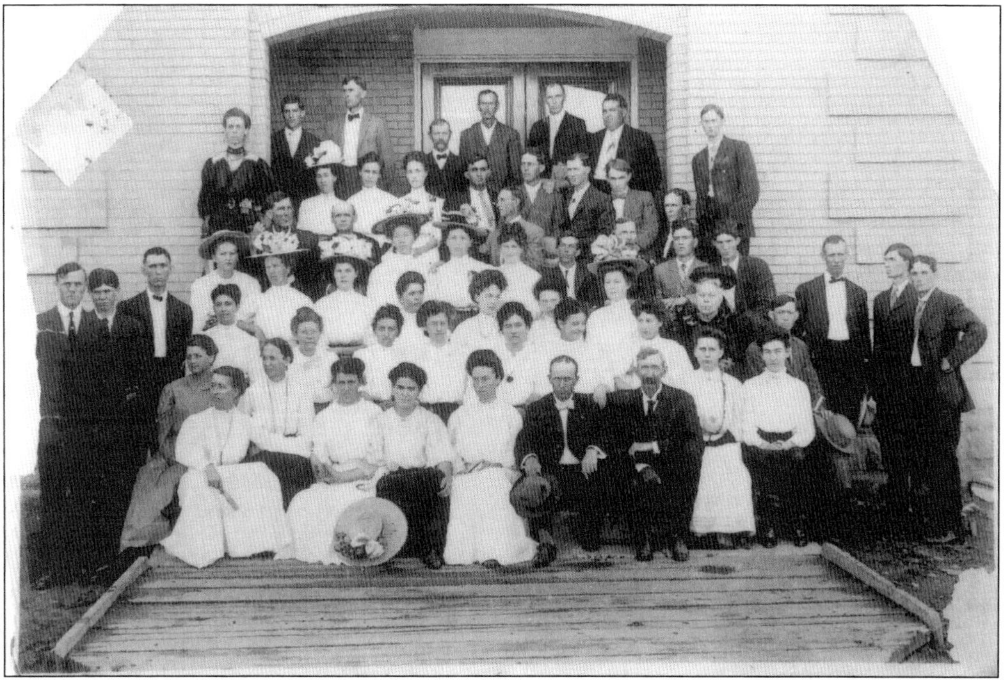

During Teachers' Examination Day in Lawrence County, participants took time out for a group photograph (above) on the steps of the county courthouse at Powhatan in 1880. Decades later, in the 1920s, rumors of statewide cheating on teacher exams would lead many to question the credibility of the entire teacher examination process. Delta residents have always depended upon and demanded a strong moral compass to guide them through life, as demonstrated in the dress and posture of those students and teacher in the *c.* 1890 photograph below. (Courtesy of Arkansas History Commission.)

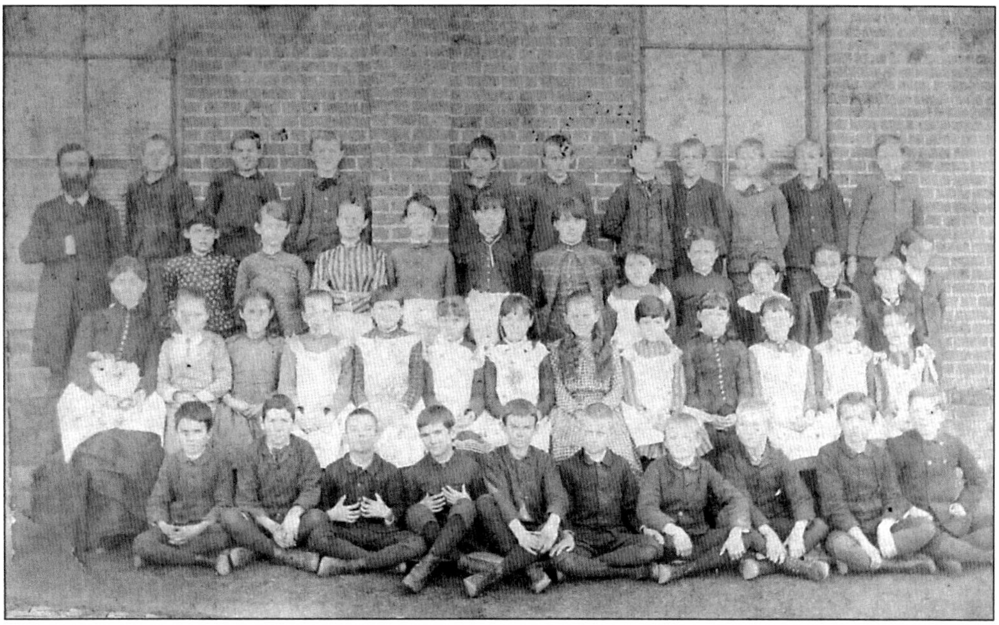

AUDITOR'S OFFICE,
LITTLE ROCK, ARKANSAS.
20 March 1846.

To the county School Commissioners of county,

Arkansas:

GENTLEMEN:—I have the honor to submit to you a statement of the prices at which the Board of county School Commissioners will dispose of the School books, slates and slate pencils, purchased by the Auditor under "An act to appropriate the whole of the common school fund to the purchase of books for common schools" approved January 7th 1845.

These books are designed for *schools organized under the common school law of this State approved 3rd February* 1843, *and such as will be governed by that law;* of which you are no doubt fully aware. The kinds of books &c. procured and the prices at which they will be sold are as follows:

KINDS OF BOOKS &C.	PRICE OF EACH BOOK. DOL. CTS.
United States Primer,	05
Webster's Spelling book,	06¼
Sequel to Webster's spelling book,	25
Goodrich's Reader No. 1,	10
Goodrich's Reader No. 2,	15
Goodrich's Reader No. 3,	25
Willard's History of the United States,	30
Gallaudet's Dictionary	30
Morse's Geography,	50
Davie's Arithmetic, first lessons, No. 1,	15
Davies' Arithmetic, No. 2,	25
Slates 7 by 11 inches; each to be sold for	15
Slate pencils at ½ of a cent each, or per dozen	06
Bullion's English Grammar, per copy	15
Root's copies, for the whole series No. 1, No. 2, No. 3 and No. 4	30

For future reference to the prices of these books, it would perhaps be well to have this communication recorded in the journal of the Board of School Commissioners or in the Clerk's office of your county.

I am gentlemen, most respectfully,

your obedient servant,

ELIAS N. CONWAY, *Auditor of Arkansas.*

Following passage of the 1843 Common Schools Law, many Arkansas communities began to organize schools. As part of this process, the state auditor would offer books for purchase to common schools. The 1846 auditor's report reflects that the emphasis at the time was on history, geography, reading, writing, and mathematics. (Courtesy Arkansas History Commission.)

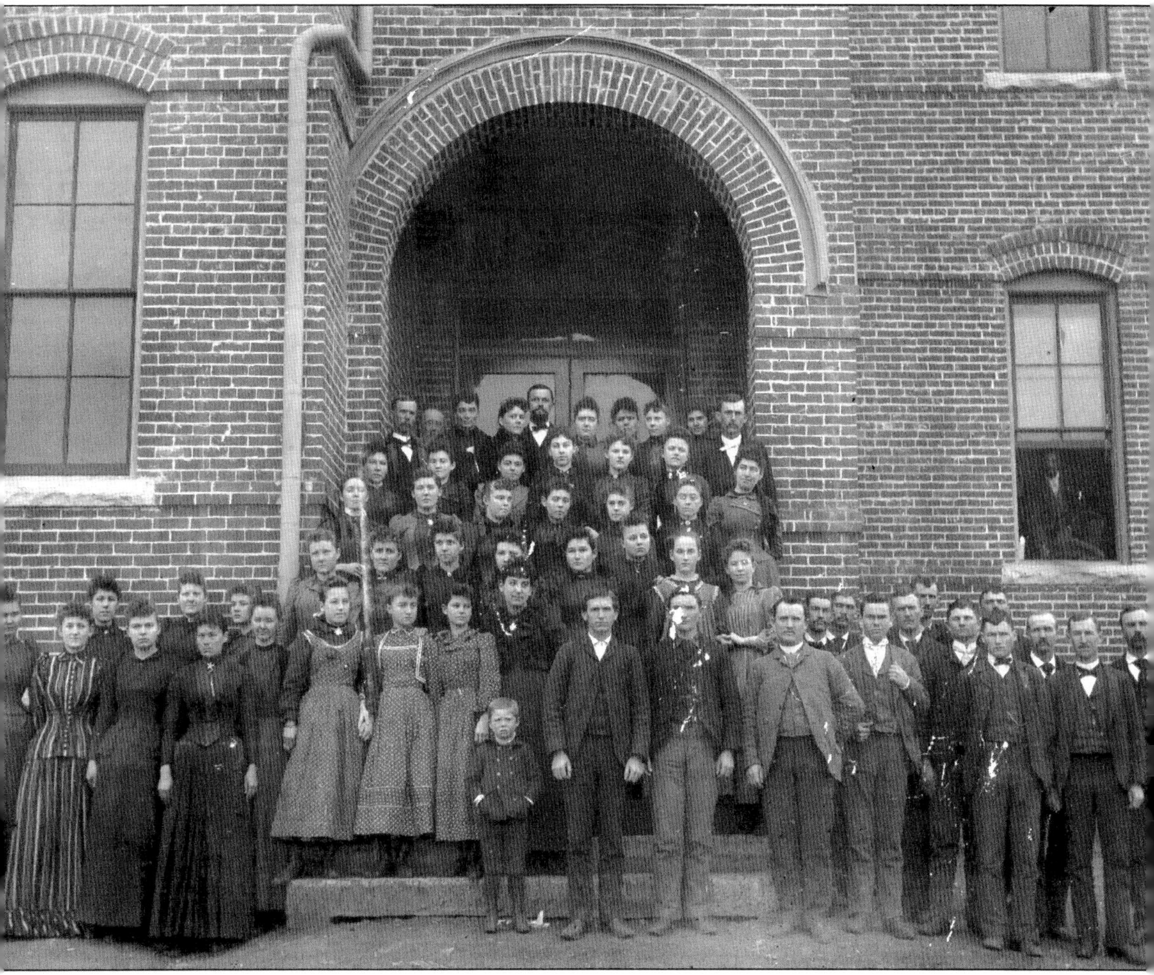

Founded in 1886, the Jonesboro Academy, shown in this *c.* 1890 photograph, existed as a private school. Clearly, for the time it attracted a large number of students. With the development of public schools in the mid-1890s, the need for private schools lessened. The rural areas around Jonesboro could not take advantage of the academy because of transportation. Note that all of the boys are wearing traditional suits, while the girls are all in ankle-length dresses. (Courtesy of Arkansas State University Museum.)

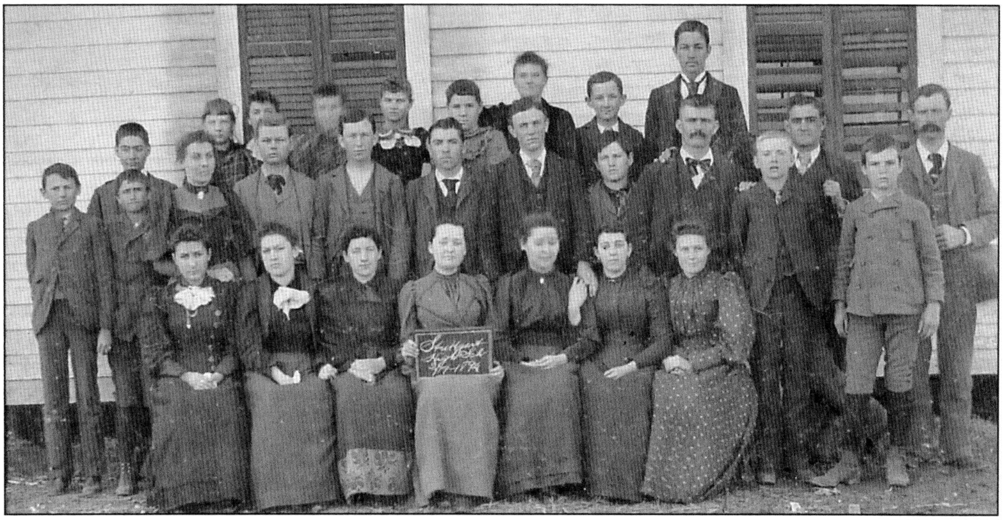

Stuttgart, Arkansas County, was one of the larger communities in the late-nineteenth century Delta. This 1894 photograph of the high school class, among the first in the region, reflects the unusually large size of the class as well as the predominantly male composition of the student body. Both of these are unique characteristics for early Delta schools. (Courtesy of Arkansas History Commission.)

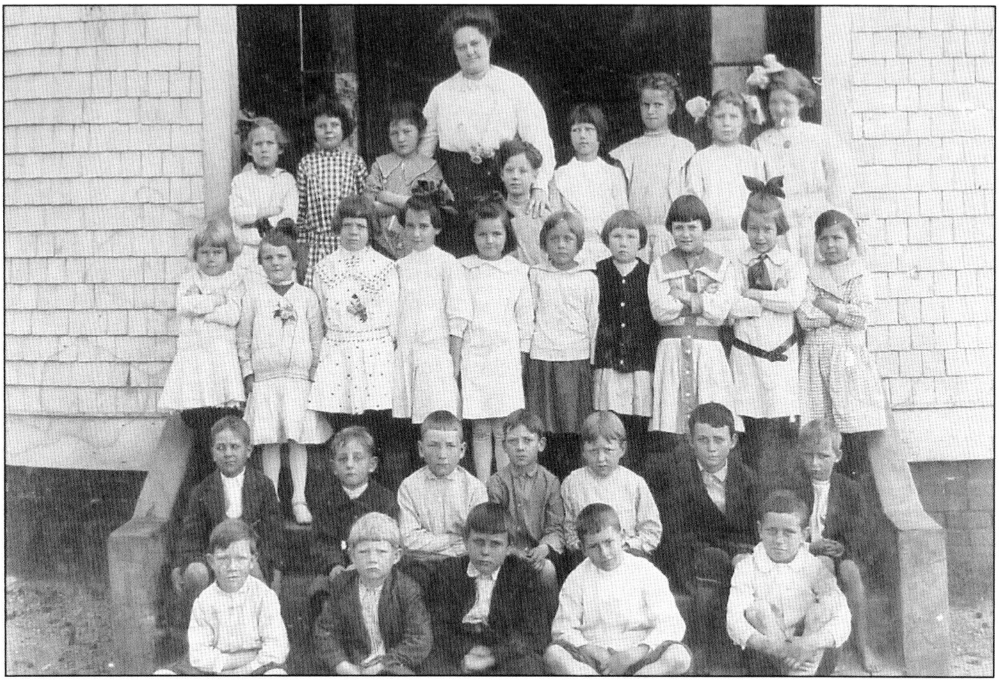

This photograph, perhaps better than any other, epitomizes late-nineteenth century education in the Arkansas Delta. These students of multiple grade levels are assembled outside of a one-room schoolhouse, left in charge of a female teacher. Another characteristic that was germane to the Delta was the disparity, although not of a tremendous degree, of wealth evident in these students' attire, with some children wearing coats, hats, and pretty dresses, while others were barefoot and ill-clad. (Courtesy Arkansas History Commission.)

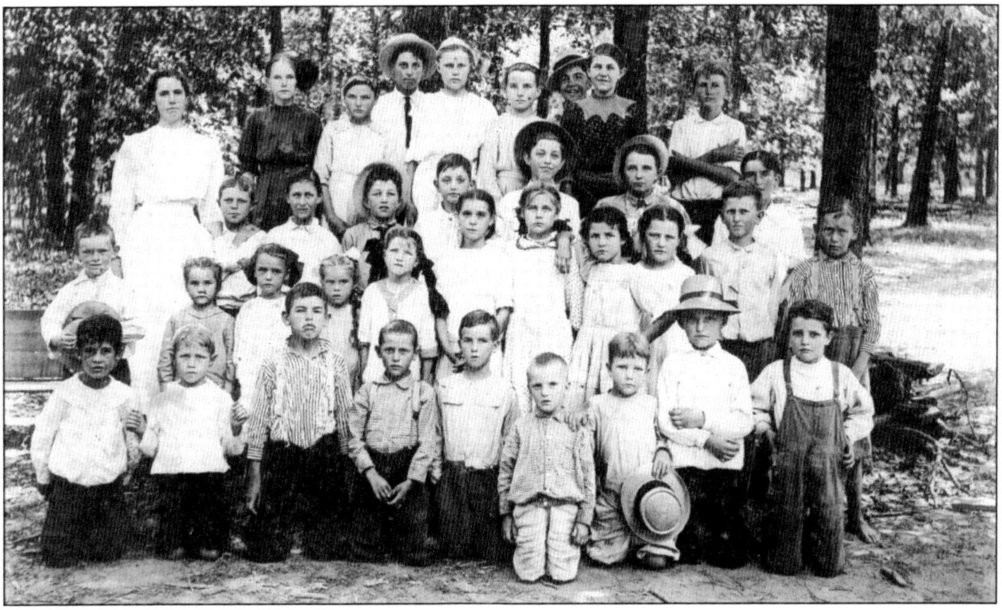

The Greensboro School, Craighead County, was established just north of Jonesboro. This *c.* 1900 school group shows students from the first grade through the eighth grade. While the girls appear well dressed, the boys' attire ranges from pants and shirts through bib overalls, to ties and hats. (Courtesy of Arkansas State University Museum.)

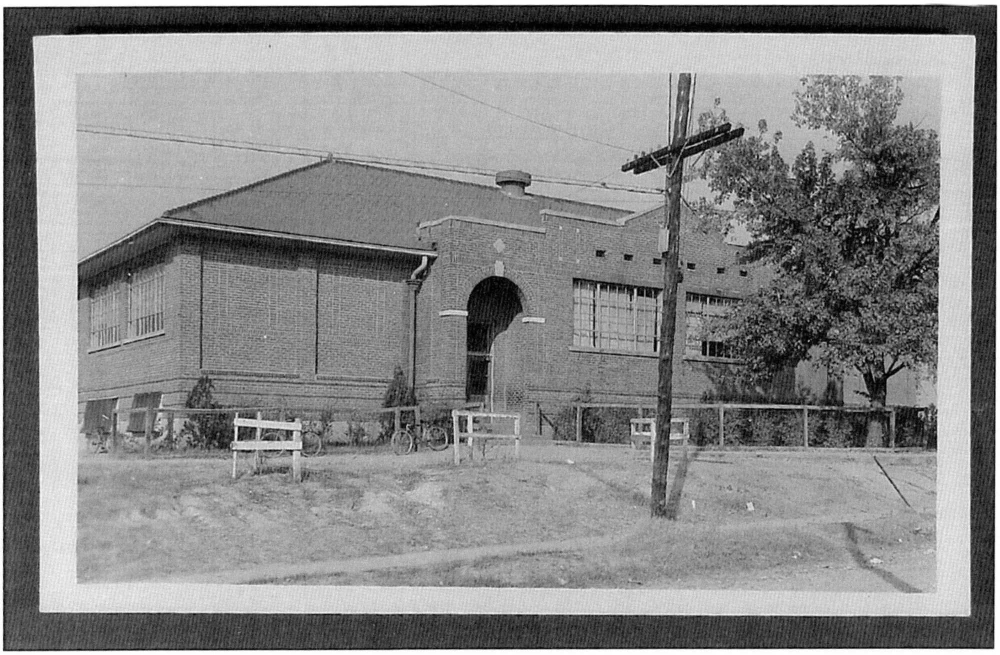

Identified as the first free school in Jonesboro, Craighead County, this building opened its doors in 1886. Although private schools had been established for two decades, a public school was clearly needed. Jonesboro would become a trade center for a large region in northeastern Arkansas after the coming of the automobile, but it was already the largest community in the region. The school was located on North Fisher Street. (Courtesy Arkansas History Commission.)

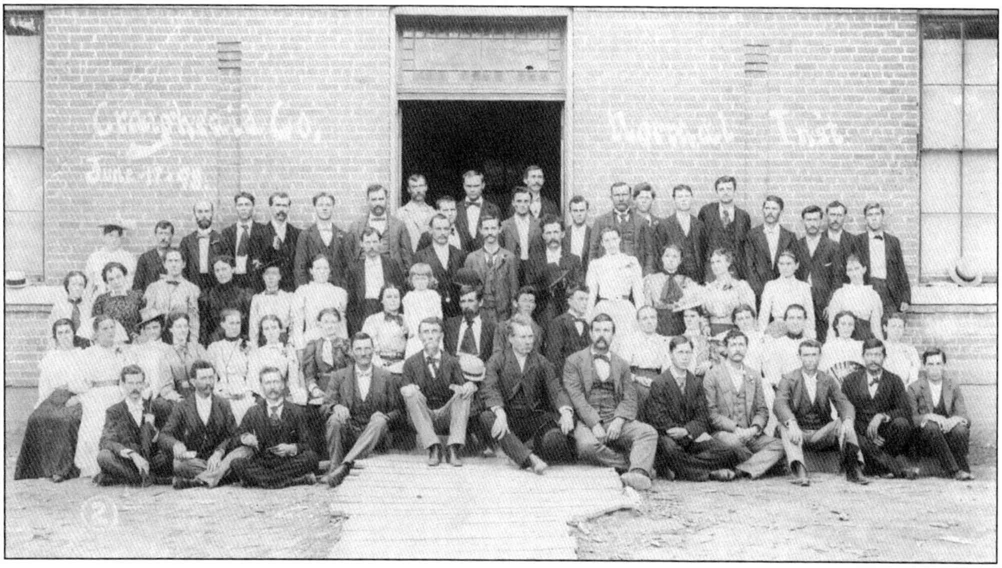

The Craighead County Normal Institute, located in Jonesboro, opened its doors in 1892. Although one local historian has indicated that numerous residents in the region acquired their college education at the Normal school, it appears that the institution was still short-lived. Students in the above photograph were among the last to graduate from the institute. In the photograph below, one will also note from the "JSN" on the dress of some of the female students, that in the early history of the school it was known as the Jonesboro Normal School. (Courtesy of Arkansas State University Museum.)

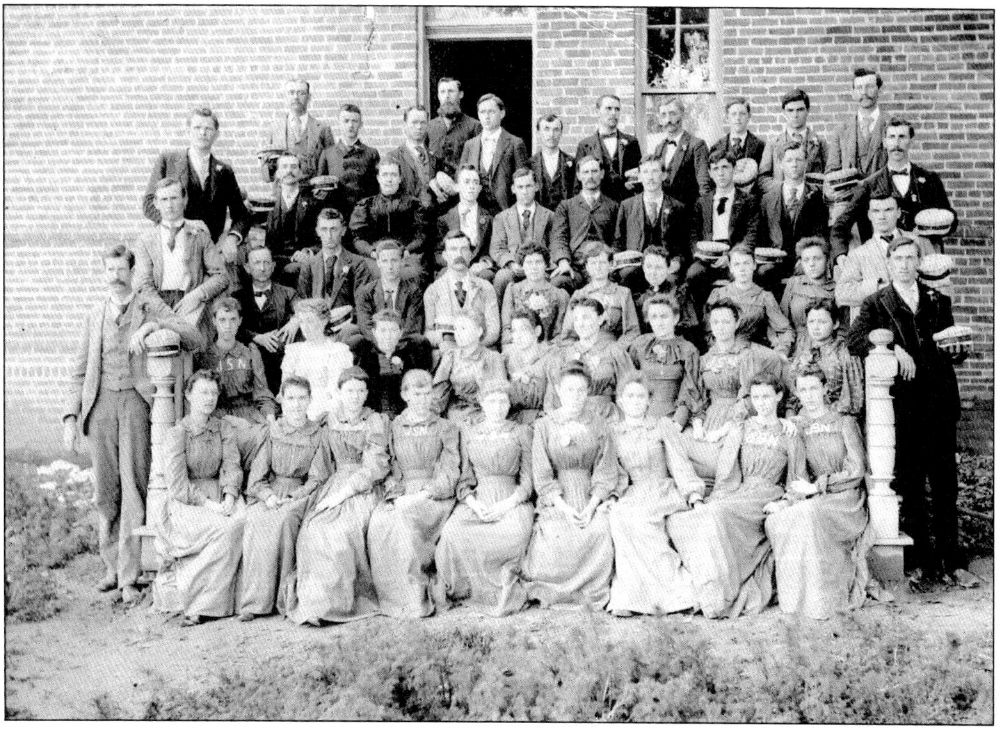

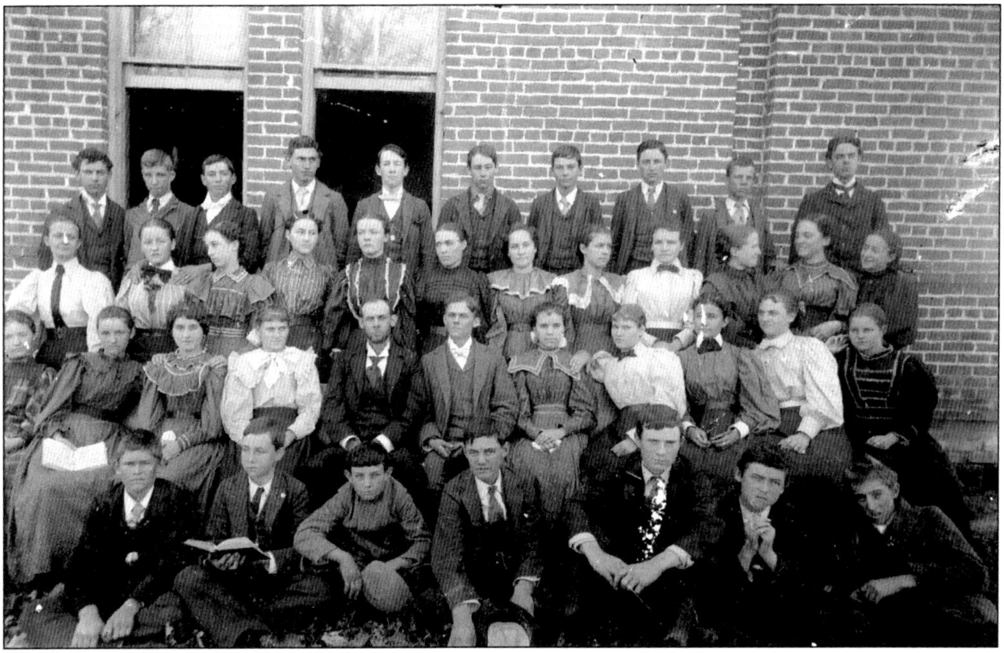

For years, many of Jonesboro's most wealthy and powerful residents sent their children to Jonesboro Academy. While some have suggested this type of institution served to further segregate residents according to their socio-economic status, this remains conjecture. What is known, however, is that the academy maintained a very high enrollment throughout the nineteenth century. (Courtesy of Arkansas State University Museum.)

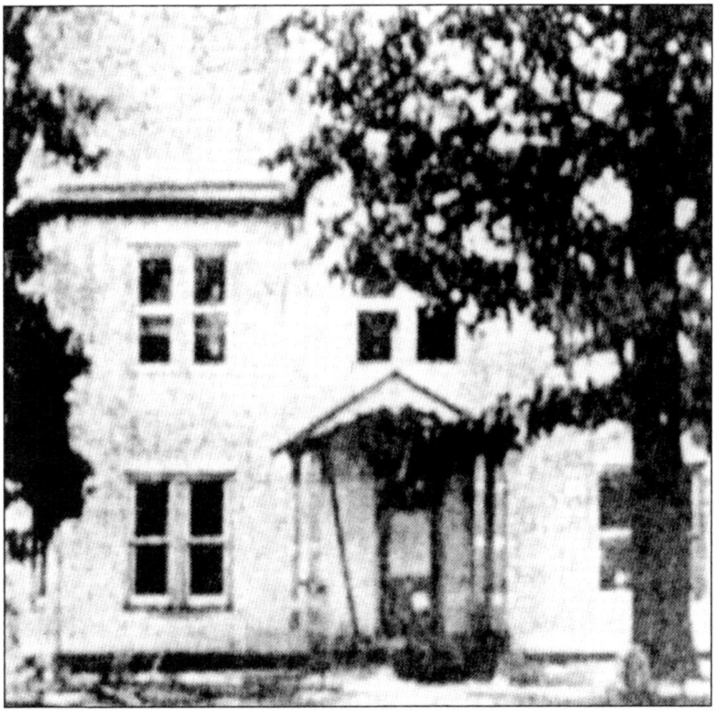

Although there seems to be general agreement over the fact that the first public high school in Jonesboro opened in 1886, local residents disagree over the location of the two-story brick house with seven rooms. Records indicate that the school, pictured at left, was either located at the corner of Church and Strawn Streets or at the corner of Oak and Madison. Either way, the building signifies Jonesboro's first attempt to provide local residents with a public education. (Courtesy of the Roselyn Horner Collection.)

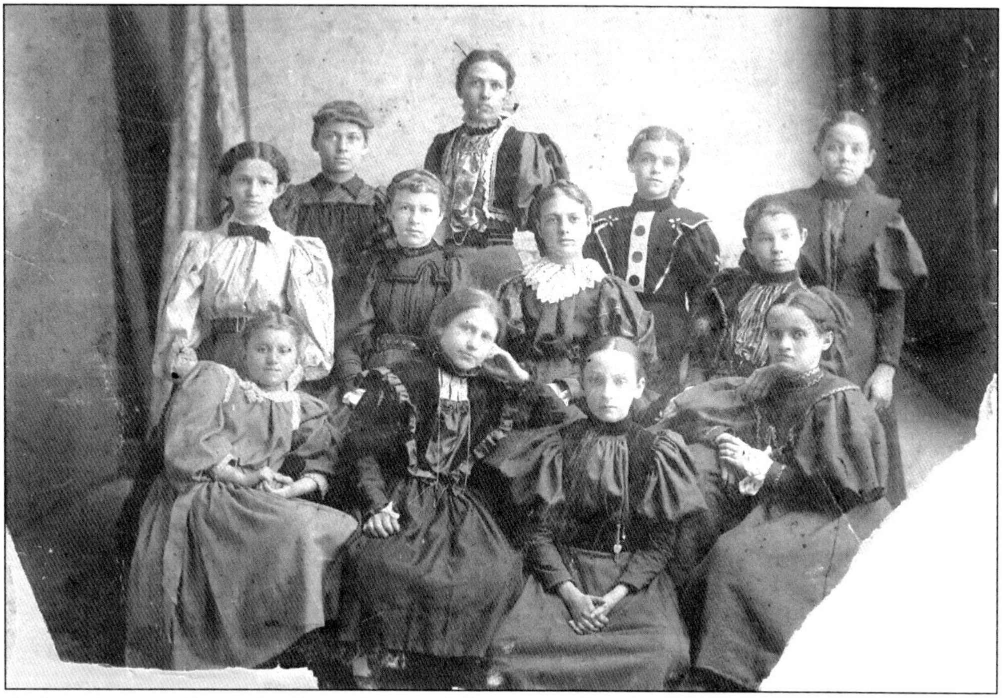

A Jonesboro public school teacher and her very dignified students pose for this 1900 photograph. The teacher looks very stern, while the young ladies look somewhat solemn. The girls' attire clearly reflects the more urban and wealthy citizenry found in Jonesboro during the late nineteenth century. The small size of the class, however, also reflects that education in this period was still considered a luxury for the select few in the city. (Courtesy of Arkansas State University Museum.)

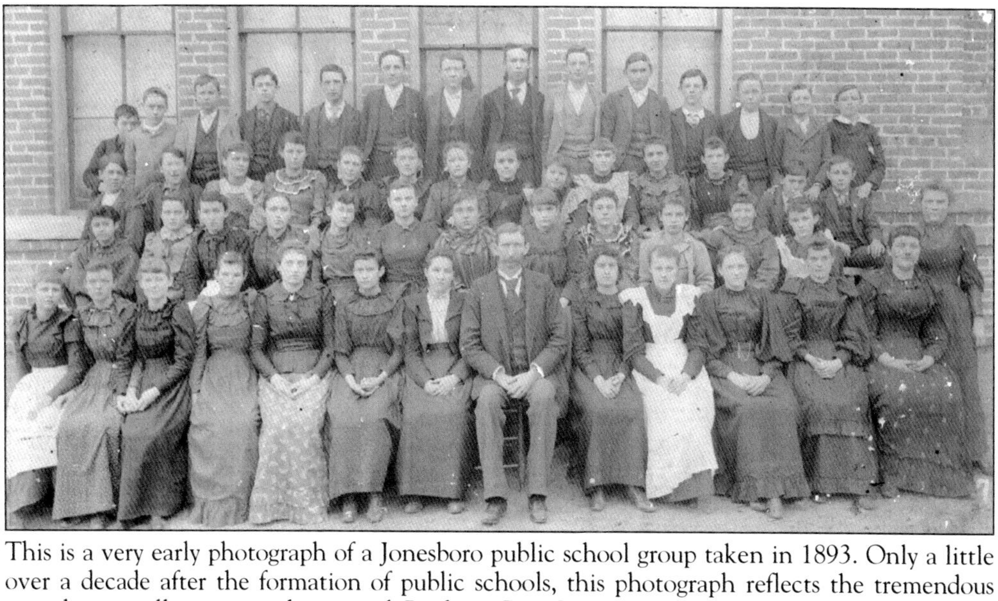

This is a very early photograph of a Jonesboro public school group taken in 1893. Only a little over a decade after the formation of public schools, this photograph reflects the tremendous growth in enrollment over that period. Professor D.T. Rogers, an early leader in Jonesboro public schools, sits in the middle of the front row. (Courtesy of Arkansas State University Museum.)

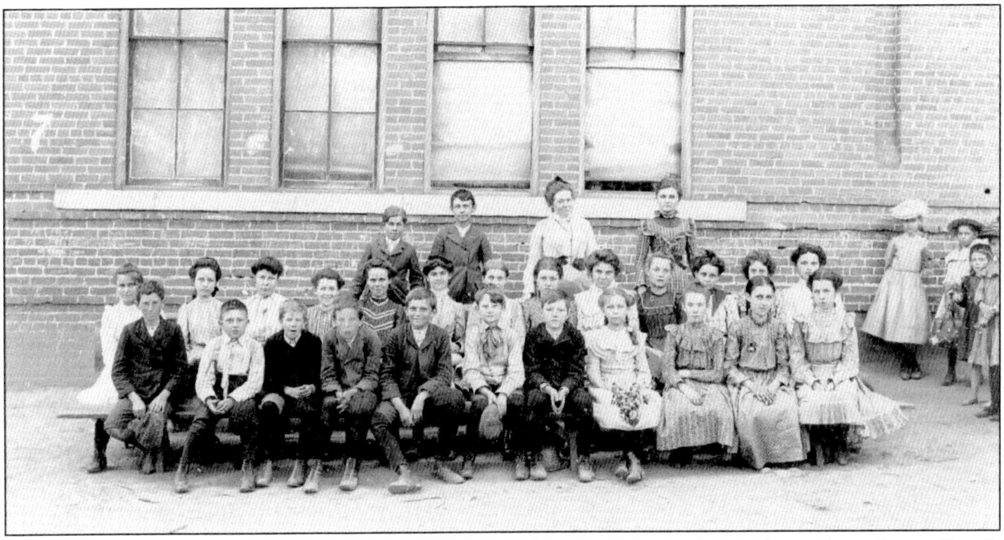

As was common practice in the late nineteenth century, students from Jonesboro South Elementary School assemble for photographs on the same day and at the same sites as that in which the earlier photograph was taken in 1893. The teachers, who appear to be no older than the high school students in the previous composite, are standing at the back. Note the next group of elementary students who are waiting their turn to the right of this photograph. (Courtesy of Arkansas State University Museum.)

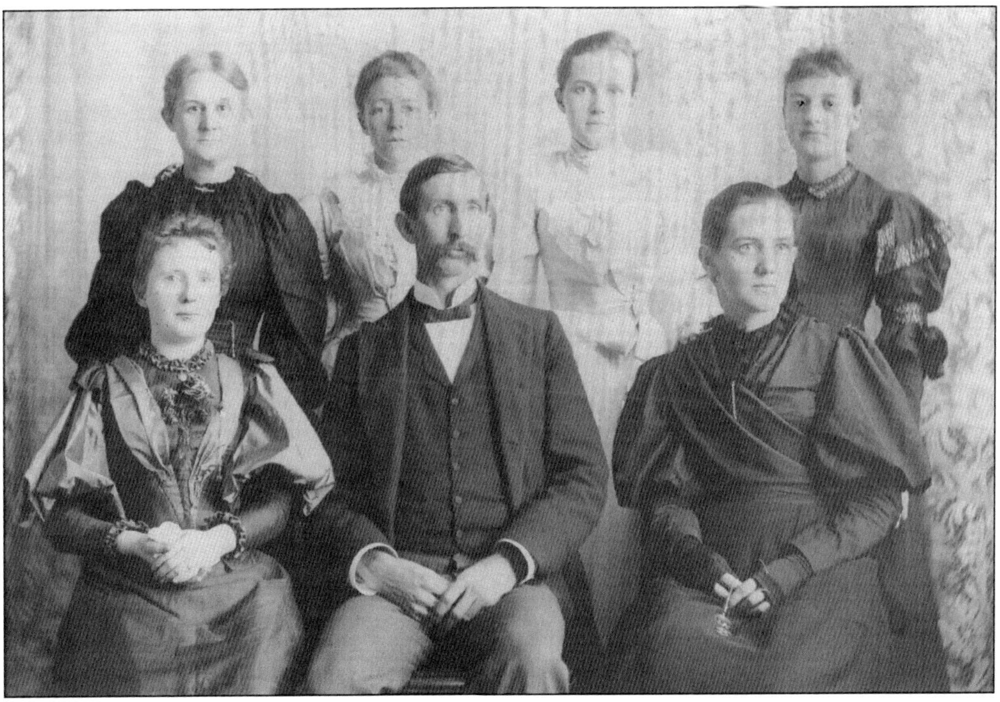

This is a formal pose by the Jonesboro public school faculty in the mid-1890s. Professor D.T. Rogers is sitting exactly in the same stiff fashion as in the earlier photo. The women teachers are all formally dressed in long sleeves. Although at the time women occupied many of the teaching positions, a male remained the school leader. (Courtesy of Arkansas State University Museum.)

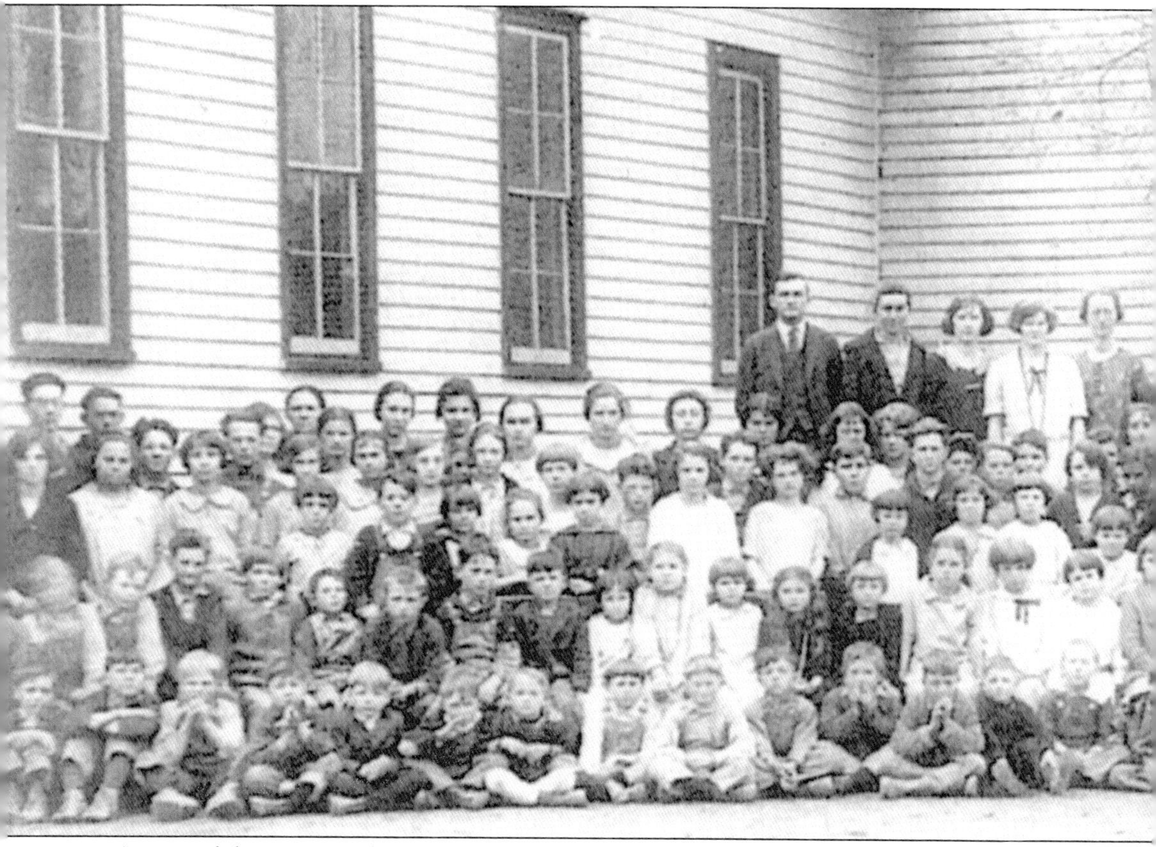

A turn-of-the-century photograph of the first Bay School, located on Allen Street, reveals much. The entire student body, as well as the faculty, assembles for this autumn class photo. Unlike the earlier composites of Jonesboro public schools of the same period, the Bay students

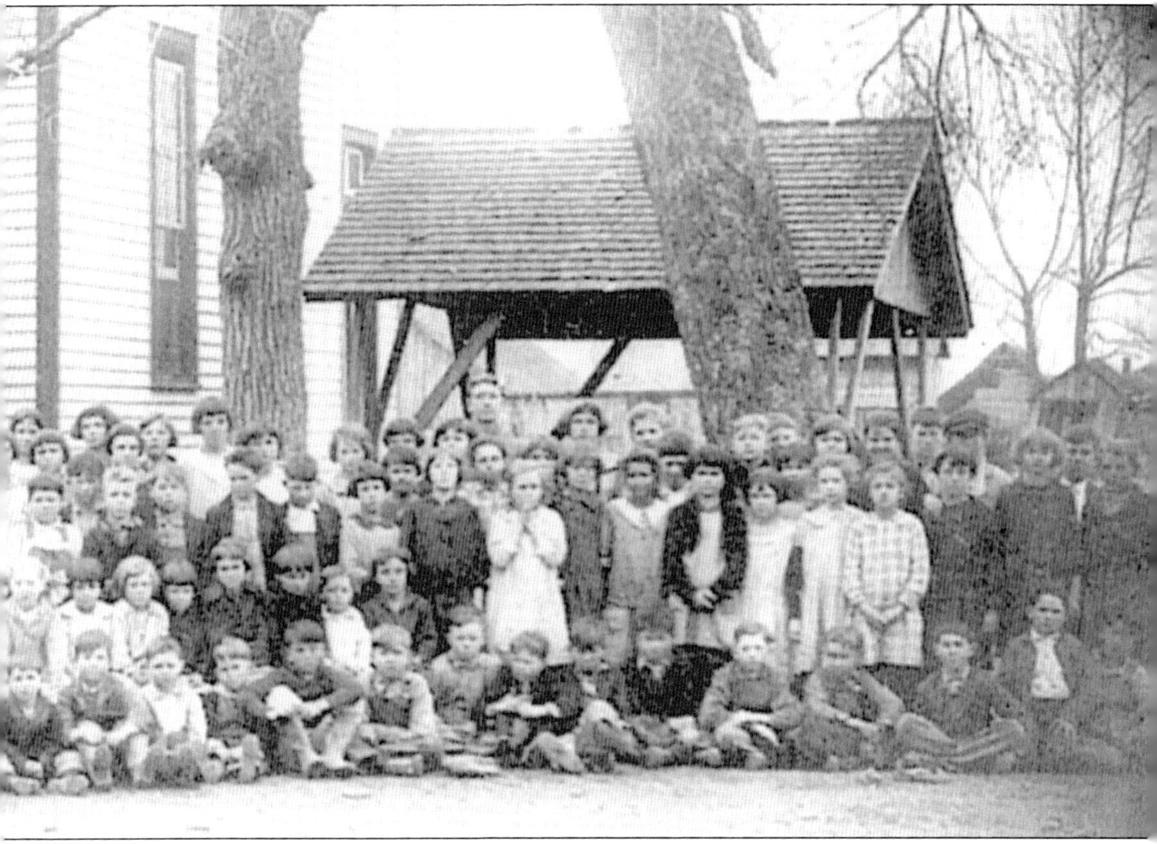

are less formally dressed and posed. The difference might be explained by the contrast in size and wealth of the two towns. (Courtesy of the Edgar Morrison Collection.)

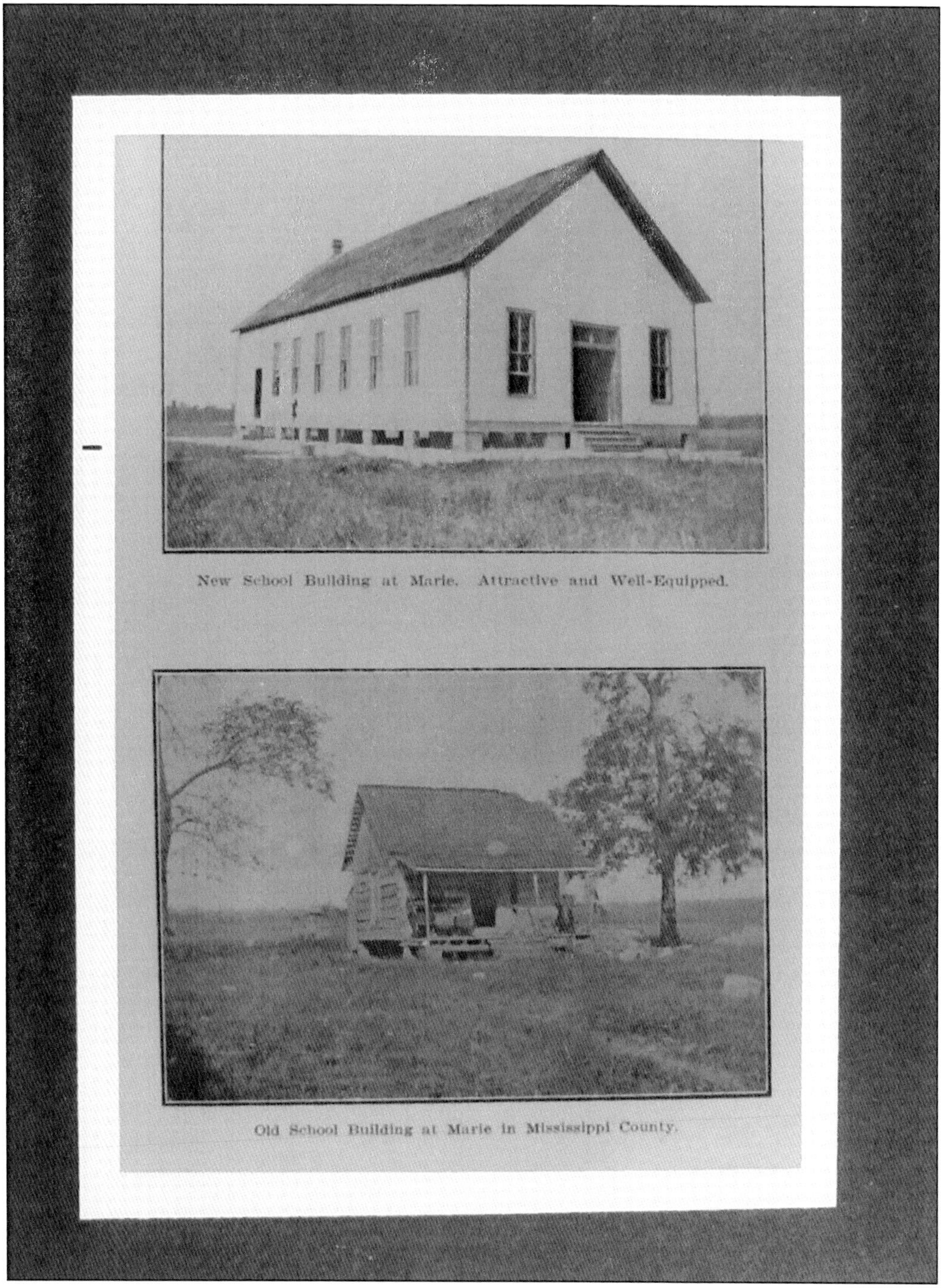

The evolution in schooling in Marie, Mississippi County, is displayed in this photograph of the two school buildings located in that community. The lower photograph is of the first one-room school building built in the late nineteenth century, while the top one is from the early twentieth century. The new school, as the caption notes, was much more "Attractive and Well-Equipped," offering multiple classrooms. (Courtesy of Arkansas History Commission.)

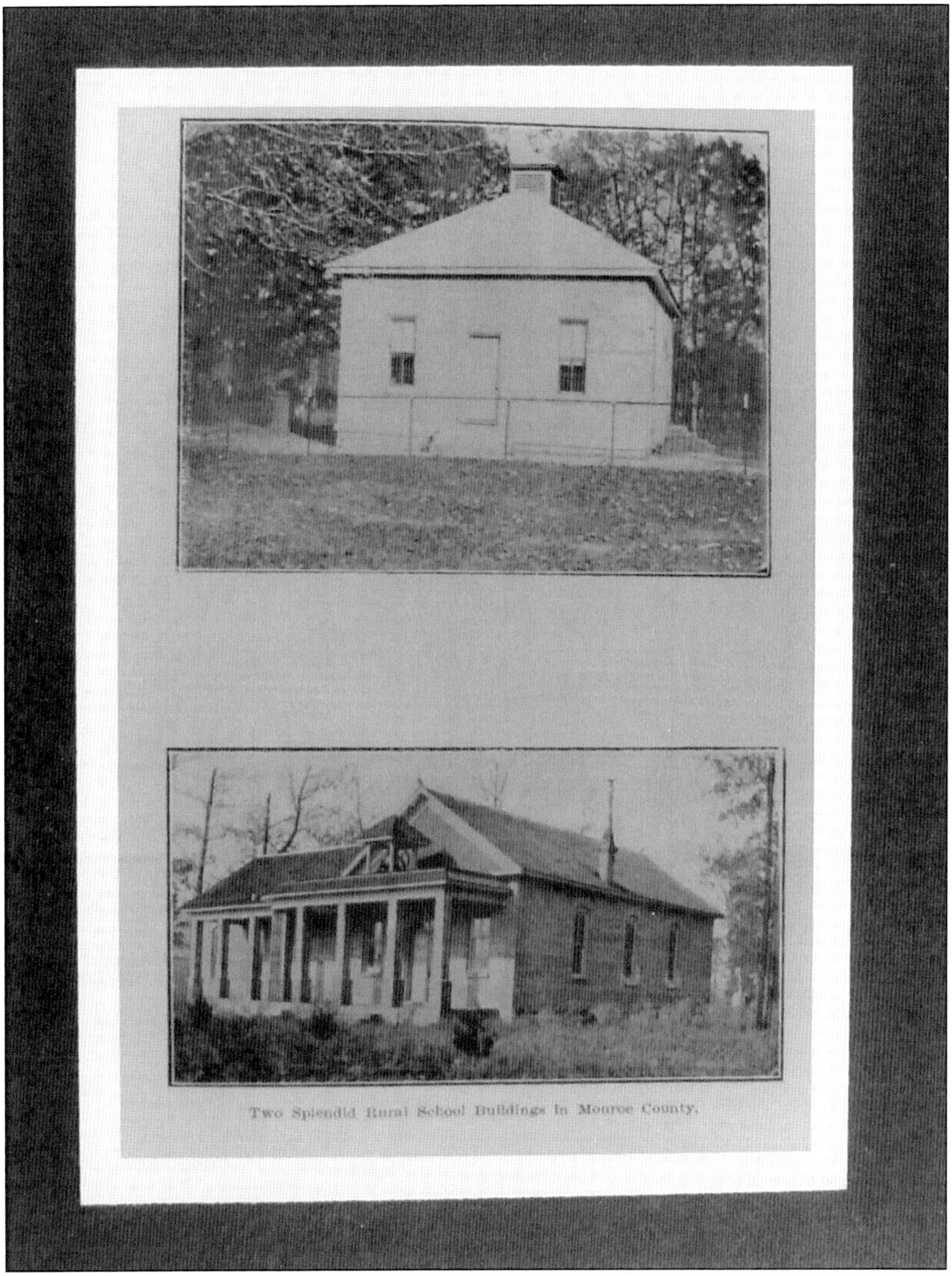

Although Monroe County was predominantly rural in the late nineteenth and early twentieth centuries, it did not impede the development of numerous schools throughout the county. Community residents were quite proud of their schools, as is evident in the caption on the photo that reads, "Two Splendid Rural Schools in Monroe County." You will note the school bell in the cupola of the building at the bottom. Both schools, however, represent some of the most well designed and ornate structures to be found outside of the larger communities during this period. (Courtesy Arkansas History Commission.)

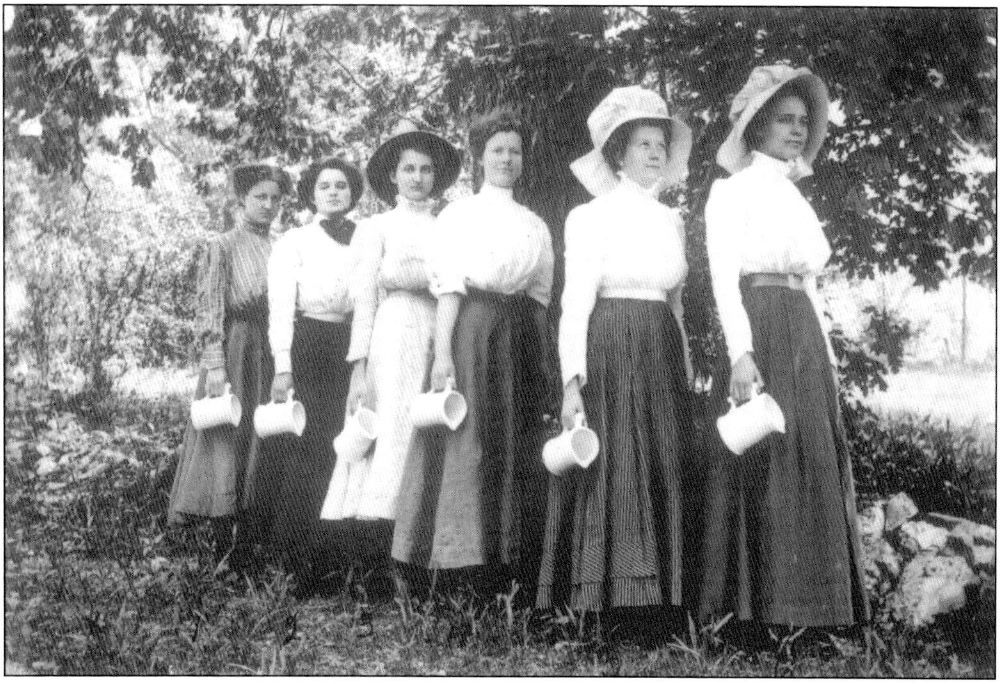

Ravenden is a small community in the northern part of the Arkansas Delta, in Randolph County. These rather well dressed young ladies were students at Ravenden Springs School. Note that all but two of them were dressed in long dark skirts with long-sleeved white blouses. Two students also have on bonnets, a common headgear worn by women in the late nineteenth and early twentieth centuries. (Courtesy Arkansas History Commission.)

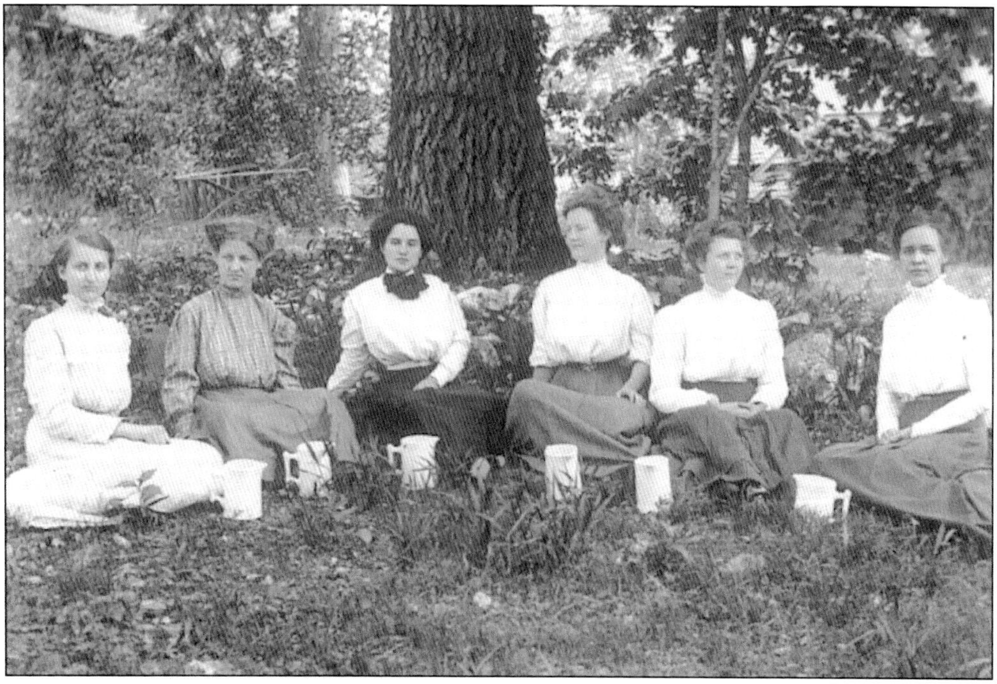

Three

Turn of the Century
Laying the Foundation

By the end of the nineteenth century, the education paradigm that had dominated Arkansas thought throughout that century began to shift. Beginning in the 1880s and '90s, many Arkansans began to distance themselves from the belief that "education was as private a matter as religion." During this critical period, numerous communities throughout the Delta, for the first time, felt committed enough to invest their time, money, and support into free public education. For some communities, the first step was small but very definitive. For example, Paragould's first public school, constructed in 1883, was a simple, one-room building, which was soon followed by the establishment of the first high school in 1909. Other communities, with more population and wealth, could begin their venture into public education on a much larger scale. A case in point: Jonesboro's first free public school, established in 1886, consisted of an elaborate two-story brick building with seven classrooms. Enrollment the first year, just slightly over two hundred pupils, quickly increased by 50 percent the following year. Regardless of the size of the school building or enrollment, Delta residents universally celebrated the birth of public schools in their communities with the same degree of pride and celebration.

With the dawn of the twentieth century, an even greater number of larger communities participated in a building frenzy. The schoolhouses built in this era tended to be much larger, with some Victorian in character, while in later decades, the new structures tended to be of a more pragmatic, much simpler design.

Rural schools, however, remained in one-room buildings, facilities that were quite often used by church groups as well. Many of these one-room schools were also, at times, overcrowded. In 1908, for example, one Arkansas Delta teacher, Lily Peter, had an enrollment of 26 students on her first day of school; however, this number quickly swelled to 47 within a few short weeks. Miss Peter, who made $45 per month, remarked about her situation in that one-room schoolhouse, "they are a pretty good bunch for a kid of seventeen to manage." This illustrates another characteristic of these one-room Delta schoolhouses: many of them were left under the care and guidance of individuals, often female, who were extremely young and had very limited formal education themselves. This chapter highlights the schooling provided to turn-of-the-century Arkansas Delta residents.

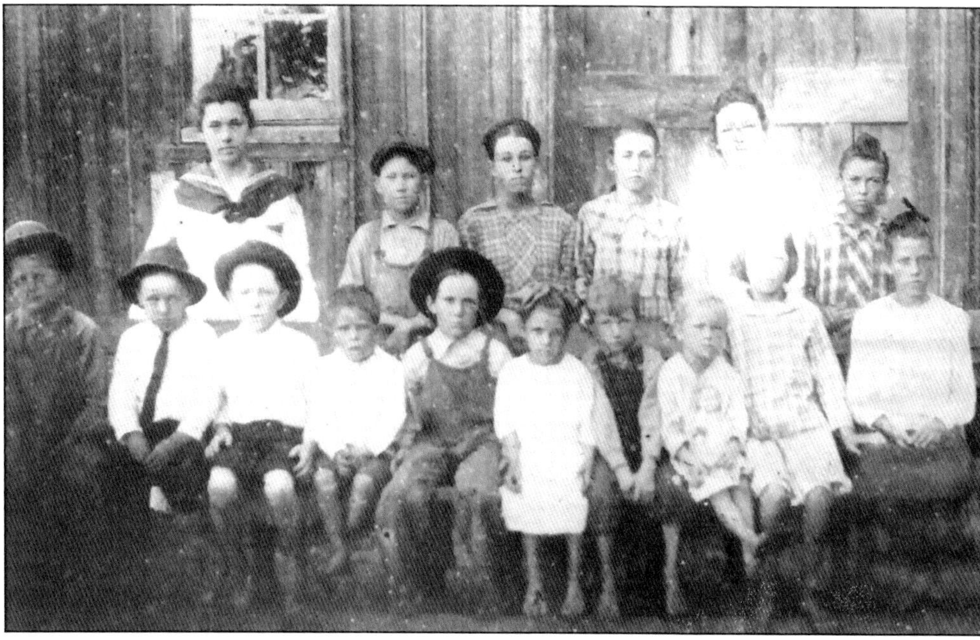

An Alsup School class gathered for this 1918 photograph. Alsup is a small community outside of Bay, in Craighead County. It is interesting to note the range of student ages. Some are clearly pre-school age, while others appear to be much closer to the end of their eighth grade education. (Courtesy of the Edgar Morrison Collection.)

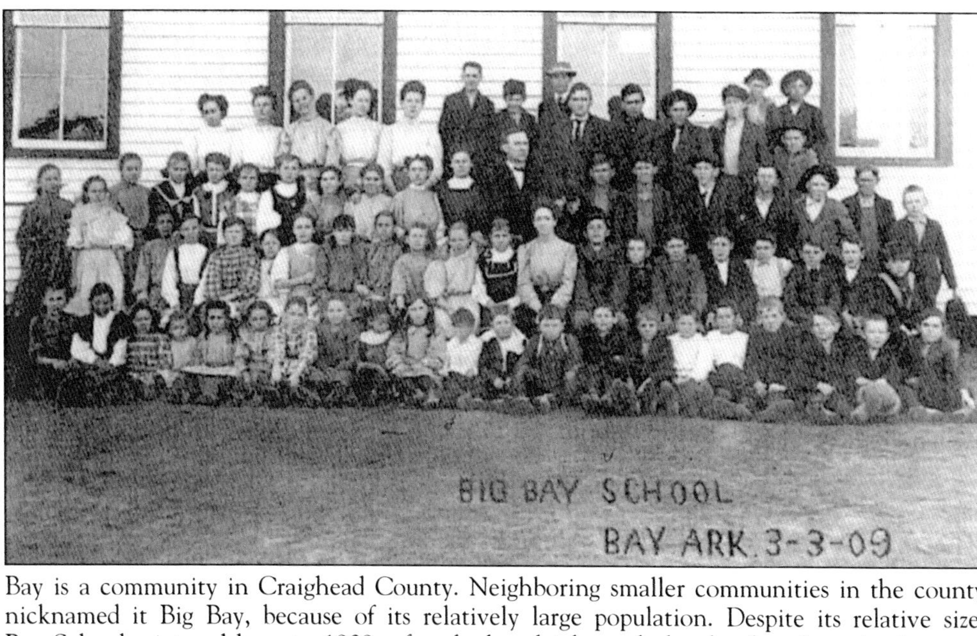

Bay is a community in Craighead County. Neighboring smaller communities in the county nicknamed it Big Bay, because of its relatively large population. Despite its relative size, Bay School, pictured here in 1909, often had multiple grade levels of students in the same classroom. (Courtesy of the Edgar Morrison Collection.)

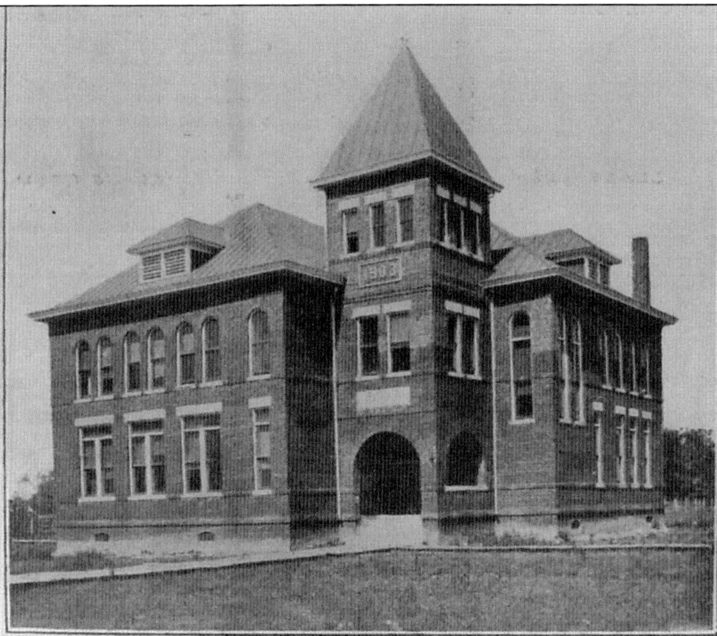

BLYTHEVILLE HIGH SCHOOL
Cost, $25,000.00; Erected, 1908; Edgar Williams, Superintendent

Blytheville High School, located in Mississippi County, is a short distance west of the Mississippi River. The first two decades of the twentieth century were part of a major building era in the Delta. One should note that relatively small communities spent a considerable amount of money for the era, constructing rather grandiose buildings. The $25,000 cost for this building would have been a significant investment for a small town in 1908. (Courtesy of Arkansas History Commission.)

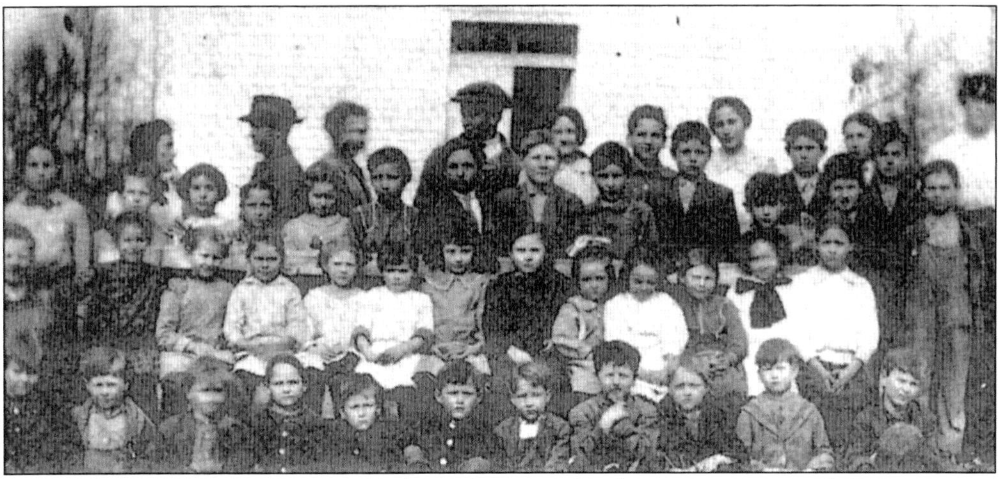

Miss Laura's class at Brown's School, located in Craighead County, is pictured above in 1912. Brown is a small community about 1 mile east of Bay. Students at Brown School range in age from first graders through what would now be considered high school. From the late nineteenth century through the mid-twentieth century, over one hundred schools dotted the countryside of Craighead County. Most of them consisted of one-room schoolhouses. (Courtesy of the Edgar Morrison Collection.)

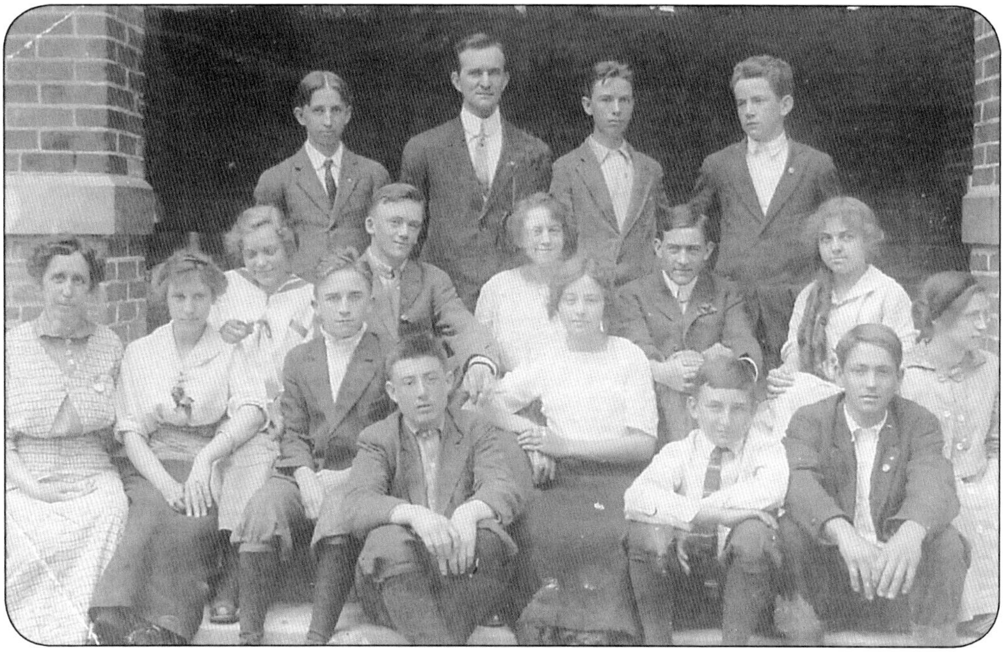

Corning is a community with a population today of slightly over three thousand. It is located in the northeastern corner of the state in Clay County. At the time this photograph of Corning's eighth grade class was taken in 1910, Corning represented one of the larger towns in the region, serving as both an economic and transportation hub for surrounding communities. (Courtesy of Arkansas History Commission.)

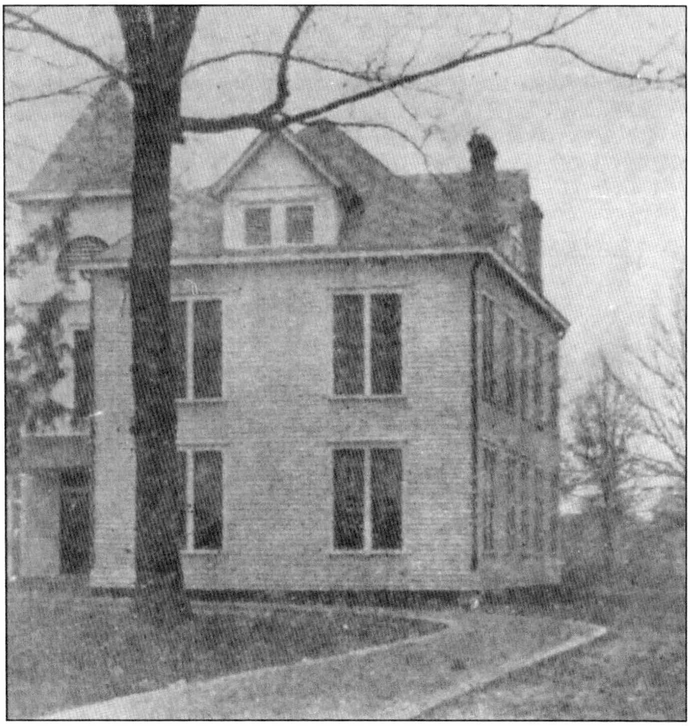

Des Arc was the largest community in Prarie County at the time of this early twentieth century photograph, thus it was named the county seat. Located on the banks of the White River, Des Arc's nearly two thousand residents proudly commemorate their history with a number of exhibits on display in the Prarie County Museum. This photograph of one of the earliest multi-classroom public schools in the region reflects an architectural hybrid design that resembles a home as well as a church in its appearance. (Courtesy of Arkansas History Commission.)

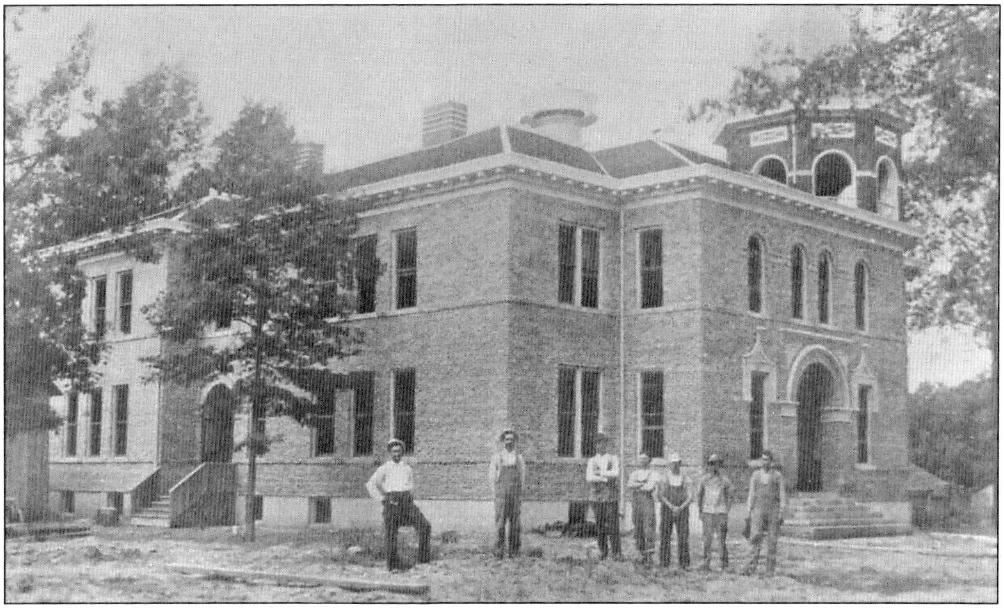

DeWitt serves as the county seat of the oldest county in the state, aptly named Arkansas County. Located on the Grand Prairie, DeWitt stands adjacent to the first permanent settlement, of European-American descent, in the lower Mississippi River Valley, at Arkansas Post. Because this region was among the first to be settled, by 1910, when DeWitt High School was constructed, residents were able to fund the $19,000 necessary to build one of the most elaborate school buildings in the entire Delta. (Courtesy of Arkansas History Commission.)

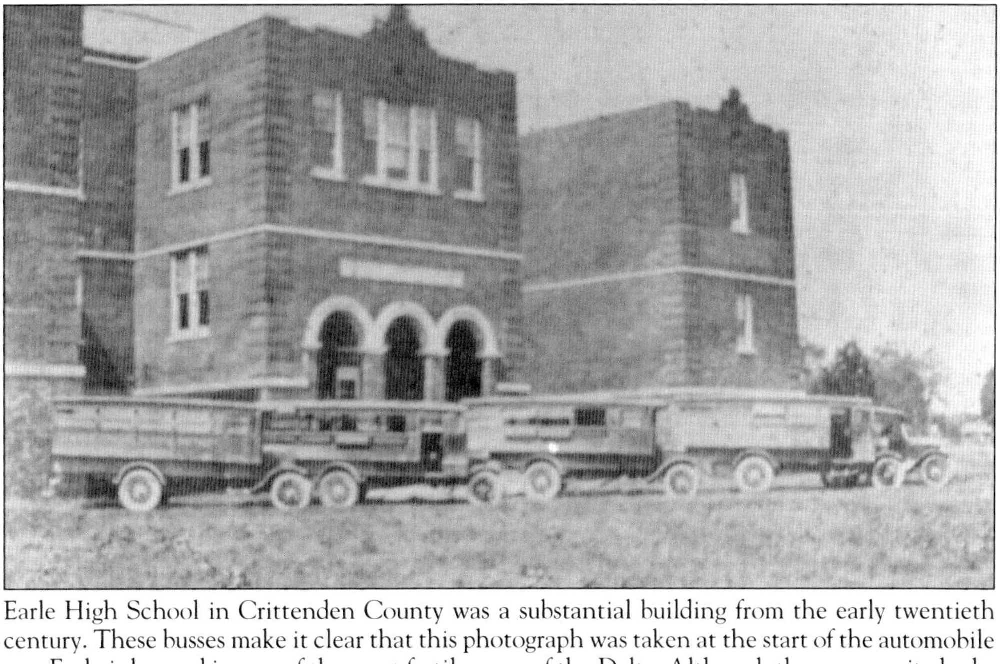

Earle High School in Crittenden County was a substantial building from the early twentieth century. These busses make it clear that this photograph was taken at the start of the automobile age. Earle is located in one of the most fertile areas of the Delta. Although the community had a large African-American population at the time, they were not allowed to attend school at this location. (Courtesy of Arkansas History Commission.)

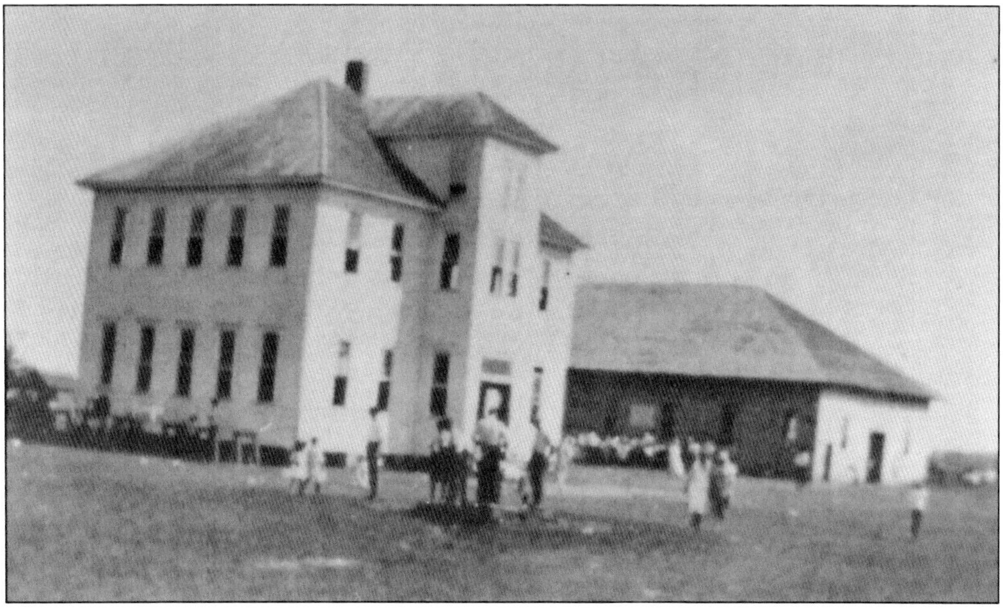

Fairview High School in St. Francis County was built during the first decades of the twentieth century. This serves to illustrate the major building movement that took place throughout the Delta, beginning in 1904 and continuing through 1920. Fairview was a small community located in an agriculturally rich area along the banks of the Mississippi River. (Courtesy of Arkansas History Commission.)

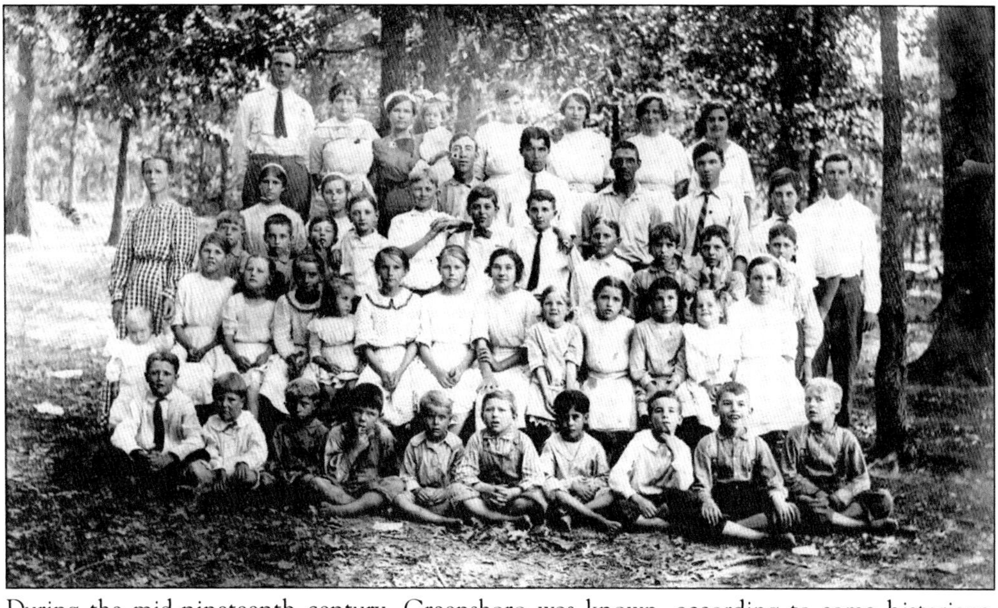

During the mid-nineteenth century, Greensboro was known, according to some historians, as the "first metropolis of northeast Arkansas." At first located in Greene County, hence the name, it was later made a part of the newly established county of Craighead in 1859. For a number of decades thereafter, Greensboro remained the largest community in the county, as evidenced in this 1903 photograph of Greensboro School students and faculty. (Courtesy of Arkansas State University Museum.)

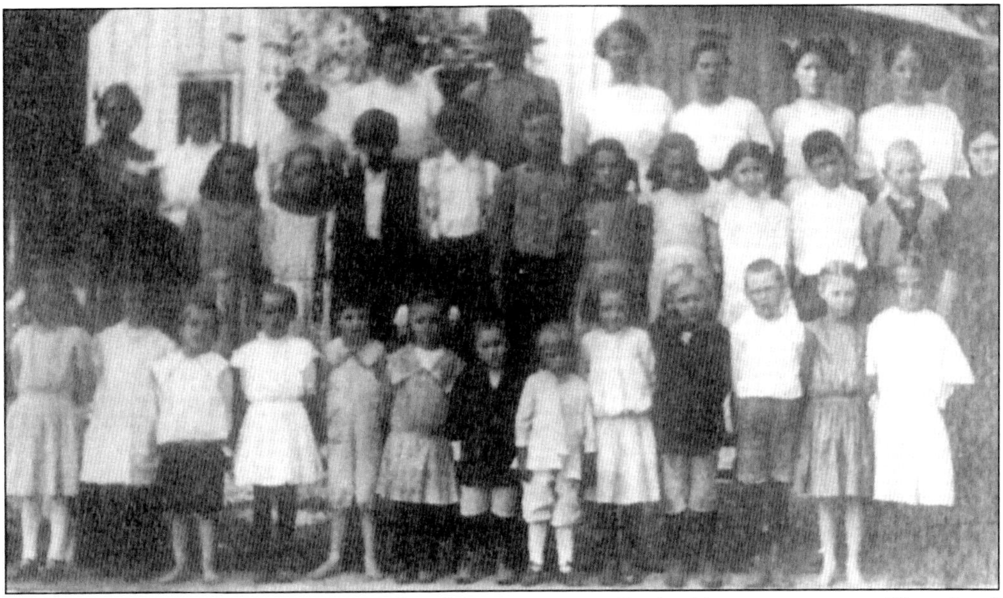

In 1912, Gum Point, located in Craighead County, was still a budding community. The school building in the background is evidence of the great effort in the early twentieth century to provide education throughout the Delta. However, many of these little communities such as Gum Point simply disappeared over time, merging with larger towns. (Courtesy of the Edgar Morrison Collection.)

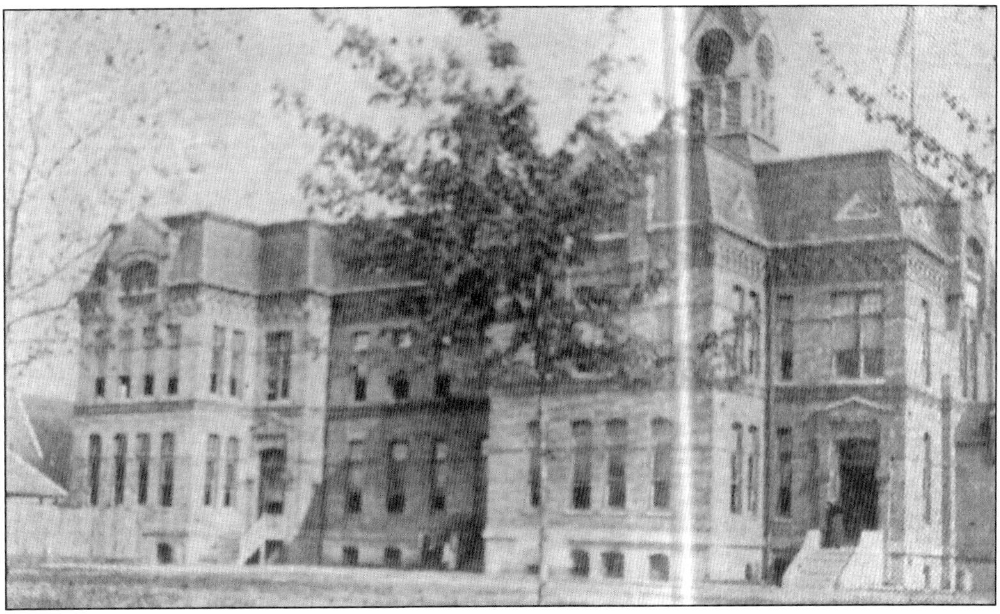

Helena is located on the Mississippi state border along the banks of the Mississippi River. Helena, with its current population of nearly seven thousand, serves as the county seat of Phillips County. This early twentieth century photograph of Helena Public Schools demonstrates the abundance of pride and wealth in the region at the time. Both of these commodities were necessary to build what some historians have referred to as the "most elegant school house in the entire Delta during the first quarter of the twentieth century." (Courtesy of Arkansas History Commission.)

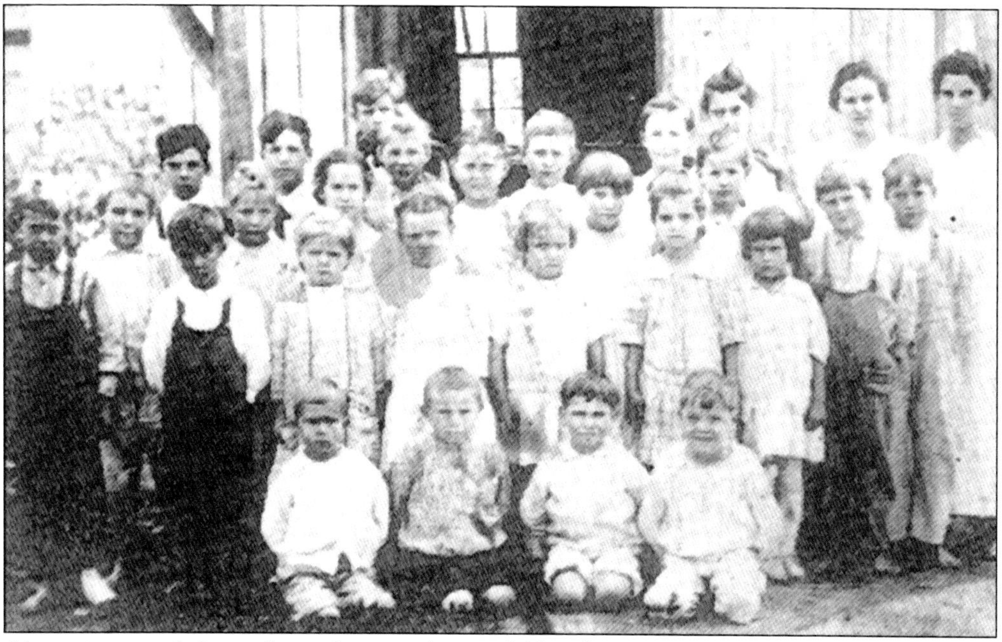

Above is one of the earliest photographs available of Herget Public School, with students assembled outside in 1917. This was the only public school to exist in the tiny community of Herget, which all but disappeared over time. With the changes in population, many small schools such as this were consolidated into larger school districts. (Courtesy of the Edgar Morrison Collection.)

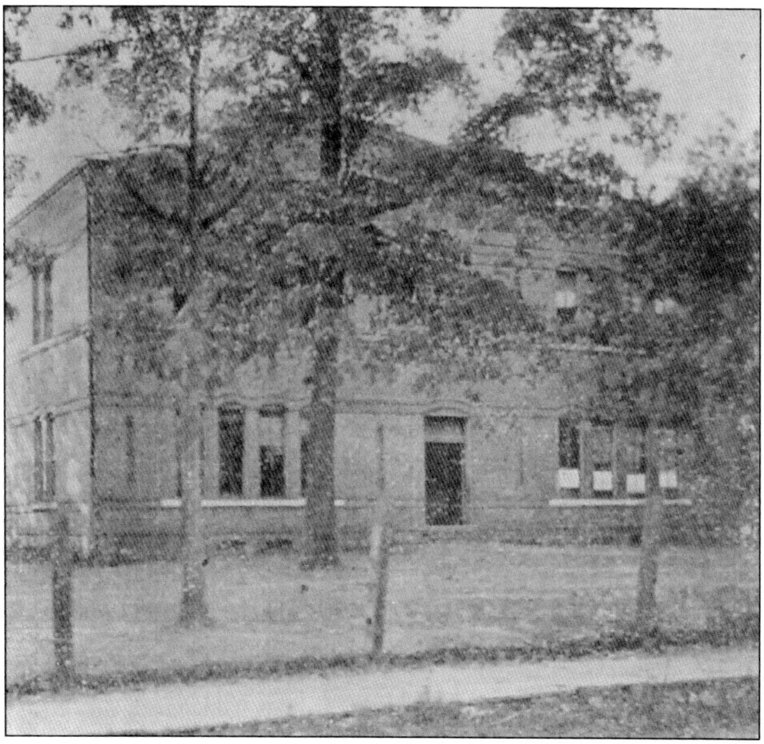

Jonesboro Public School, Craighead County, was erected at the close of the nineteenth century. The first school in Jonesboro was a family house, which opened in 1886. The city was growing rapidly enough that it quickly established several elementary schools as well as a high school within a decade. (Courtesy of Arkansas History Commission.)

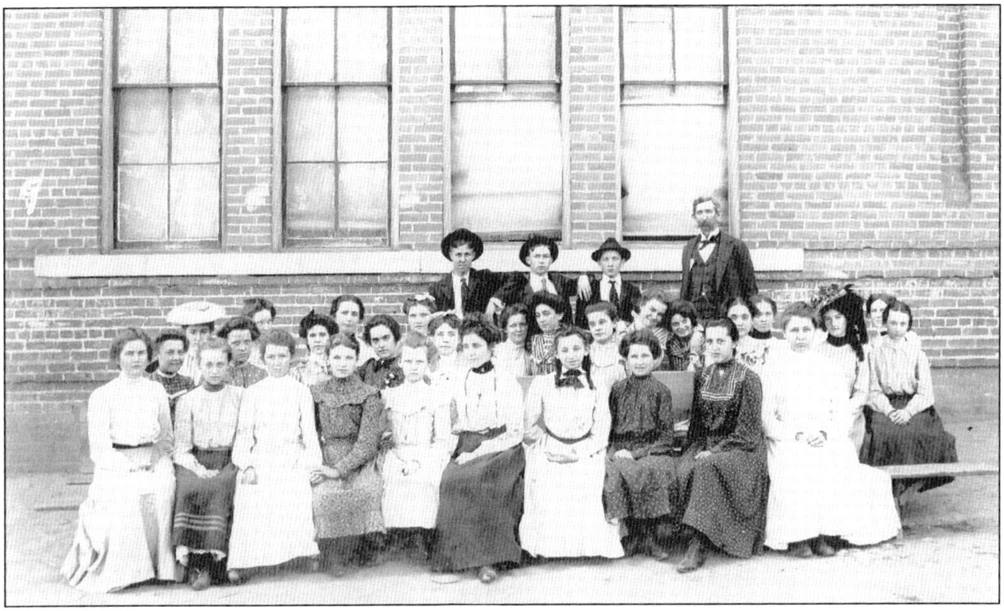

Few changes in Delta public education were ushered in with the new century. This 1902 photograph of these well-dressed middle and upper-class Jonesboro High School students serves as a reminder of the fact that a high school education was still primarily reserved for the wealthy in society. (Courtesy of Arkansas State University Museum.)

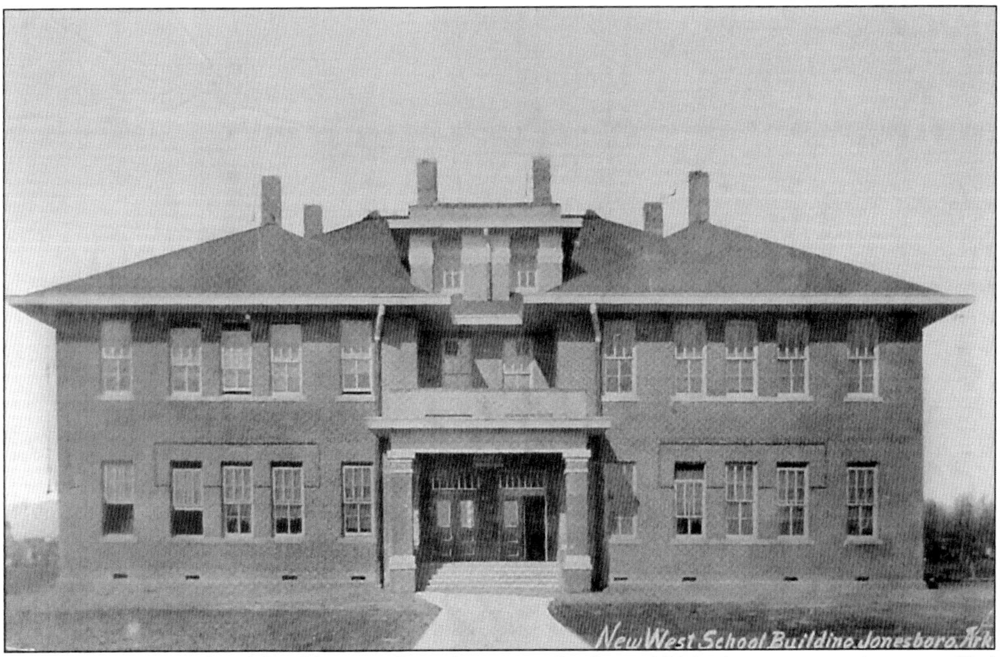

The New West School Building in Jonesboro was built in 1914. At one time it was called the James Reddman School, being named after its first principal. Students still remember the slide fire escape on the west side of the building and how much fun they had during fire drills. (Courtesy of Arkansas History Commission.)

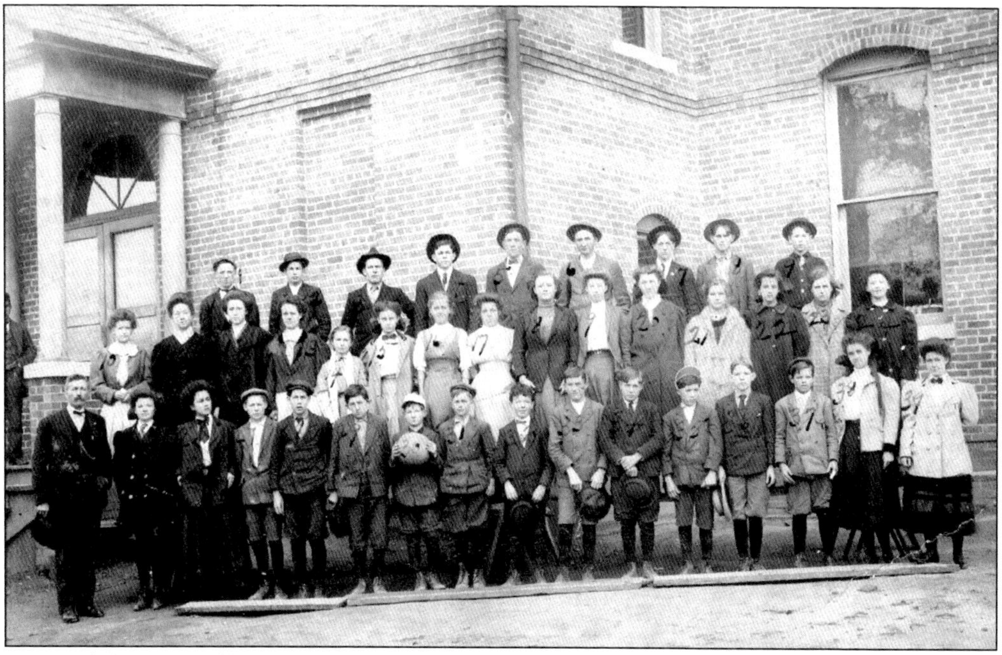

Many of the more affluent residents of Jonesboro sent their children to Old East School. This well-dressed group of students are accompanied by their principal, H.W. Wilkins, pictured on the far left, for this 1905 class photo on the front lawn of their brick, two-story school. (Courtesy of Arkansas State University Museum.)

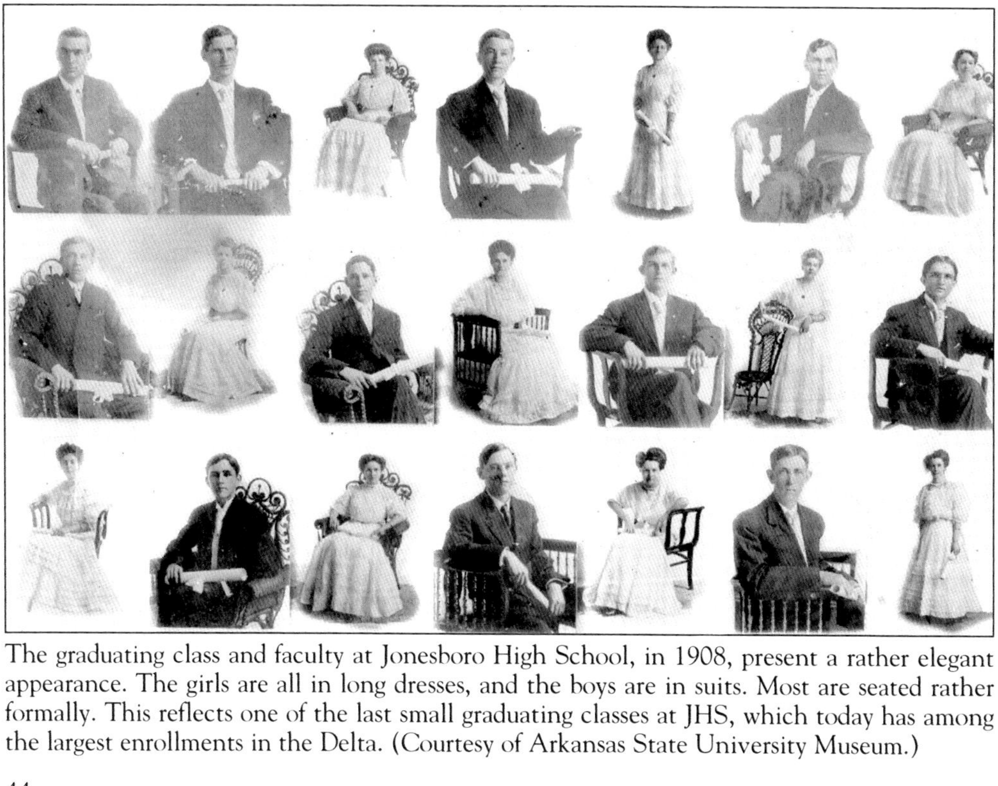

The graduating class and faculty at Jonesboro High School, in 1908, present a rather elegant appearance. The girls are all in long dresses, and the boys are in suits. Most are seated rather formally. This reflects one of the last small graduating classes at JHS, which today has among the largest enrollments in the Delta. (Courtesy of Arkansas State University Museum.)

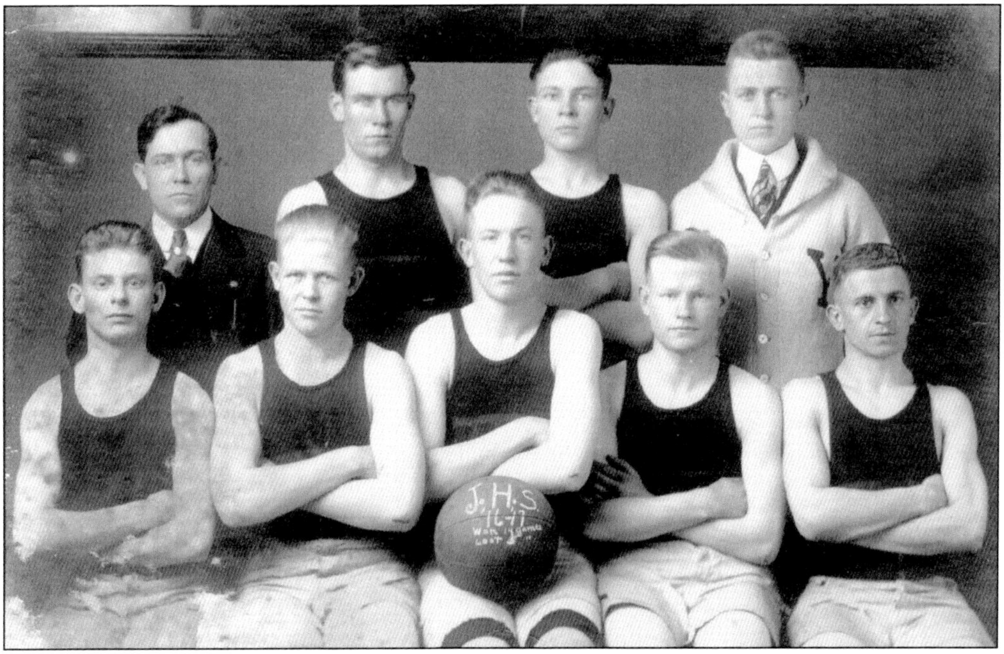

The Jonesboro High School basketball team of 1916–17 demonstrates the continuing importance of organized sports in the region. Still, the fact that there were only seven boys on the team suggests that students were not as interested as the adults. The size of the boys makes it clear that basketball was a different game in this era. (Courtesy of Arkansas State University Museum.)

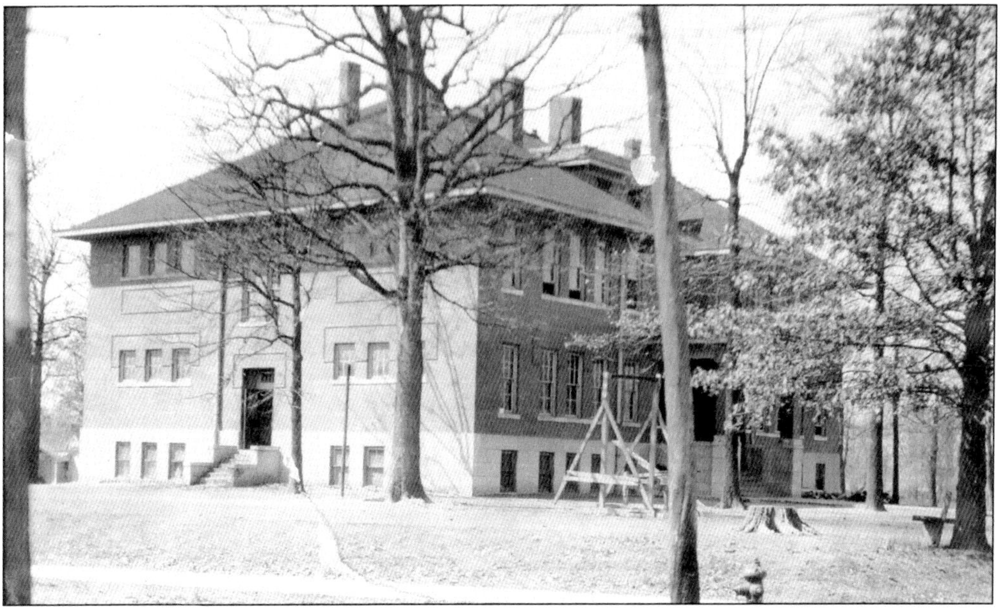

The Old South School in Jonesboro was destroyed in 1956; however, a new building was erected within a few months. This development pattern throughout the Delta seems quite common. The district built a number of structures in the early part of the century and then began to replace them in the 1950s, another period of prosperity. (Courtesy of Arkansas State University Museum.)

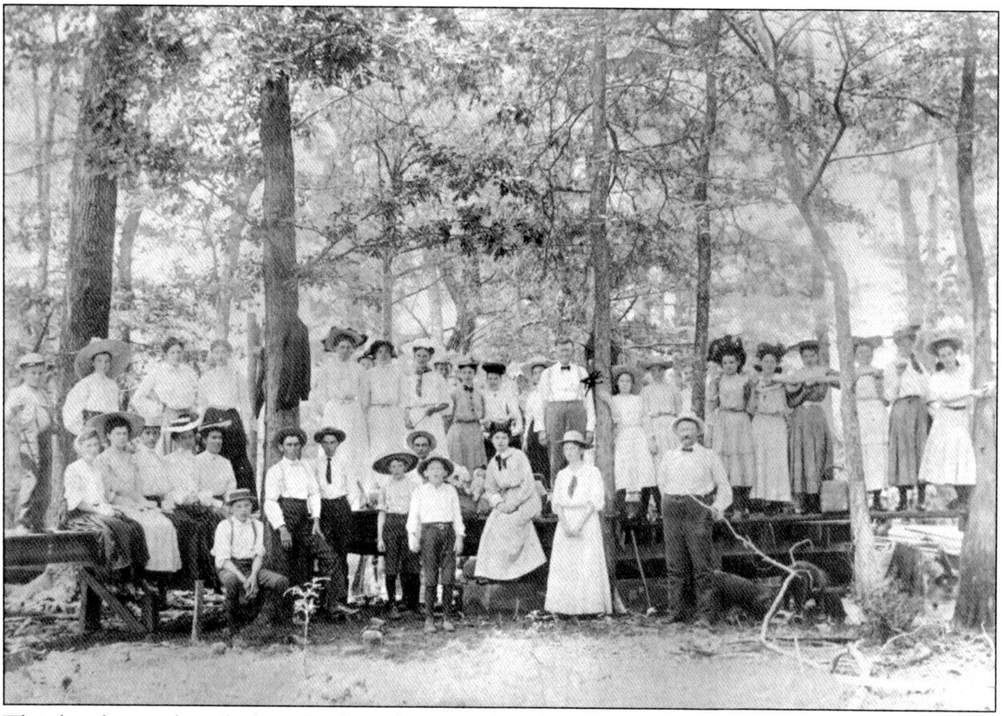

This has been identified as the Jonesboro High School senior class of 1913, although several boys in the front appear to be much younger than traditional seniors. Note the continued predominance of females in the turn-of-the-century graduating classes. (Courtesy of Arkansas State University Museum.)

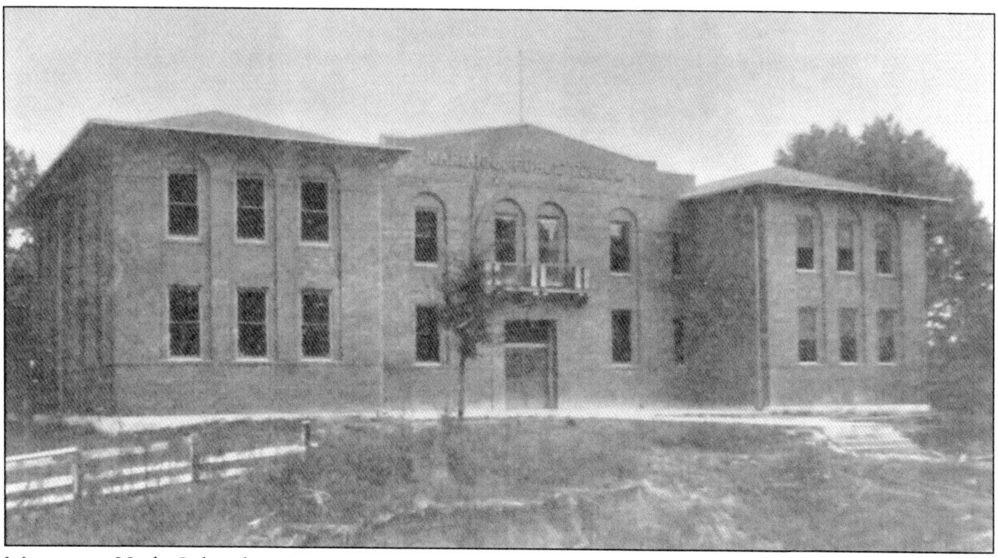

Marianna High School in Lee County is a good representation of the substantial number of traditional brick buildings that characterized the larger public schools constructed in the Delta during this period. It was erected in 1906, at a cost of $25,000. Marianna is located a few miles west of the Mississippi River in a very fertile agricultural region. (Courtesy of Arkansas History Commission.)

Marion High School in Crittenden County was built in 1912, at a cost of $35,000. Marion is a community on the banks of the Mississippi River that has benefited greatly from its rich soil and ideal location in the Delta. The fact that the Marion school district could spend $35,000 in 1912 to build a high school is an indication of great wealth. (Courtesy of Arkansas History Commission.)

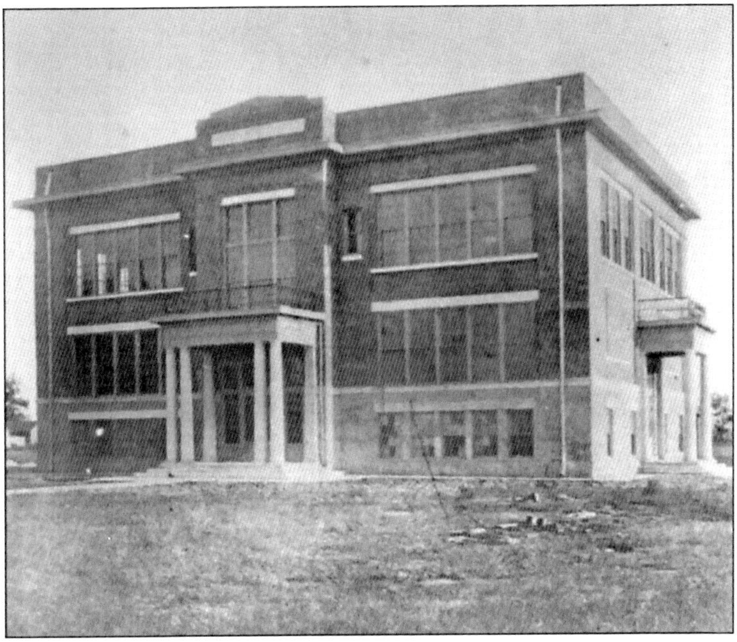

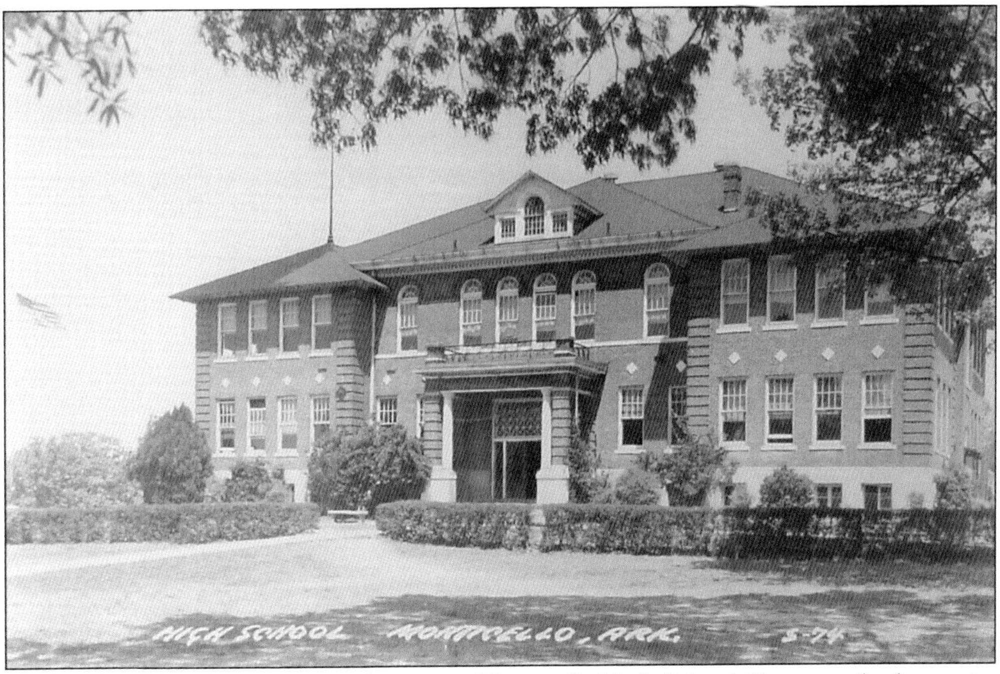

This photograph of early twentieth century Monticello High School illustrates the larger size of the community as well as the pragmatic nature of its residents. Monticello, located on the banks of the Saline River adjacent to Seven Devils Swamp, has always been one of the largest communities in the region. With a population today of well over eight thousand, it serves as the county seat of Drew County. (Courtesy of the Arkansas History Commission.)

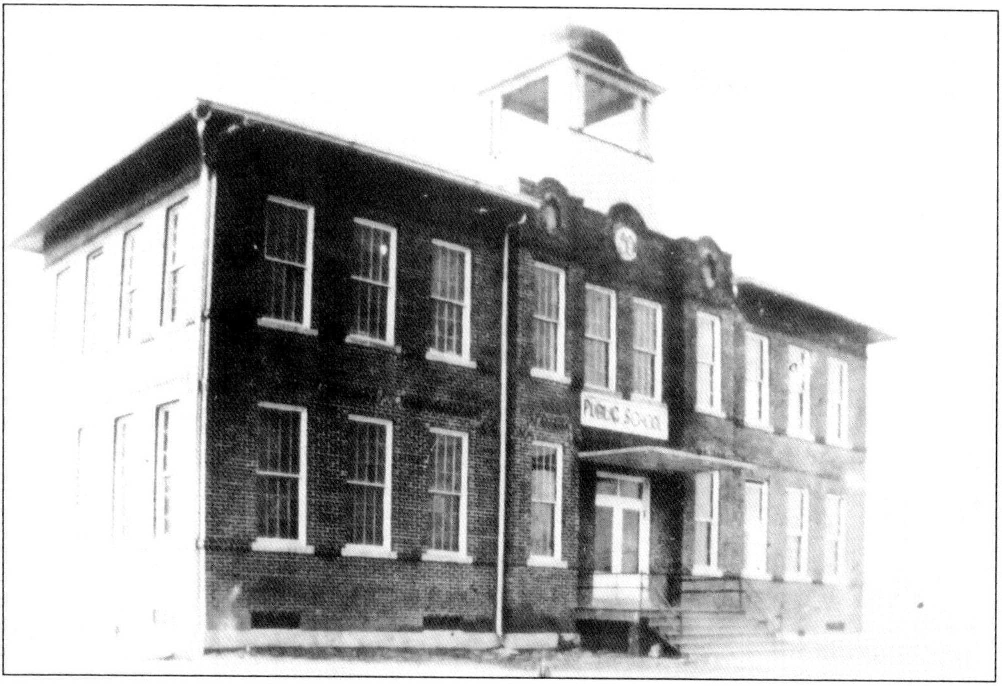

Following the 1859 creation of Craighead County, which was carved out of land taken form Greene, Poinsett, and Mississippi Counties, population in the region grew at unprecedented rates. Within a few decades, Nettleton was constructing a new public school building, pictured above, to accommodate the swelling enrollment. Pictured below is one of the first Nettleton School group photographs from 1902. (Nettleton Public Schools.)

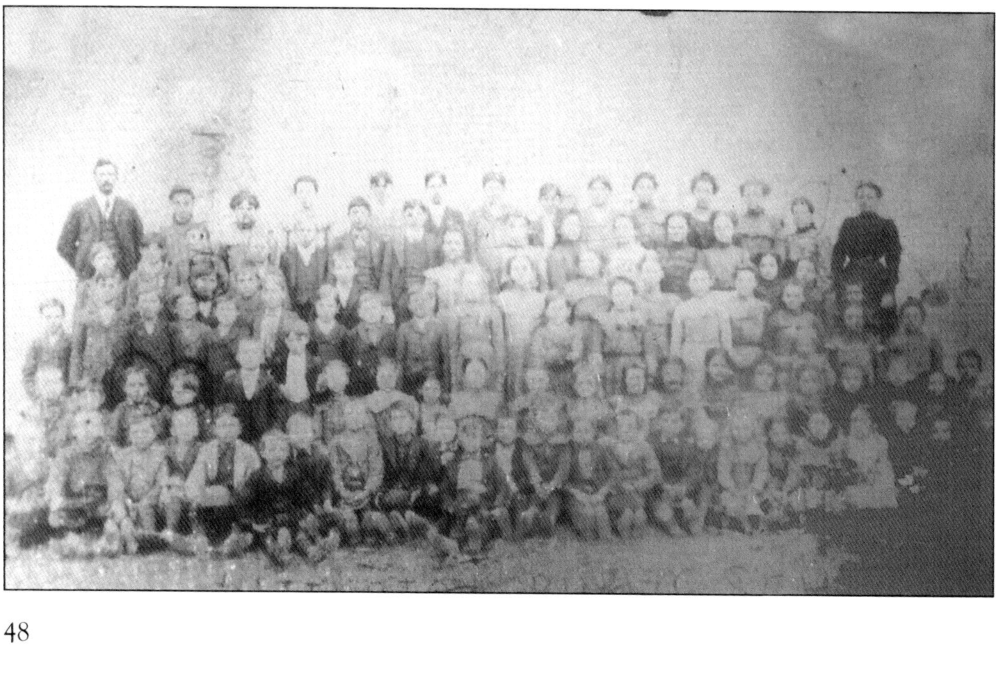

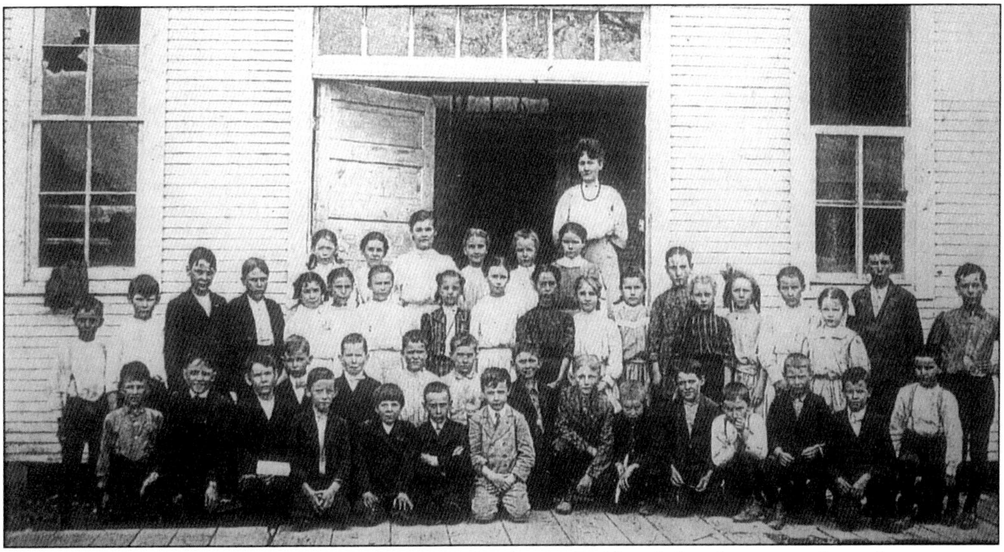

Prior to the 1908 construction of the new Nettleton Public School, pictured on the opposite page, students attended classes in this much less appealing building located on School Street. The lack of aesthetics, however, did not deter this class from proudly posing for a class photo in 1905 in front of the building. (Nettleton Public Schools.)

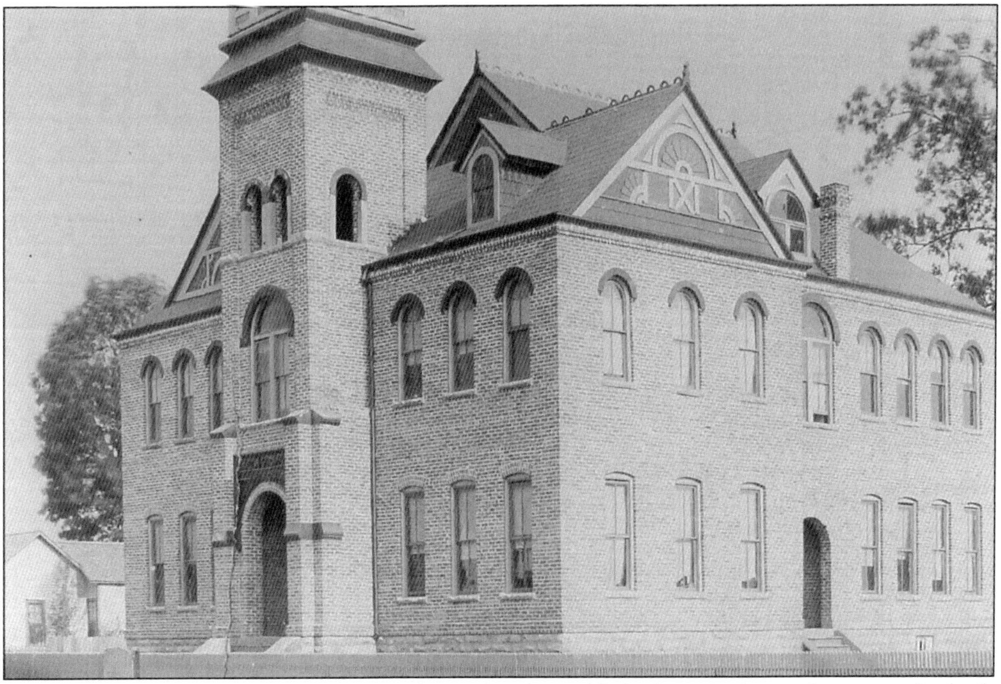

Newport School represents the first free school established in Jackson County, of which Newport serves as county seat, and among the first constructed in the Delta. Its grandness and symmetry made it the largest, most attractive building in Newport for nearly half a century. Located on the banks of the White River, Newport, today with a population just under seven thousand, serves as the political and economic center for the entire county. (Courtesy of the Arkansas History Commission.)

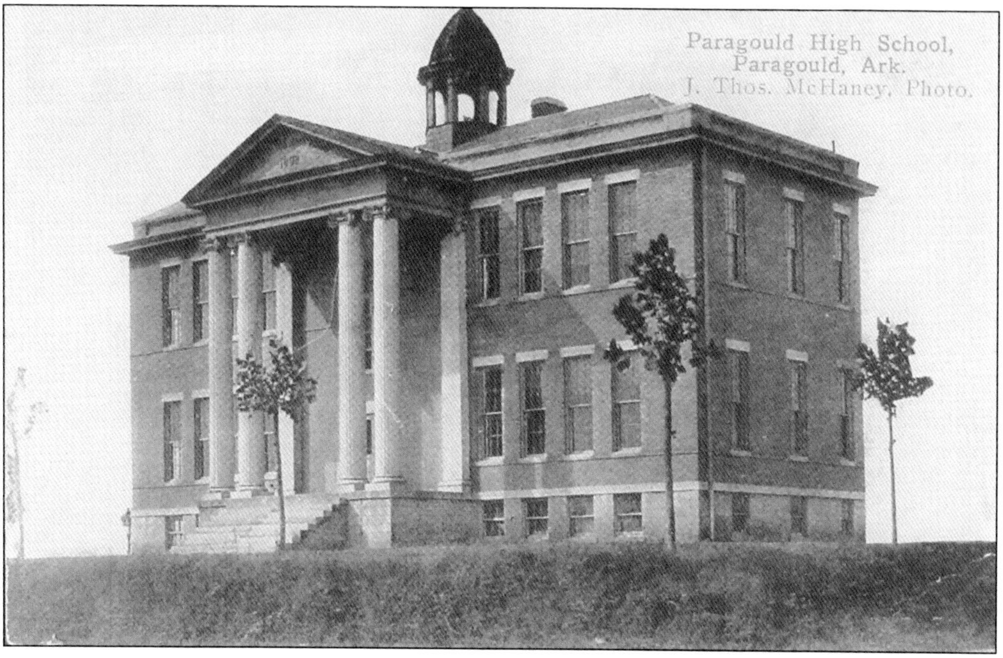

Along the banks of the St. Francis River, near the Missouri border, reside the residents of Paragould. Paragould, the county seat of Greene County, has always been among the largest communities in the Delta, with a present population of nearly 22,000. The first school in Paragould was opened in 1909. The photograph above of the "new" Paragould High School reflects the impressive, neo-classic design of other buildings erected in the early twentieth century. As Paragould continued to grow rapidly, city fathers soon found the need to expand and modernize the high school yet again, as illustrated in the photograph below. (Courtesy of the Arkansas History Commission.)

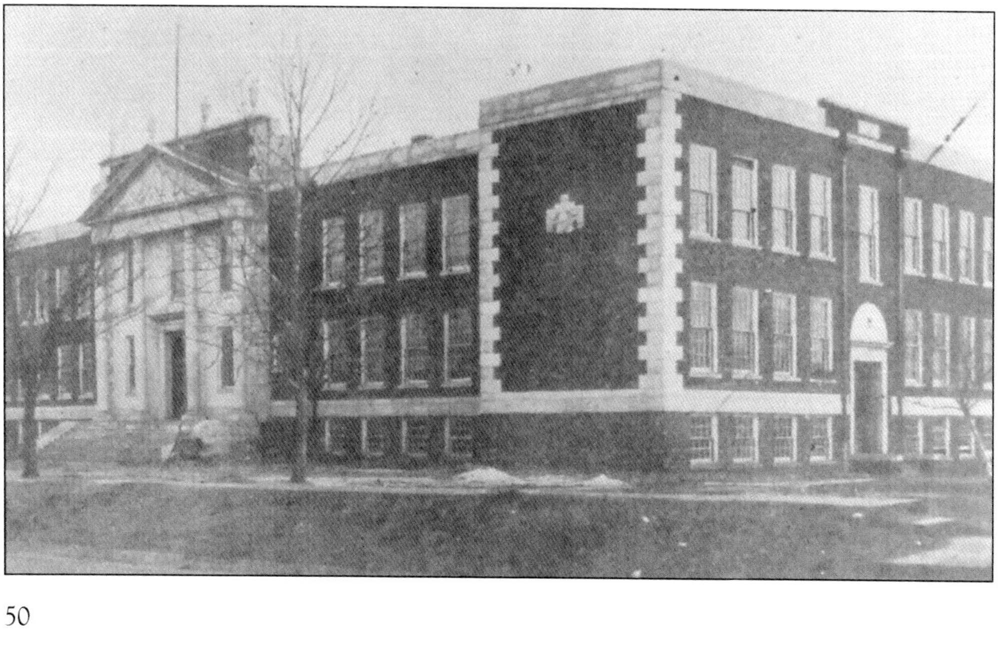

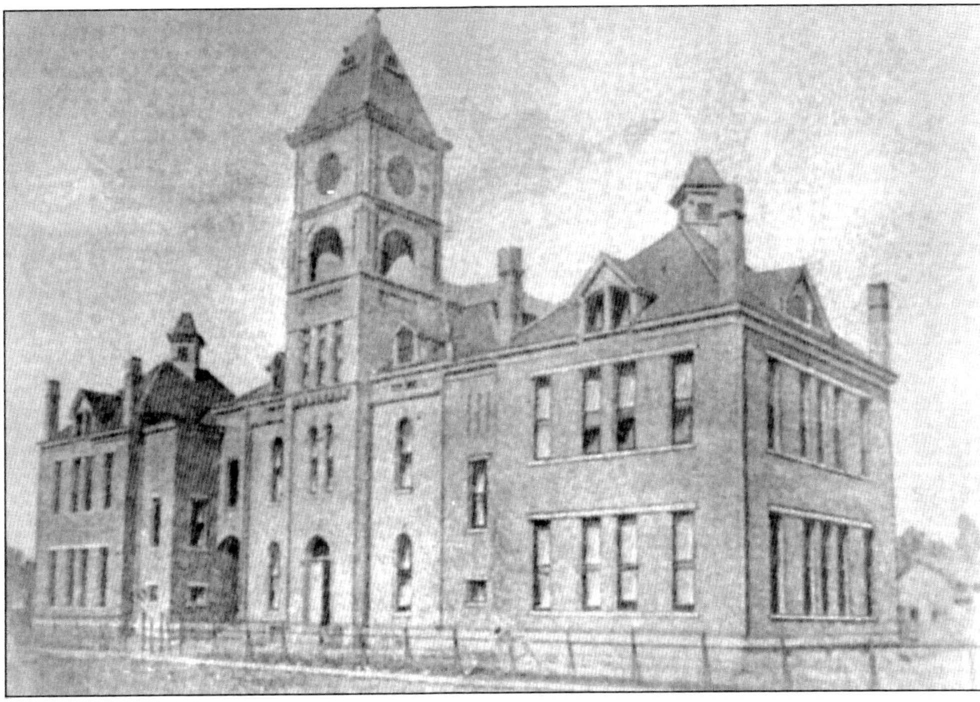

Located on the banks of the Arkansas River, Pine Bluff represents the largest city on the western edge of the Delta, with a current population of 53,000. It is also home to the second largest institution of higher learning in the Delta, the University of Arkansas at Pine Bluff. Because of its large population and the fact that it also serves as the county seat of Jefferson County, some of the first schools constructed in the southern region of the Delta were located in Pine Bluff, including Sixth Avenue School pictured above. Pine Bluff was also among the first communities in the Delta to build a high school for its residents. The postcard below illustrates the pride residents had for their city's high school. (Courtesy of the Arkansas History Commission.)

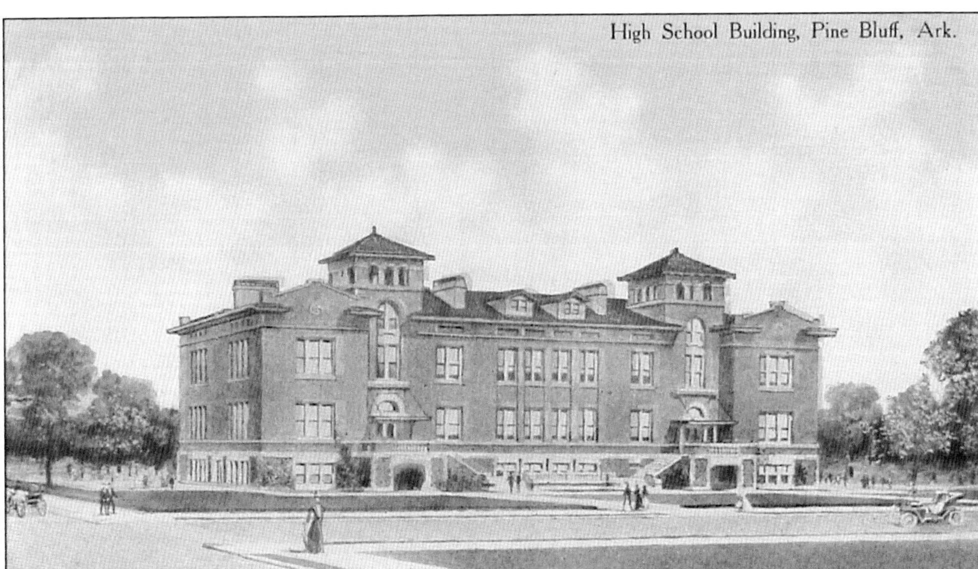

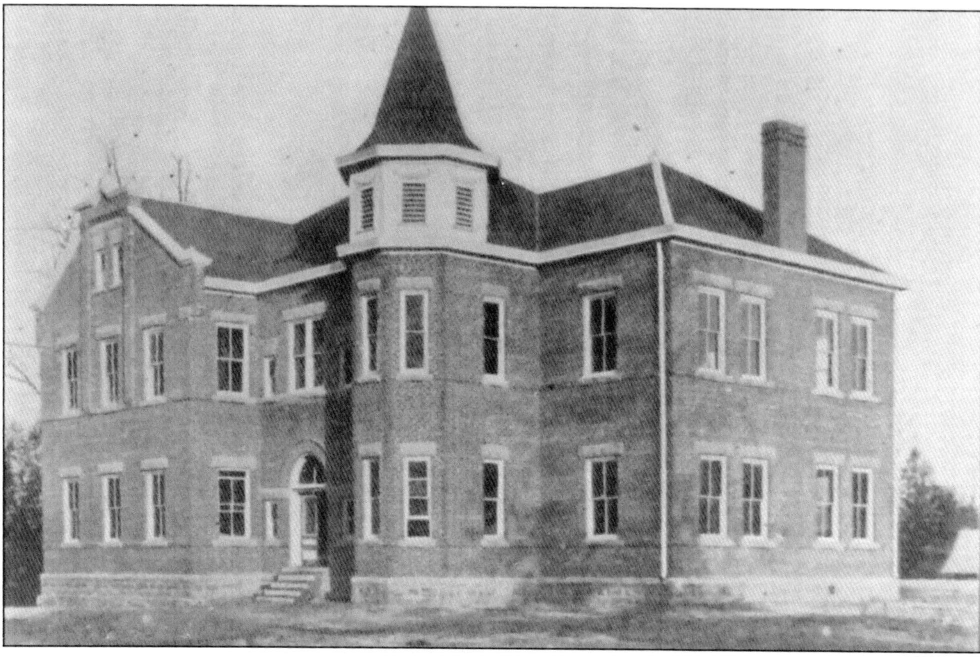

The community of Pocahontas is located on the banks of the Black River, near the Missouri border. Pocahontas, with a population today of just over 6,500, has always served as the county seat of Randolph County. The photo above depicts one of the first twentieth century schools constructed in Pocahontas, erected in 1904. Pictured below is one of the first classes to graduate from the newly constructed school. (Courtesy of Arkansas History Commission.)

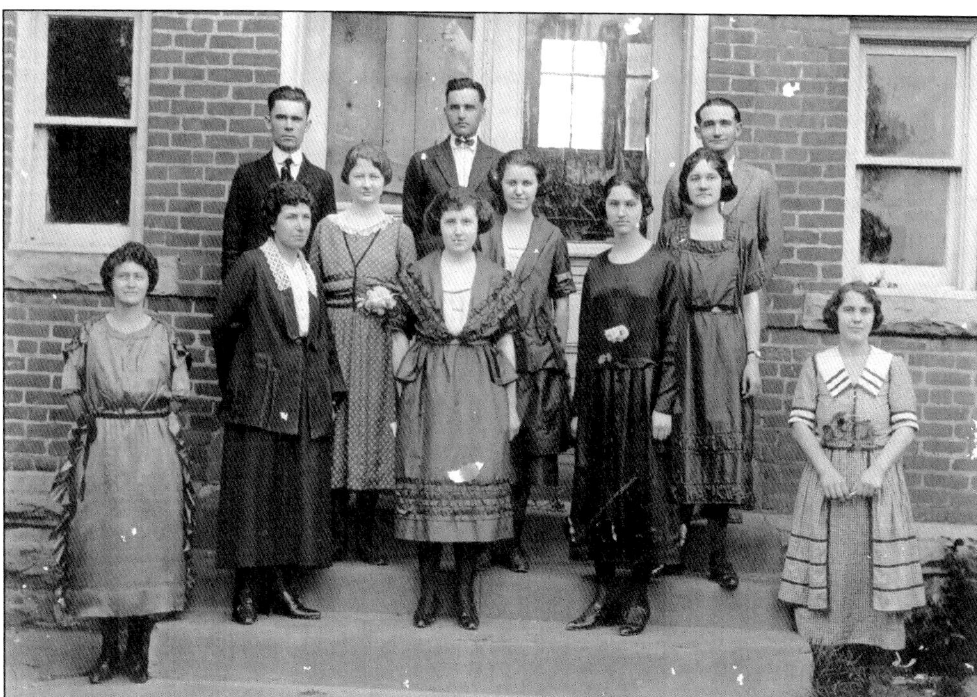

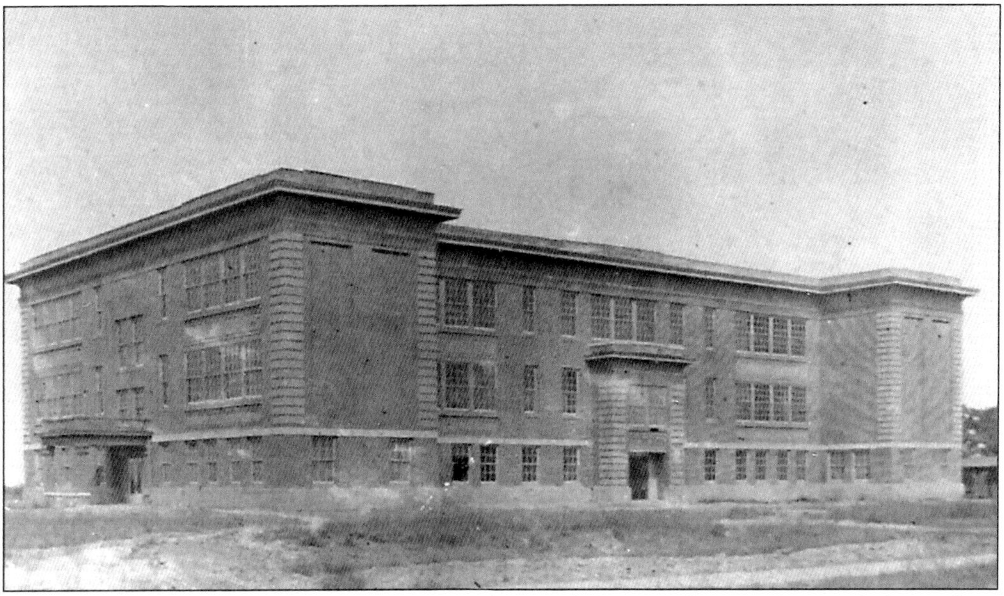

Stuttgart is a community today with a population slightly under ten thousand, located on the banks of the White River near Peckerwood Lake in Arkansas County. In 1911, due to increased enrollment, Stuttgart residents decided to construct a new school at a cost of $50,000. It would remain one of the largest in the region for nearly a decade. (Courtesy of Arkansas History Commission.)

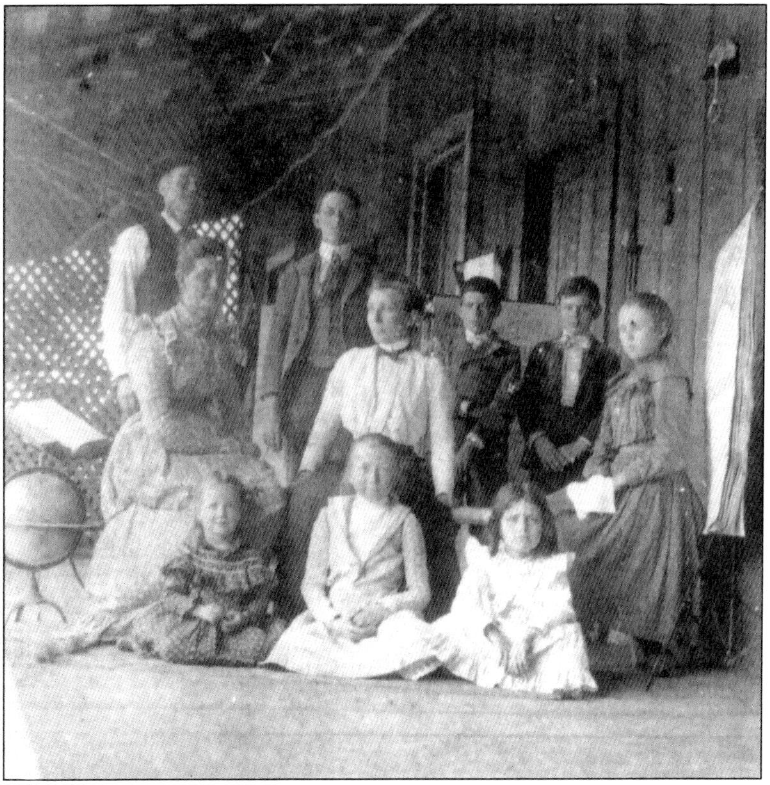

Miss Tommie Owens and her students pose on the back porch of E.M. Trippe's home, known as School Trippe, in McGhee, for this 1900 photograph. Among Miss Owens' many students at this one-room school located in Desha County were her two nieces. (Courtesy of Arkansas History Commission.)

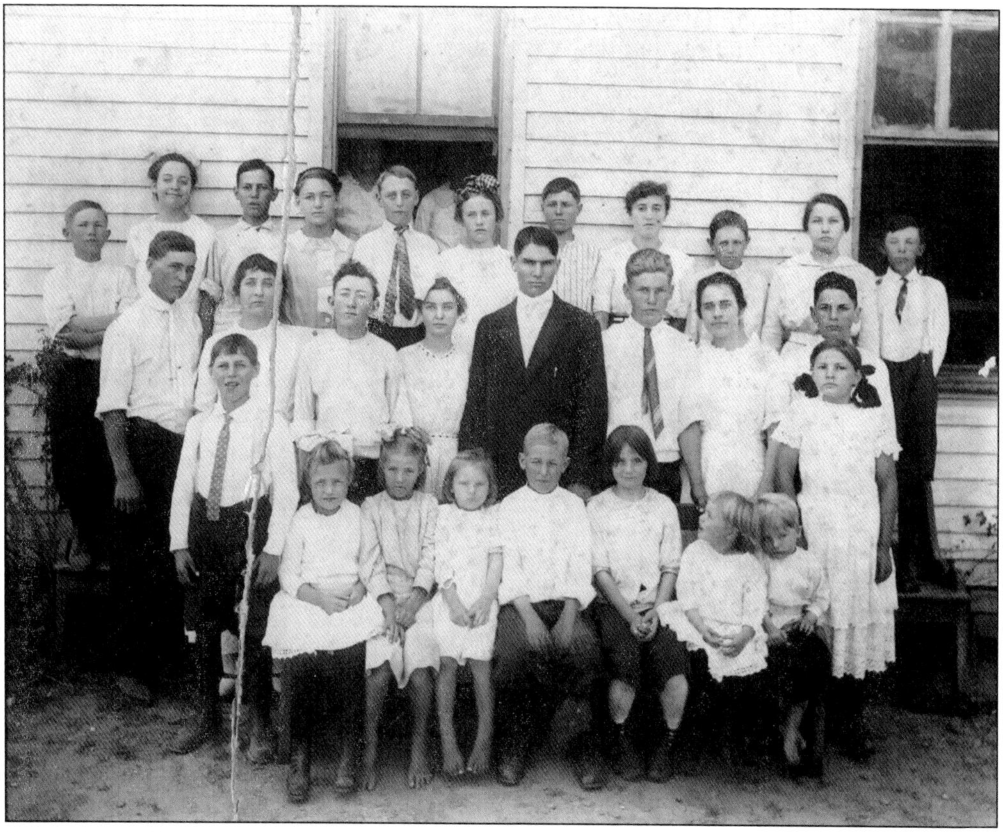

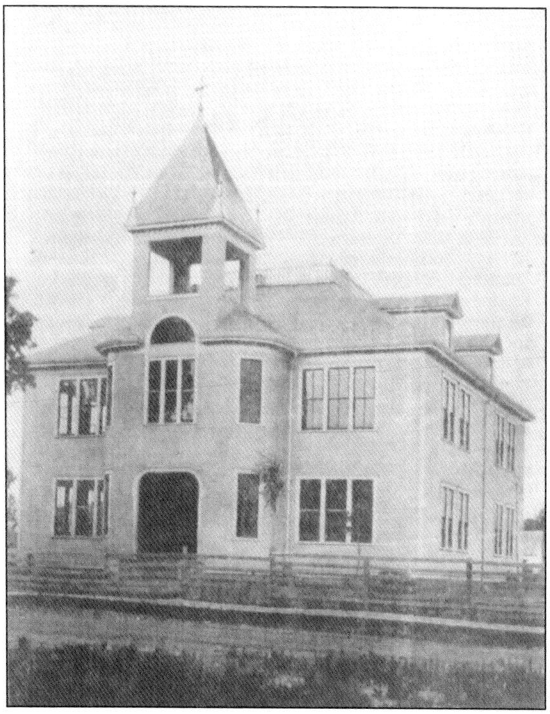

Valley View School was recently ranked second in the state on the Annual School Report Card. Although Valley View represents one of the fastest growing communities in the Delta at the close of the twentieth century, it was among the smallest in Craighead County at the time of this 1915 photograph. (Courtesy of Arkansas State University Museum.)

Constructed at the turn of the century, Warren Public School was the largest school in Bradley County, of which Warren serves as county seat, and one of the grandest schools found in the Delta at the time. Note the hybrid design of the building, which mirrors the architectural appearance of a large home and/or church. (Courtesy of Arkansas History Commission.)

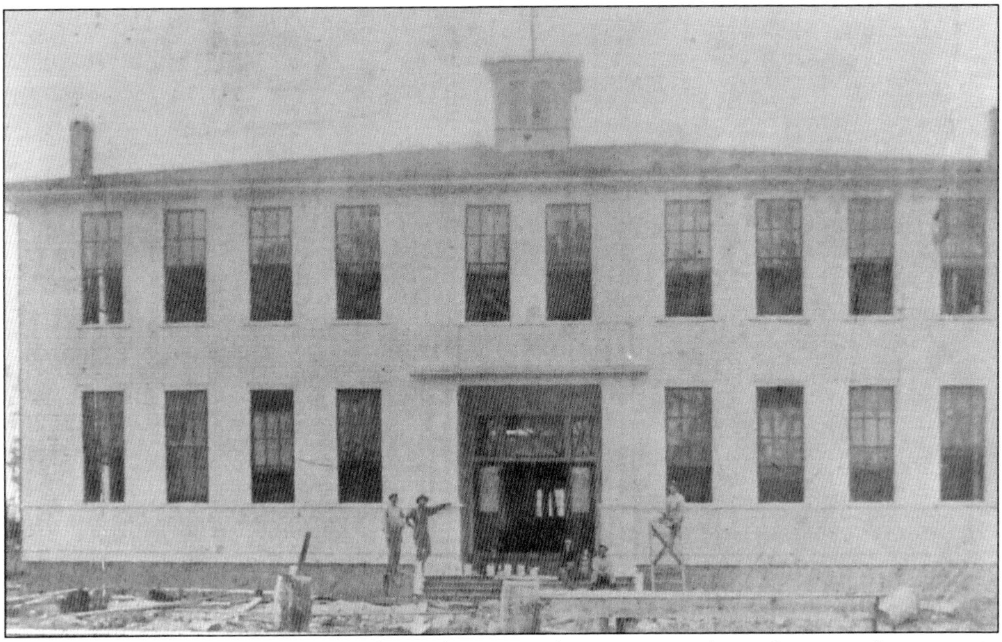

Although Warren's population in the early twentieth century was but a fraction of its near six thousand total today, its school enrollment was growing at such an incredible rate that a high school was erected in 1911, at a cost of $40,000, to accommodate the large student population at the time. (Courtesy of Arkansas History Commission.)

Wynne is located on the banks of the L'Anguille River, near the Tennessee border. It has always served as the county seat of Cross County. This postcard portrays the "modern" public school that was constructed in 1904, when E.W. Doran was serving as principal. (Courtesy of the Arkansas History Commission.)

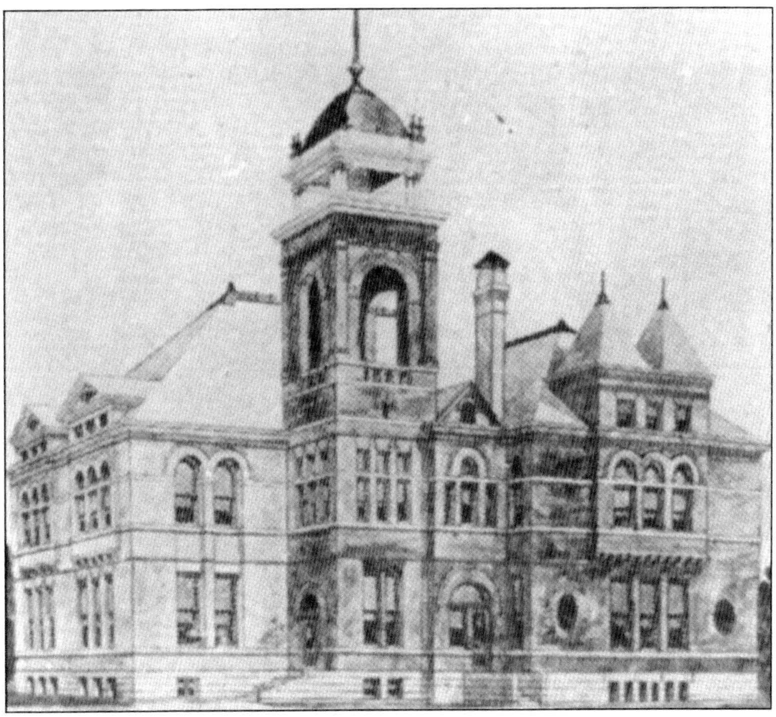

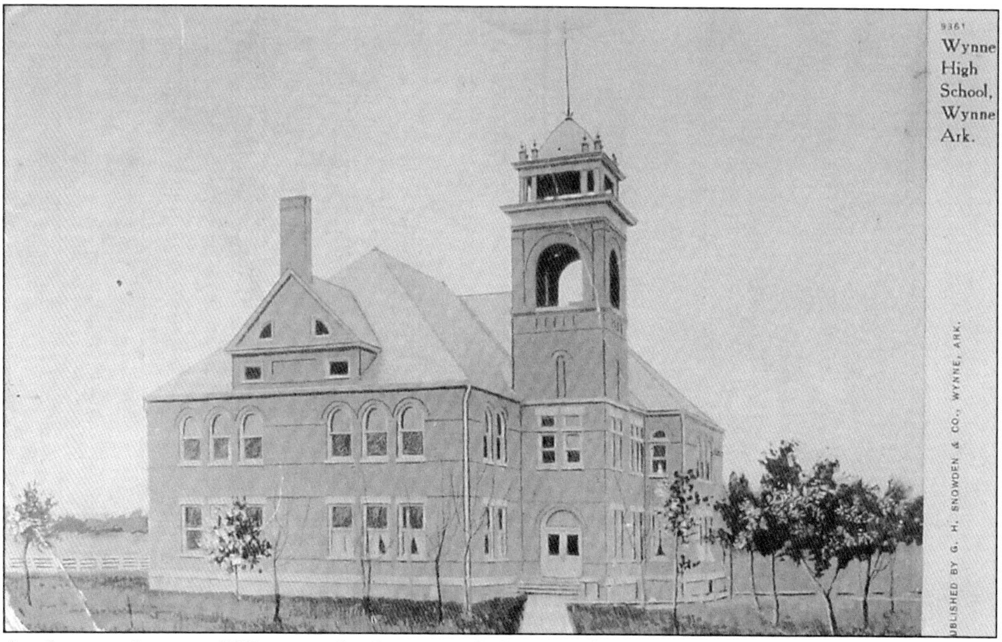

As the population of Wynne, which currently has nearly nine thousand residents, continued to grow throughout the first part of the twentieth century, the need for a new high school, pictured above, became quite apparent. Wynne High School was clearly designed to closely match the earlier public school, which now housed the elementary grades, erected in 1904. In addition to expanding its number of classrooms, Wynne also started offering more courses, such as Mrs. Annie Marks Coffin's music class, pictured below. (Courtesy the Arkansas History Commission.)

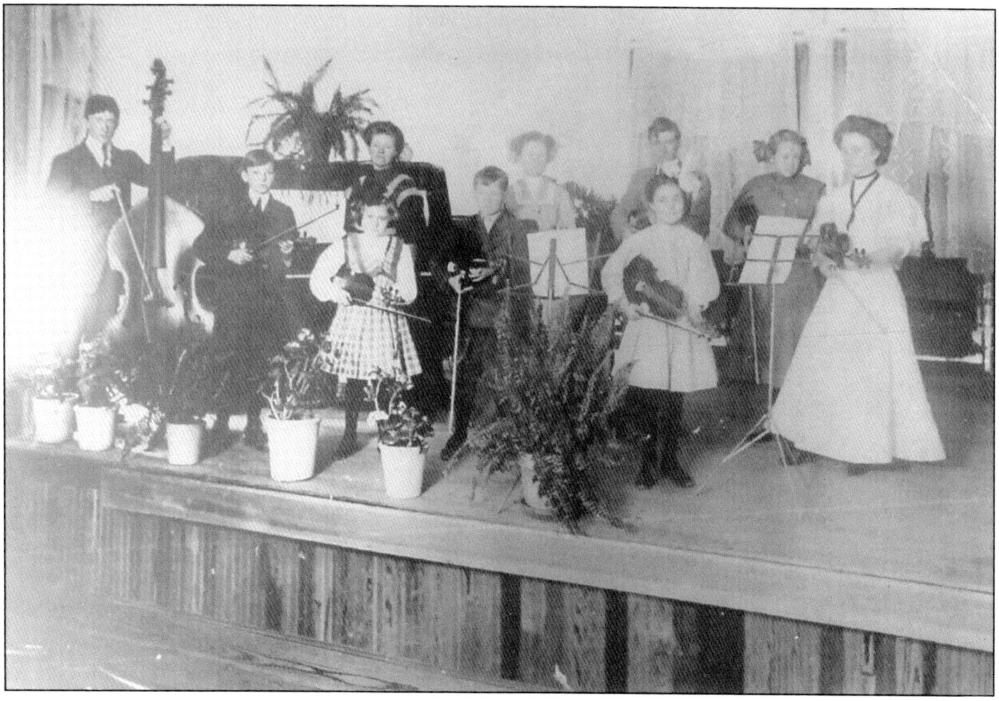

Four

1920s
The "Building Twenties"

During the 1920s, the Arkansas Delta witnessed a period of continued growth. The construction of school buildings during this period was second only to the building boom that ushered in the twentieth century. This time, however, the buildings were perhaps a bit less majestic and more pragmatic. Community pride in the local schools was perhaps more evident during this period than any other in the history of the Arkansas Delta. Students were afforded more opportunities than ever before to become involved in co-curricular activities, such as the arts and sports.

It is also during the "building twenties" that the Delta began to develop a more standardized framework for hiring teachers and implementing their curricula. Despite the fact that teacher contracts from this period reflect a seemingly high degree of rigor, a shortage of well-trained and experienced teachers in the region meant that the majority of those individuals hired to teach in Delta schools had little training beyond the upper grade levels they were often expected to teach. In addition, one-room schools remained the most common type of structure in which these pedagogues practiced.

One of the most significant developments during the 1920s, however, was the increased number of women who were entrusted with the education of Delta children. Perhaps the life of one teacher in particular, Elsie Dawson, best illustrates the advances made by some Delta women during this decade. In the late 1920s, when Elsie completed the eighth grade, she decided to return to the one-room school for an additional year, which was common practice. The next year, she was hired to teach in a one-room school of her own. Although she would leave the profession for short periods of time, Elsie would serve as a Delta teacher for the next four decades. During her tenure, the state requirements for teachers would change several times, requiring Elsie to attend night classes at Arkansas State University, where she eventually completed her degree, while at the same time raising her children. Elsie's story is not unlike the countless other women who would witness the evolution of education in the Delta from the one-room schoolhouses they would start their teaching careers in during the 1920s and '30s, to the modern facilities they would retire from in the 1960s and '70s. The teachers, students, and schools they would pass through during the 1920s serve to form the focus of this chapter.

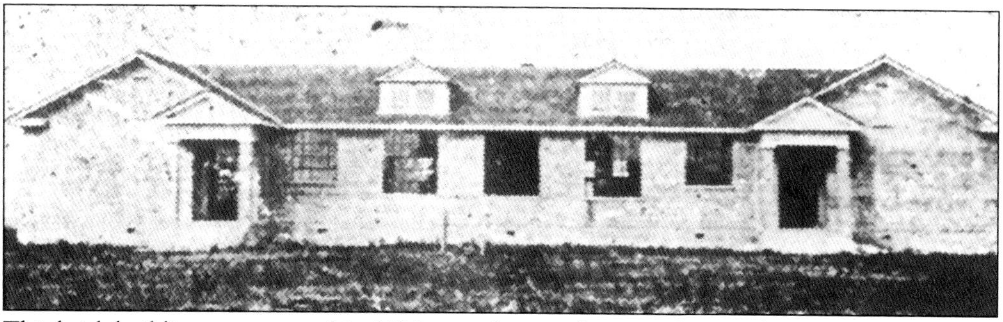

This brick building, constructed in 1928, soon became home to Bay High School in Craighead County. It was a small building with six classrooms, clearly indicating the size of the community as well as the growing enrollment. Shortly after this building was completed, the communities of Bay and Brown consolidated schools. (Courtesy of the Edgar Morrision Collection.)

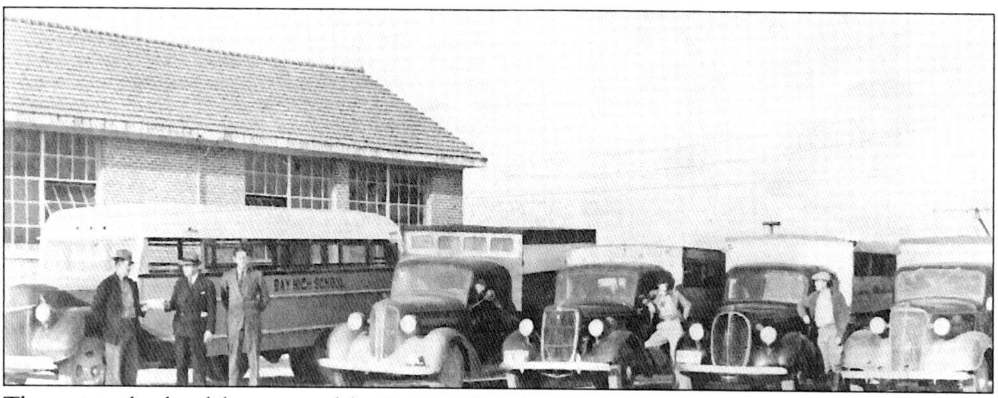

The original school busses used by Bay High School are on display. During the 1930s, Bay consolidated with most of the small schools in the area, leaving one teacher remaining in the small schools to teach the primary grades. This required a fleet of busses, cars, and trucks such as these to transport students to the consolidated high school. (Courtesy of the Edgar Morrison Collection.)

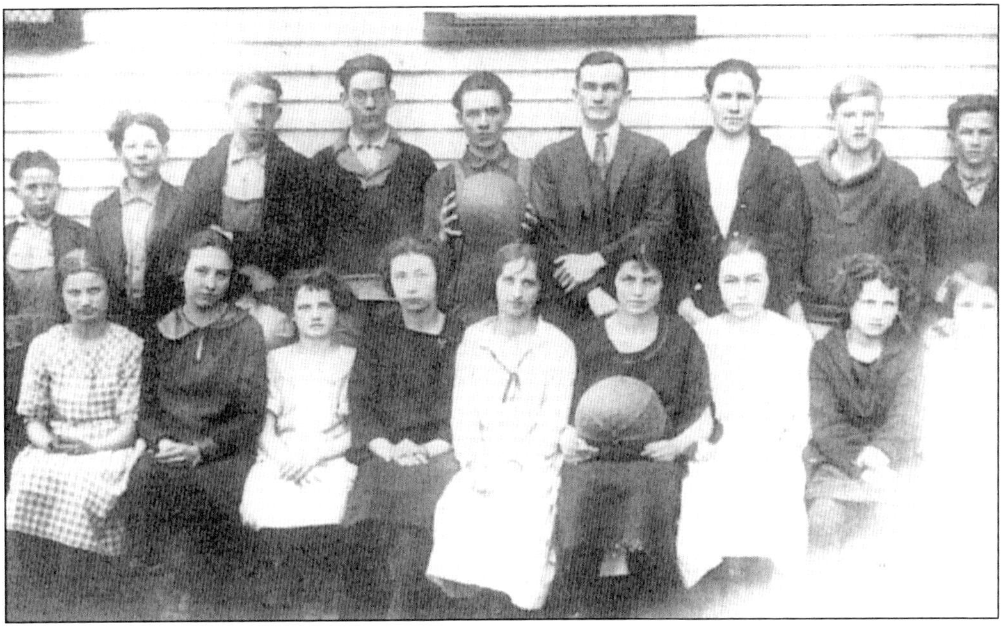

At the time these photographs were taken in the early 1920s, Bay School District was still referred to as "Number 21," a legacy of the late nineteenth century when it was first constructed on a section of land with that number designation. The Bay Public School eighth grade class, the terminal education level of most Bay students, posed for this 1924 photograph, while a lower elementary group of Bay students from the same period take a recess to sit for the class composite below. (Courtesy of the Edgar Morrison Collection.)

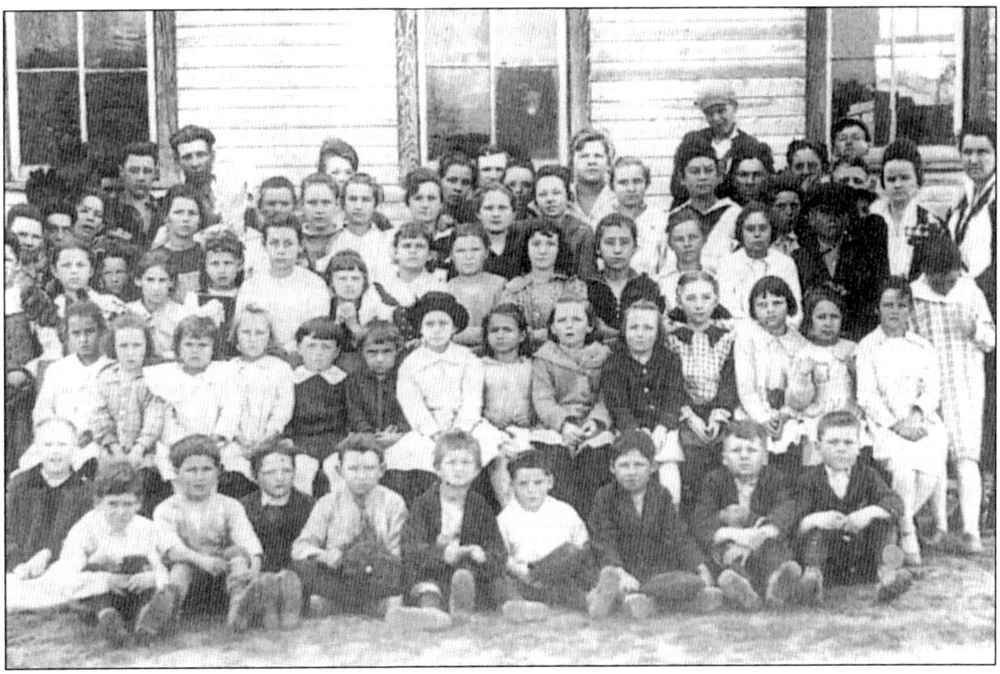

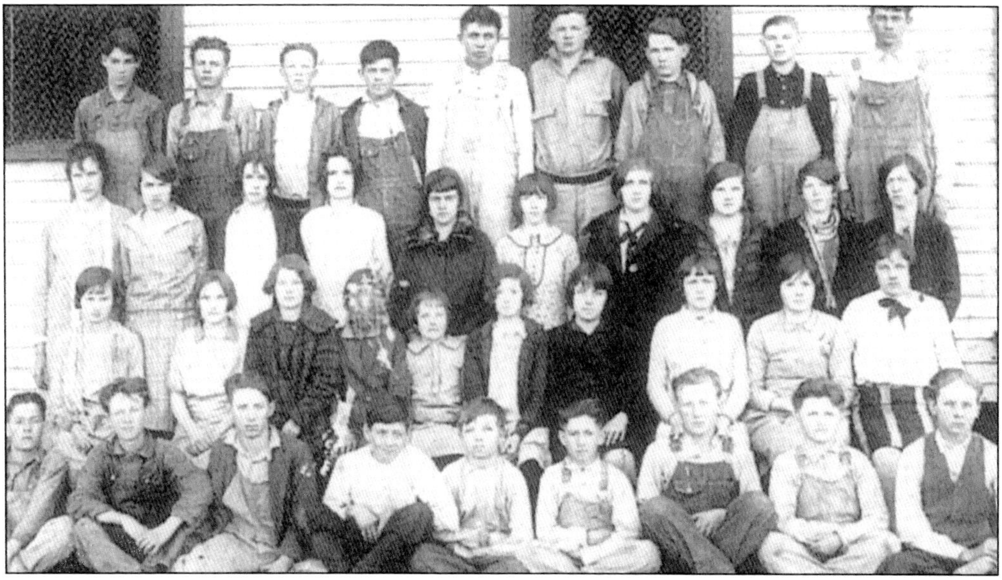

In addition to their children receiving an education, the dividends residents received from having a local school included a heightened sense of community identity and pride. Students at Bay Public, pictured above in a 1926 photograph, not only went to school together, but they also attended church, community picnics, and sporting events alongside each other. Almost certainly, Bay residents would have cheered on the girls basketball team pictured below as they played a game of half-court basketball, which remained the standard for girls basketball in Arkansas for the next half-century. (Courtesy of the Edgar Morrison Collection.)

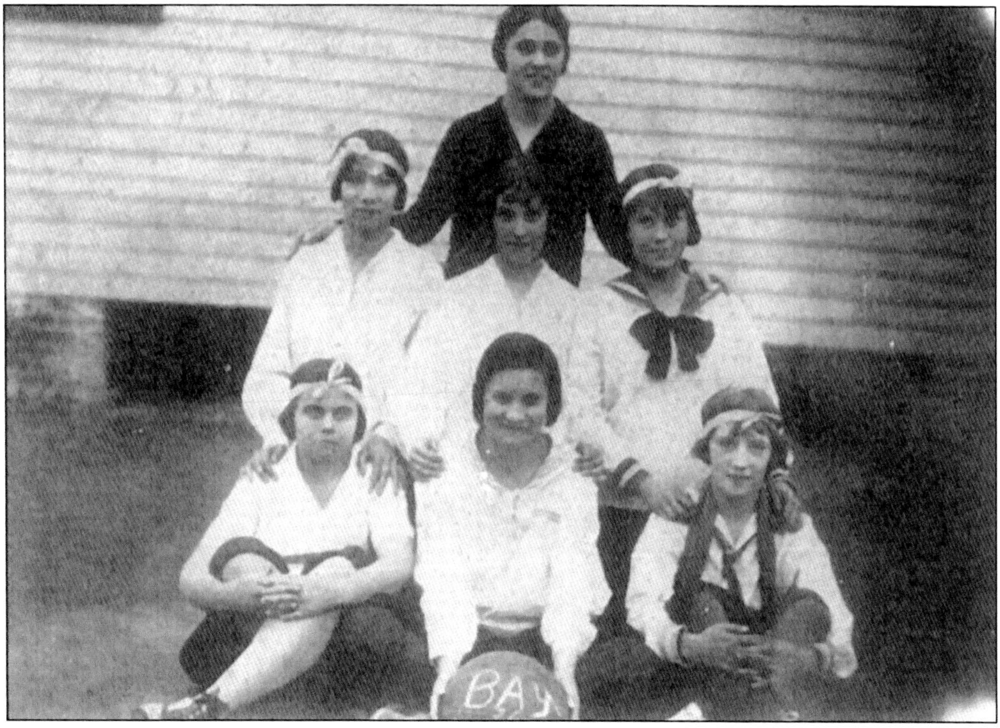

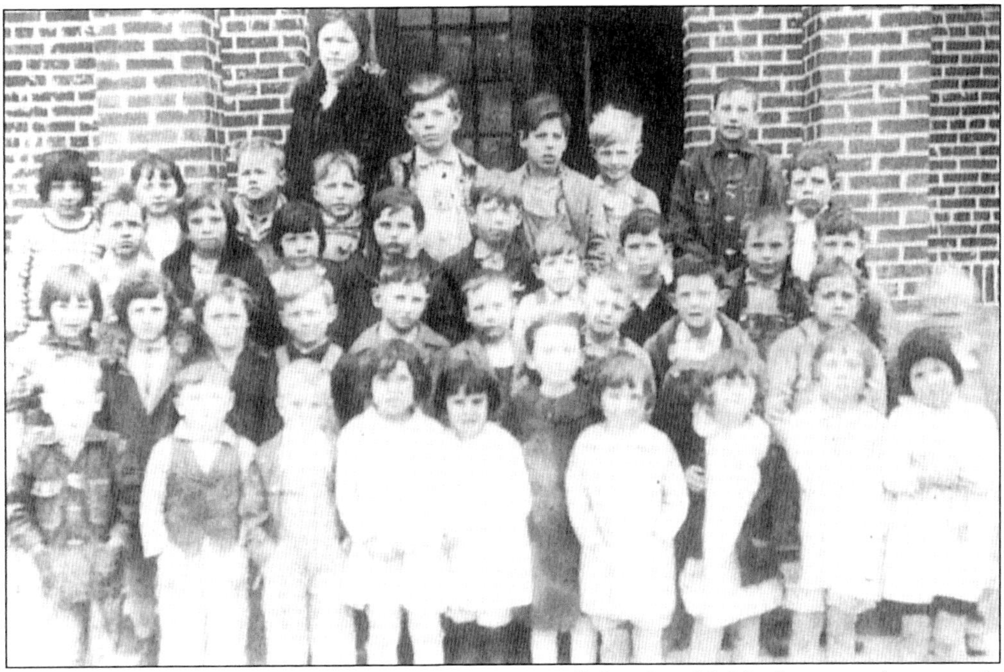

Little did anyone know when this early 1929 picture of Miss Cary Holt's class was taken outside of the Bay School's new facility that the start of the Great Depression loomed on the horizon. At the time of this photo, Bay School had an enrollment of 295 students and employed 11 teachers. (Courtesy of the Edgar Morrison Collection.)

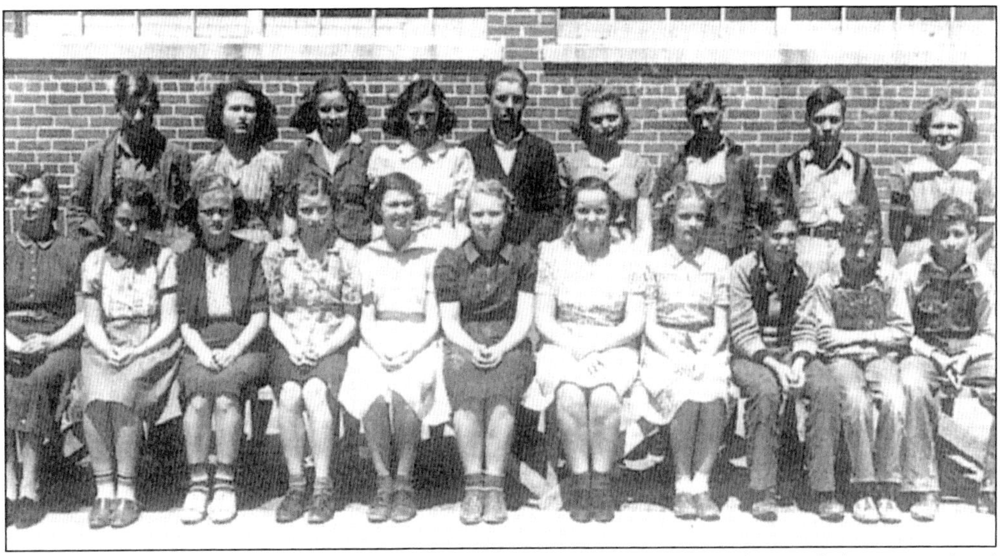

By the time this photograph of Bay school students was taken in front of the new school building c. 1930, consolidation with Brown was already underway. By the mid 1950s, the Bay enrollment was over 1,300. As agriculture changed and the migration of sharecroppers and workers out of state commenced, enrollment fell dramatically until the late 1960s. Enrollment reached a low point at that time of fewer than eight hundred students, a 40 percent reduction. (Courtesy of the Edgar Morrison Collection.)

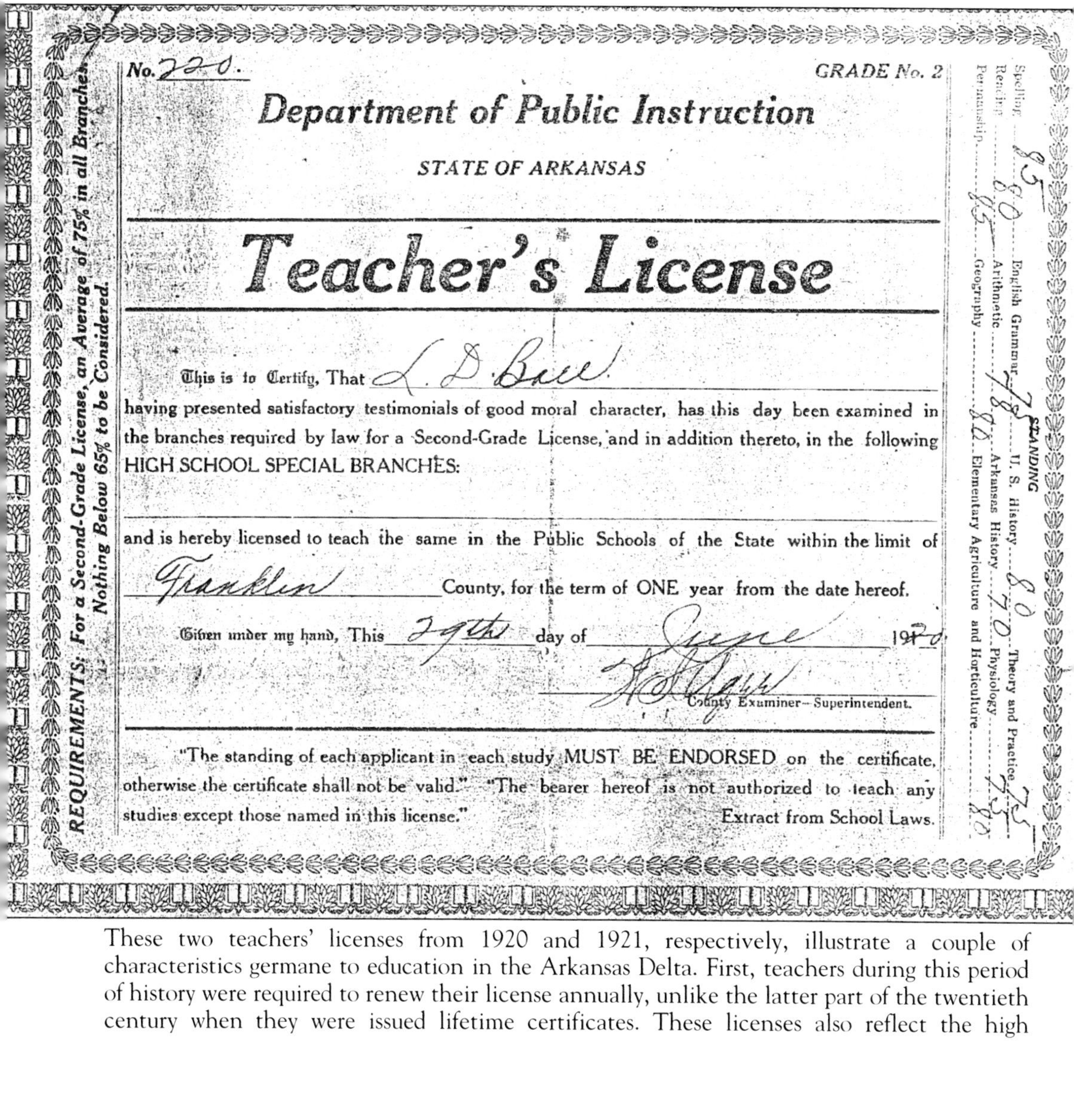

No. 220.

GRADE No. 2

Department of Public Instruction

STATE OF ARKANSAS

Teacher's License

This is to Certify, That L. D. Ball

having presented satisfactory testimonials of good moral character, has this day been examined in the branches required by law for a Second-Grade License, and in addition thereto, in the following HIGH SCHOOL SPECIAL BRANCHES:

and is hereby licensed to teach the same in the Public Schools of the State within the limit of Franklin County, for the term of ONE year from the date hereof.

Given under my hand, This 29th day of June 1920

County Examiner—Superintendent.

"The standing of each applicant in each study MUST BE ENDORSED on the certificate, otherwise the certificate shall not be valid." "The bearer hereof is not authorized to teach any studies except those named in this license." Extract from School Laws.

REQUIREMENTS: For a Second-Grade License, an Average of 75% in all Branches. Nothing Below 65% to be Considered.

STANDING

Spelling 85, Reading 80, Penmanship 85, English Grammar 78, Arithmetic 78, Geography 80, U. S. History 80, Arkansas History 70, Elementary Agriculture and Horticulture 80, Theory and Practice 75, Physiology 75

These two teachers' licenses from 1920 and 1921, respectively, illustrate a couple of characteristics germane to education in the Arkansas Delta. First, teachers during this period of history were required to renew their license annually, unlike the latter part of the twentieth century when they were issued lifetime certificates. These licenses also reflect the high

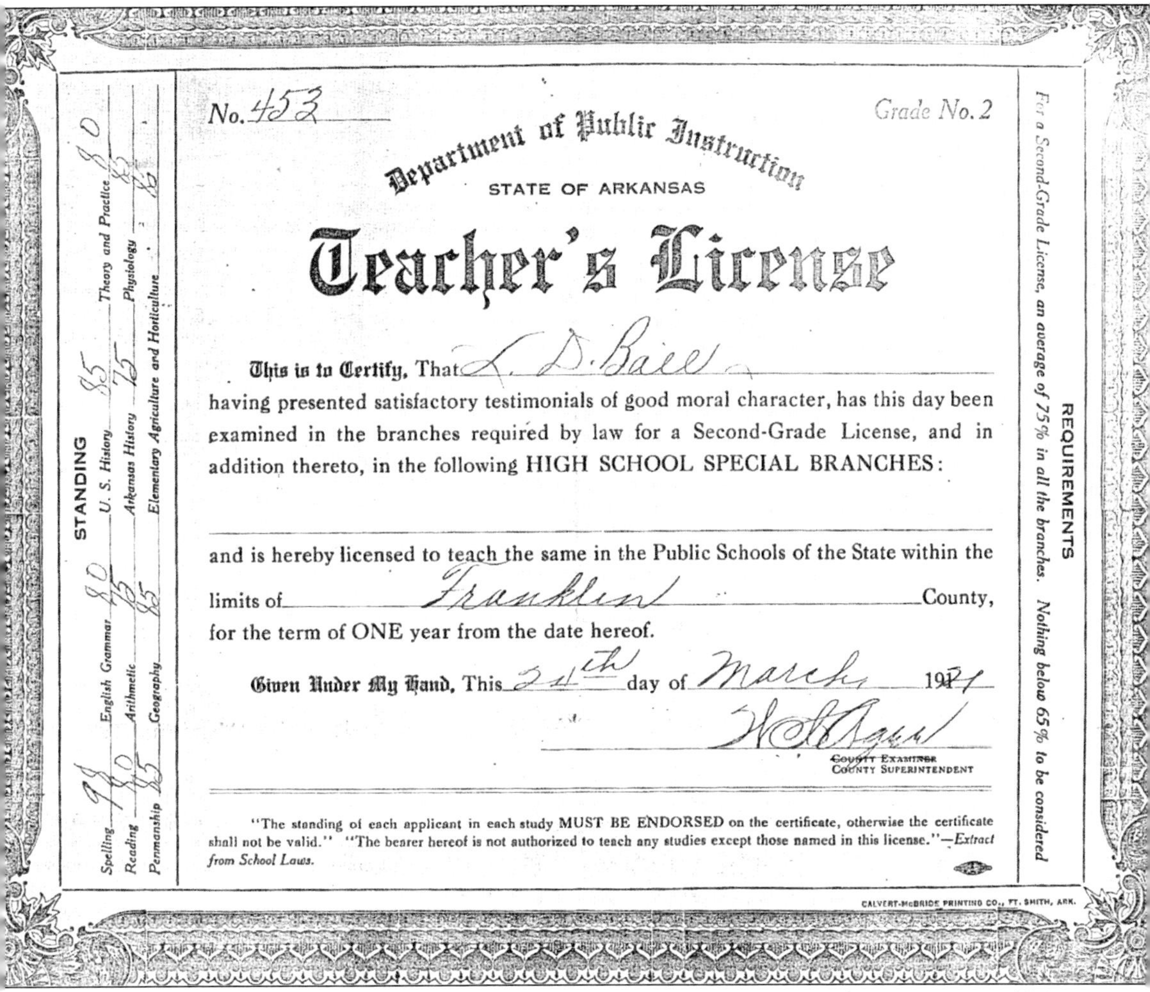

No. 453 Grade No. 2

Department of Public Instruction

STATE OF ARKANSAS

Teacher's License

This is to Certify, That L. D. Ball having presented satisfactory testimonials of good moral character, has this day been examined in the branches required by law for a Second-Grade License, and in addition thereto, in the following HIGH SCHOOL SPECIAL BRANCHES:

and is hereby licensed to teach the same in the Public Schools of the State within the limits of Franklin County, for the term of ONE year from the date hereof.

Given Under My Hand, This 24th day of March 1921

COUNTY EXAMINER
COUNTY SUPERINTENDENT

"The standing of each applicant in each study MUST BE ENDORSED on the certificate, otherwise the certificate shall not be valid." "The bearer hereof is not authorized to teach any studies except those named in this license."—*Extract from School Laws.*

STANDING

Spelling 90 English Grammar 80 U. S. History 85 Theory and Practice 80

Reading 90 Arithmetic 75 Arkansas History 75 Physiology 85

Penmanship 85 Geography 85 Elementary Agriculture and Horticulture 85

REQUIREMENTS

For a Second-Grade License, an average of 75% in all the branches. Nothing below 65% to be considered

CALVERT-McBRIDE PRINTING CO., FT. SMITH, ARK.

standards the state established for teachers, requiring them to score a cumulative average of 75 percent or higher, with no individual test score below 65 percent being considered. (Courtesy of the Larry Ball Collection.)

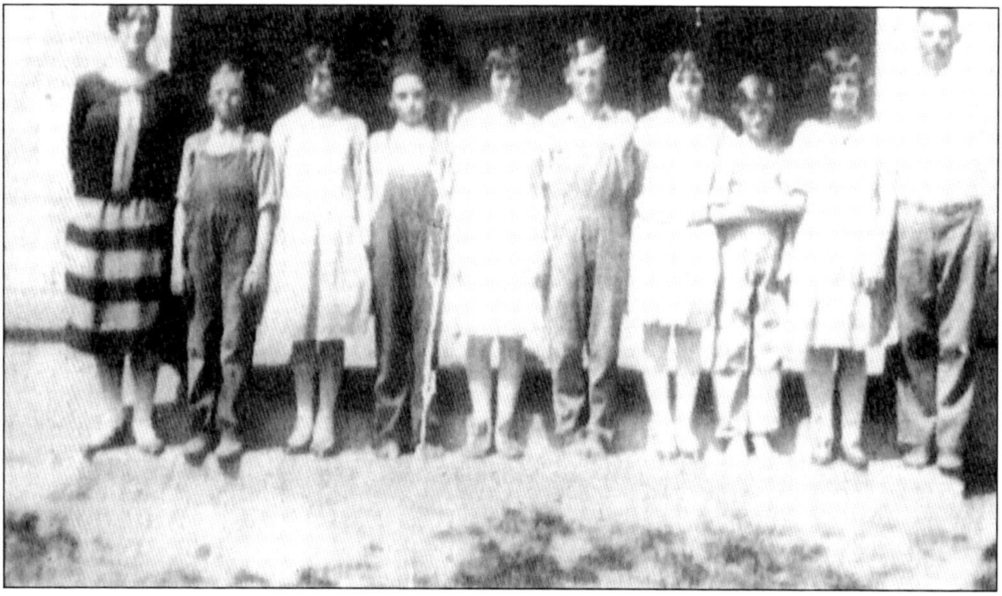

During the 1920s, most Delta schools operated with an average school tax of six to eight mills, receiving no state aid. While many schools would eventually close their doors due to a lack of available funding and decreasing enrollment, others survived the consolidation movement that was taking place during this period. Elementary students at Brown, pictured in these two photographs along with their teachers, for example, continued to attend their local school at the lower grade levels, avoiding traveling to their newly consolidated secondary school at Bay. (Courtesy of the Edgar Morrison Collection.)

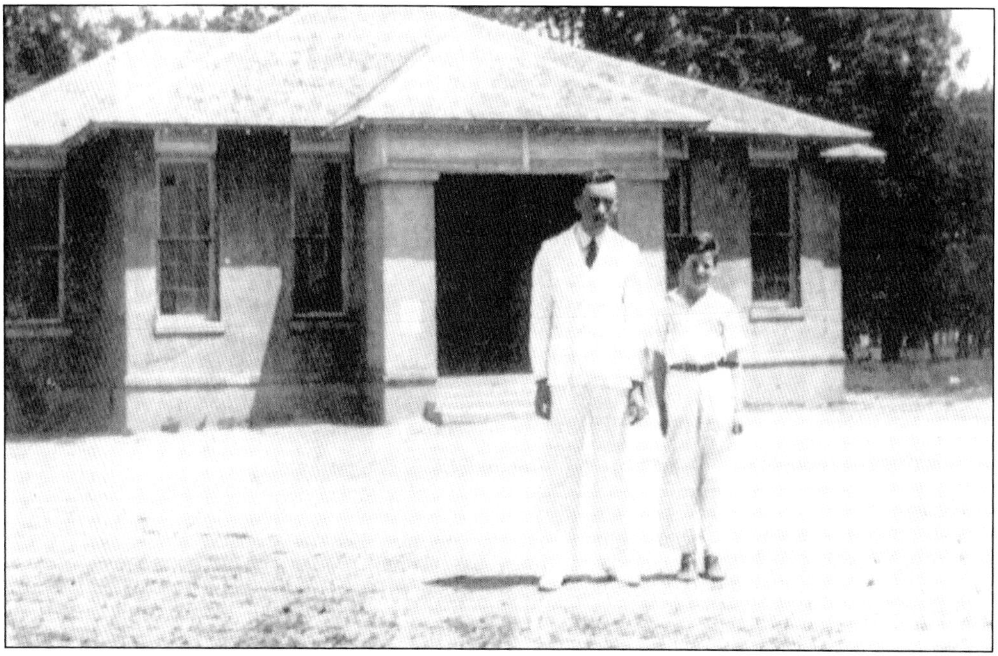

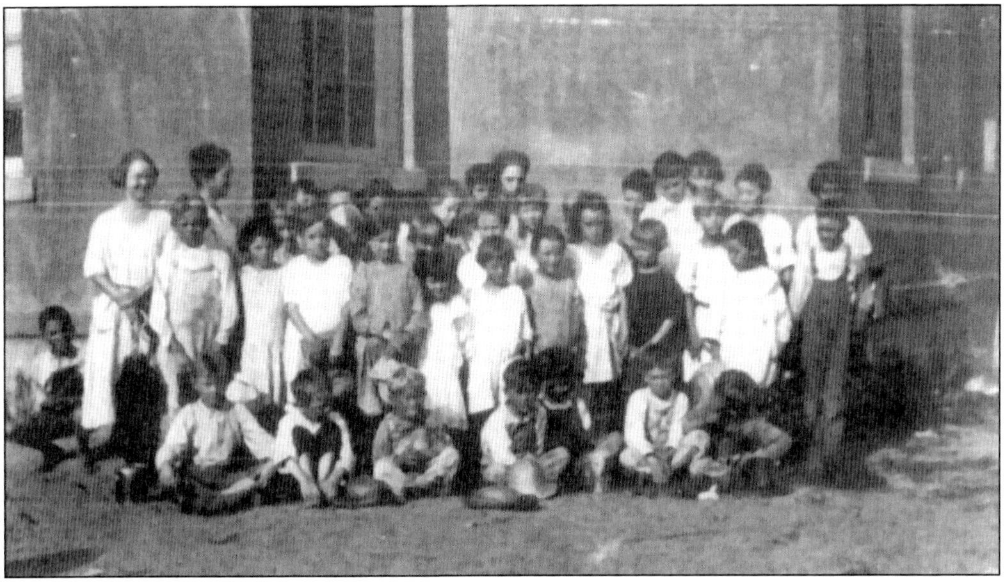

Among the primary books used by Mrs. Lydia Baker Ridge in her Brown Elementary School, pictured below, were the *Blue-Black Speller*, *Ray's Arithmetic*, and *McGuffey's Reader*. It was during the 1920s, as well, that many students, such as those pictured above outside of their new Brown School building, made the transition from one-room schoolhouses to more modern two-room facilities with characteristic "little" and "big" rooms. (Courtesy of the Edgar Morrison Collection.)

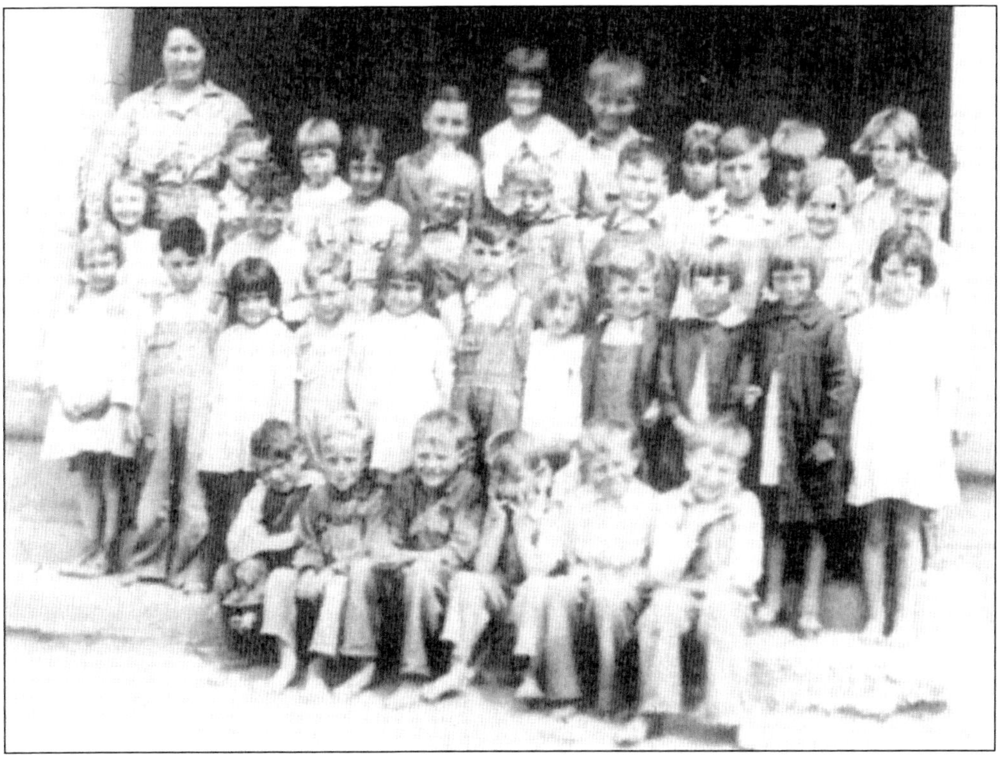

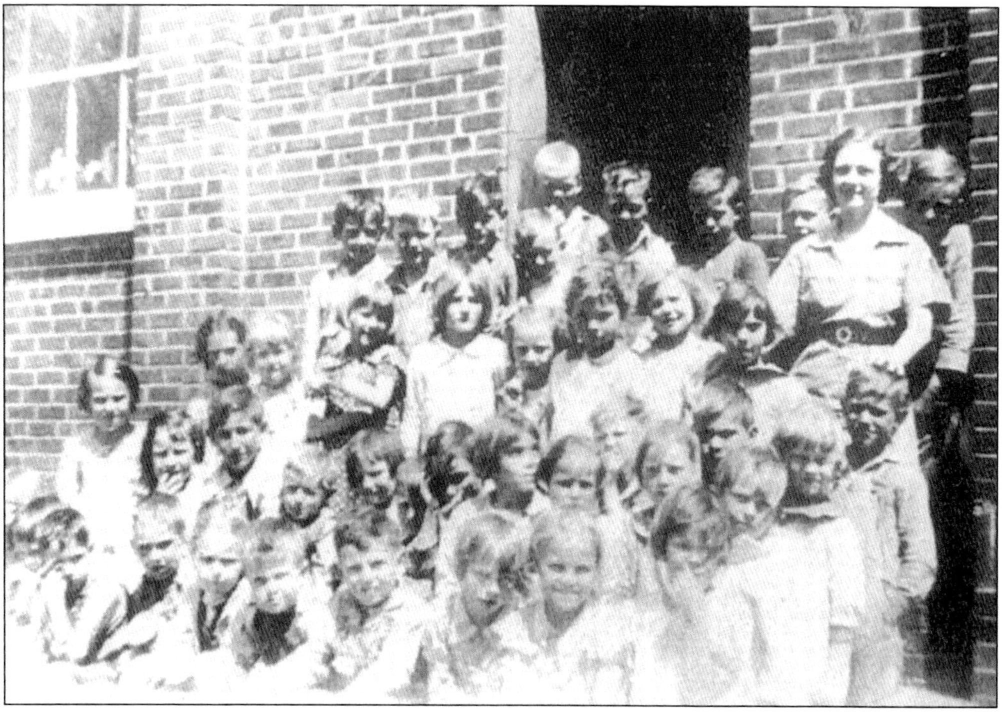

Miss Mattie Isbell and her students at Lunsford School take time to pose for this *c.* 1920 photograph outside of their schoolhouse. Although Lunsford School served a remote, rural area outside of present-day Bay in Craighead County, it had a large enough enrollment to allow it to survive longer than other rural schools before being consolidated. (Courtesy of the Edgar Morrison Collection.)

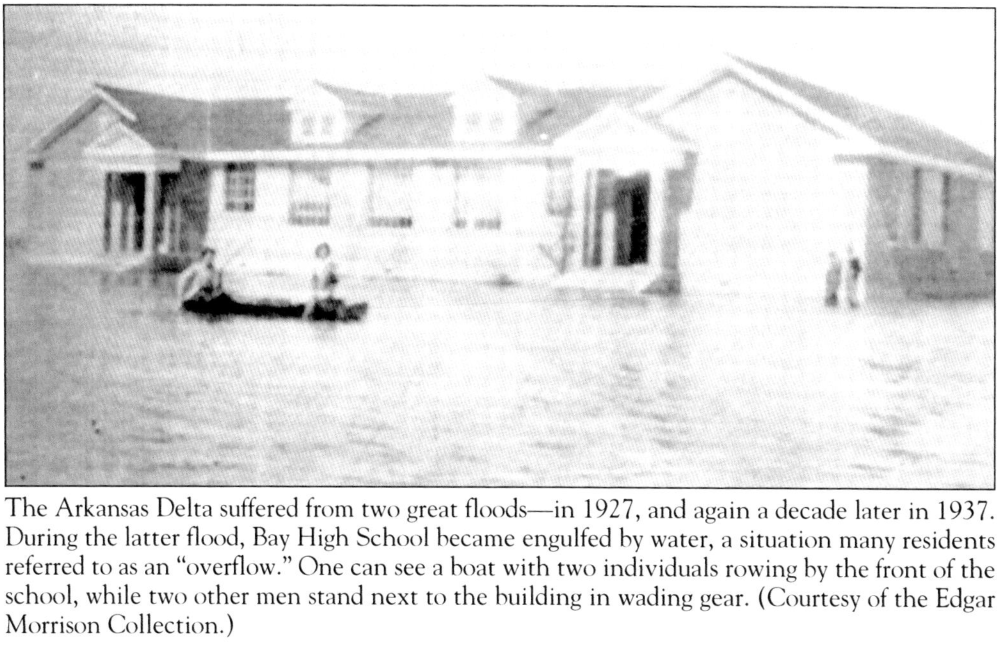

The Arkansas Delta suffered from two great floods—in 1927, and again a decade later in 1937. During the latter flood, Bay High School became engulfed by water, a situation many residents referred to as an "overflow." One can see a boat with two individuals rowing by the front of the school, while two other men stand next to the building in wading gear. (Courtesy of the Edgar Morrison Collection.)

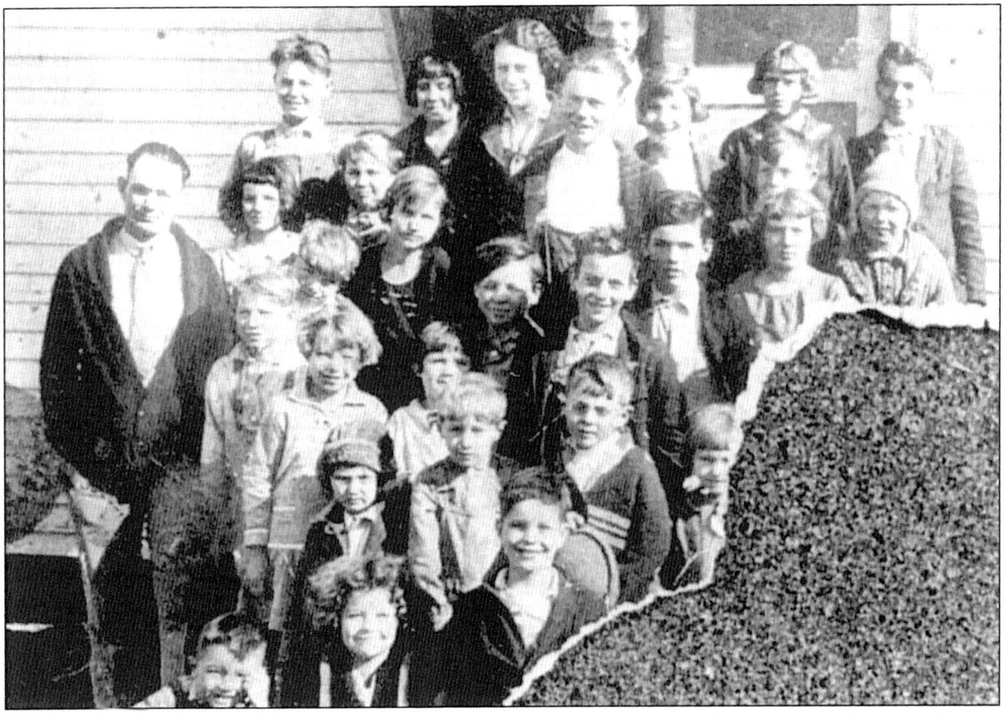

Davis Spur was a community that evolved out of a strong agricultural center that developed over time in Craighead County. A number of sharecroppers and farmers would send their children to Davis Spur School in order to learn the three Rs and then quickly resume their roles on the family farm. At the time of this photograph there existed another school in the area for the children of the African-American sharecroppers. (Courtesy of the Edgar Morrison Collection.)

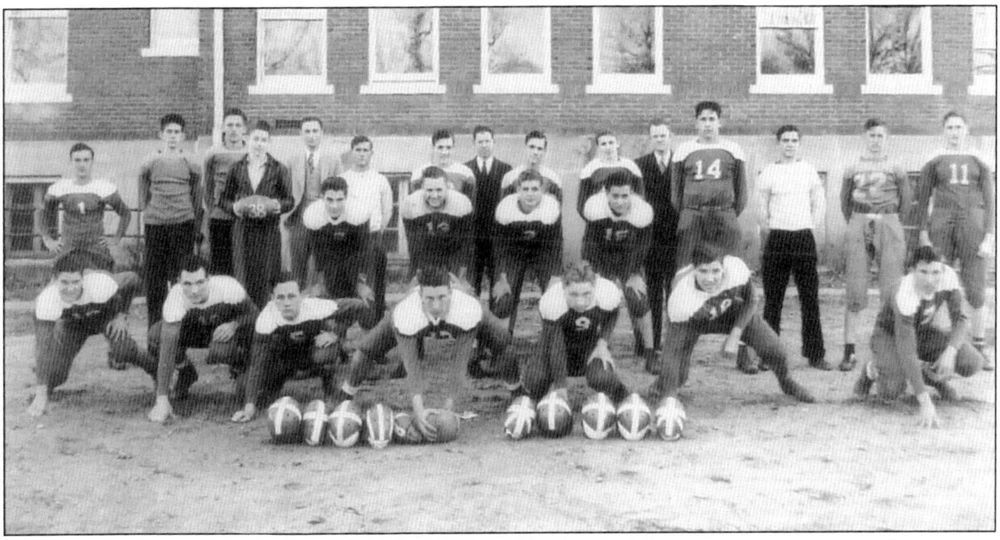

Sporting events, as well as spelling matches and school debates, were quite popular among the students and community residents during the 1920s and '30s. This group of East Warren football players pose in an intimidating as possible fashion given the uniforms of the day, outside their high school. (Courtesy Arkansas History Commission.)

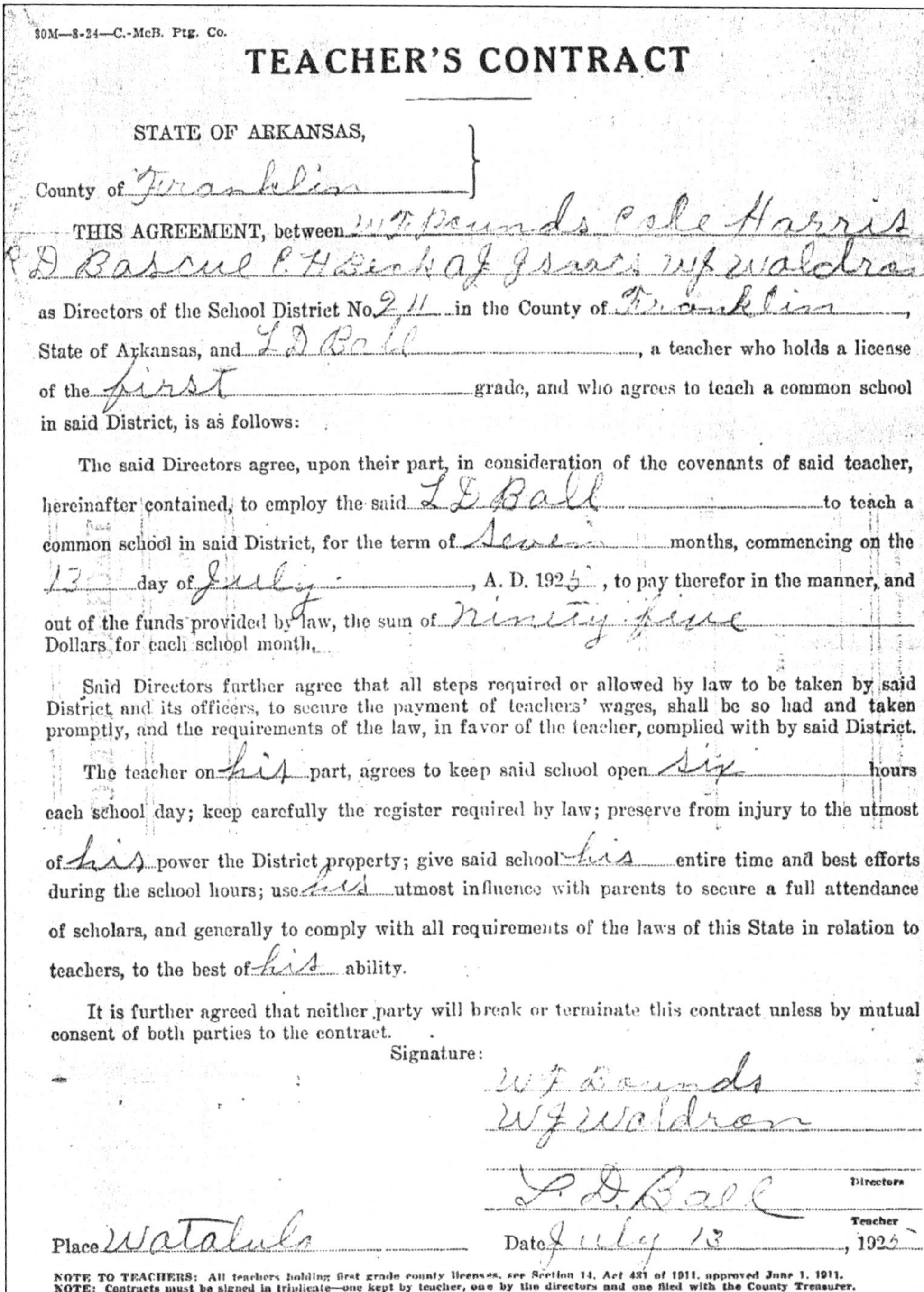

30M—8-24—C.-McB. Ptg. Co.

TEACHER'S CONTRACT

STATE OF ARKANSAS,
County of Franklin

THIS AGREEMENT, between W. F. Pounds, Cole Harris, D Bascue, C. H. Beck, A. J. Isaacs, W. F. Waldron as Directors of the School District No. 211 in the County of Franklin, State of Arkansas, and L. D. Ball, a teacher who holds a license of the first grade, and who agrees to teach a common school in said District, is as follows:

The said Directors agree, upon their part, in consideration of the covenants of said teacher, hereinafter contained, to employ the said L. D. Ball to teach a common school in said District, for the term of Seven months, commencing on the 13 day of July, A. D. 1925, to pay therefor in the manner, and out of the funds provided by law, the sum of Ninety-five Dollars for each school month.

Said Directors further agree that all steps required or allowed by law to be taken by said District and its officers, to secure the payment of teachers' wages, shall be so had and taken promptly, and the requirements of the law, in favor of the teacher, complied with by said District.

The teacher on his part, agrees to keep said school open six hours each school day; keep carefully the register required by law; preserve from injury to the utmost of his power the District property; give said school his entire time and best efforts during the school hours; use his utmost influence with parents to secure a full attendance of scholars, and generally to comply with all requirements of the laws of this State in relation to teachers, to the best of his ability.

It is further agreed that neither party will break or terminate this contract unless by mutual consent of both parties to the contract.

Signature:
W. F. Pounds
W. F. Waldron
Directors
L. D. Ball
Teacher

Place Watalula Date July 13, 1925

NOTE TO TEACHERS: All teachers holding first grade county licenses, see Section 14, Act 481 of 1911, approved June 1, 1911.
NOTE: Contracts must be signed in triplicate—one kept by teacher, one by the directors and one filed with the County Treasurer.

These two teacher contracts from the 1920s Arkansas Delta are quite revealing. First it becomes apparent that even at this early date, the state government was already heavily involved with education, issuing a standard contract for all schools within Arkansas to utilize. A second observation is, despite a certain degree of uniformity, that there was tremendous disparity in the

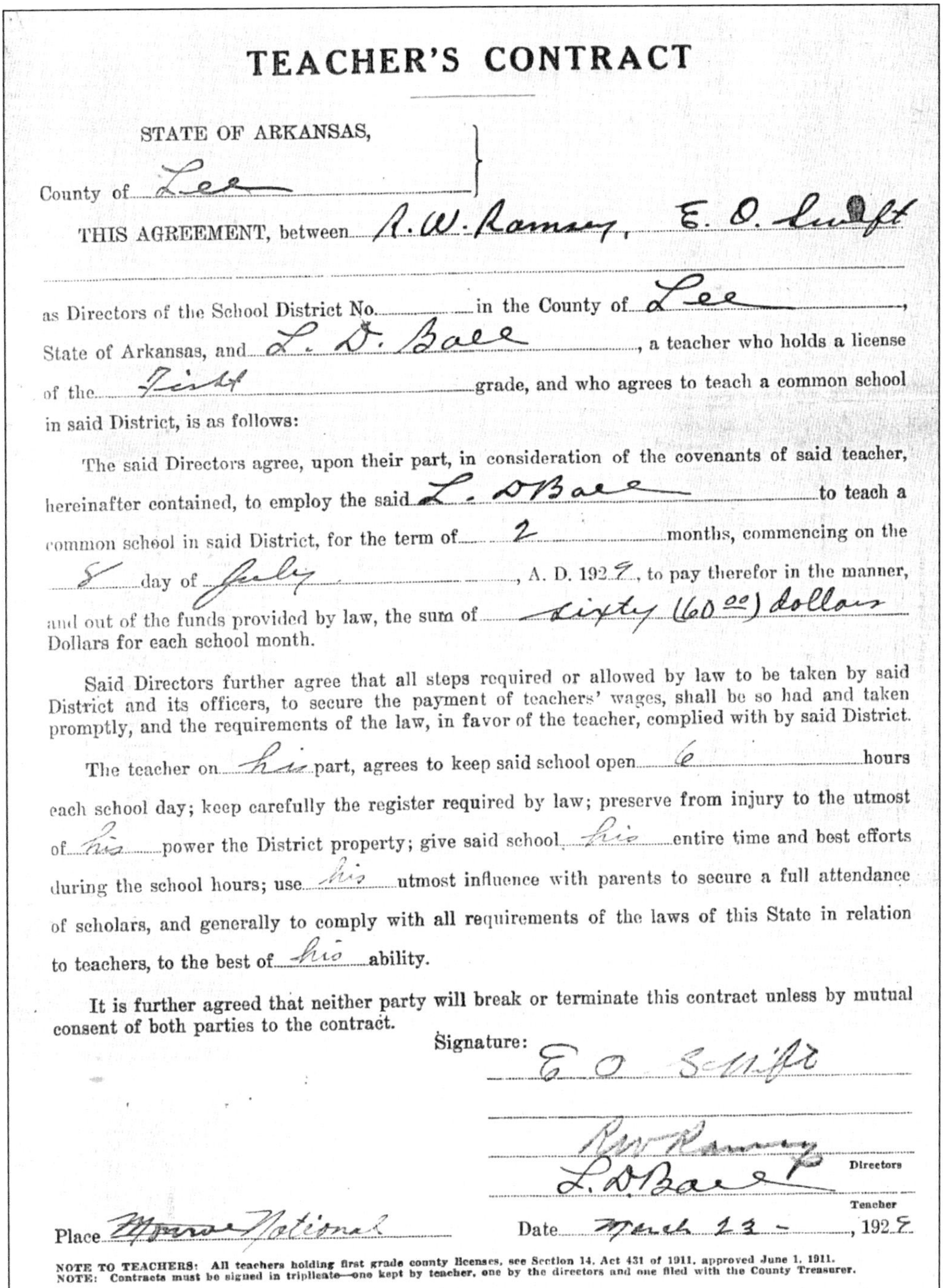
TEACHER'S CONTRACT

STATE OF ARKANSAS,
County of Lee

THIS AGREEMENT, between R. W. Ramsey, E. O. Swift

as Directors of the School District No. ____ in the County of Lee, State of Arkansas, and L. D. Ball, a teacher who holds a license of the First grade, and who agrees to teach a common school in said District, is as follows:

The said Directors agree, upon their part, in consideration of the covenants of said teacher, hereinafter contained, to employ the said L. D Ball to teach a common school in said District, for the term of 2 months, commencing on the 8 day of July, A. D. 1929, to pay therefor in the manner, and out of the funds provided by law, the sum of sixty (60.00) dollars Dollars for each school month.

Said Directors further agree that all steps required or allowed by law to be taken by said District and its officers, to secure the payment of teachers' wages, shall be so had and taken promptly, and the requirements of the law, in favor of the teacher, complied with by said District.

The teacher on his part, agrees to keep said school open 6 hours each school day; keep carefully the register required by law; preserve from injury to the utmost of his power the District property; give said school his entire time and best efforts during the school hours; use his utmost influence with parents to secure a full attendance of scholars, and generally to comply with all requirements of the laws of this State in relation to teachers, to the best of his ability.

It is further agreed that neither party will break or terminate this contract unless by mutual consent of both parties to the contract.

Signature: E O Swift

R W Ramsey

Directors

L. D Ball

Teacher

Place Monroe National Date March 23 - , 1929

NOTE TO TEACHERS: All teachers holding first grade county licenses, see Section 14, Act 431 of 1911, approved June 1, 1911.
NOTE: Contracts must be signed in triplicate—one kept by teacher, one by the directors and one filed with the County Treasurer.

salaries teachers received across the Delta. Case in point, a Franklin County teacher received a salary of $95 a month in 1925, while four years later a Lee County (a not as prosperous region) teacher received $60 a month. (Courtesy of Larry Ball Collection.)

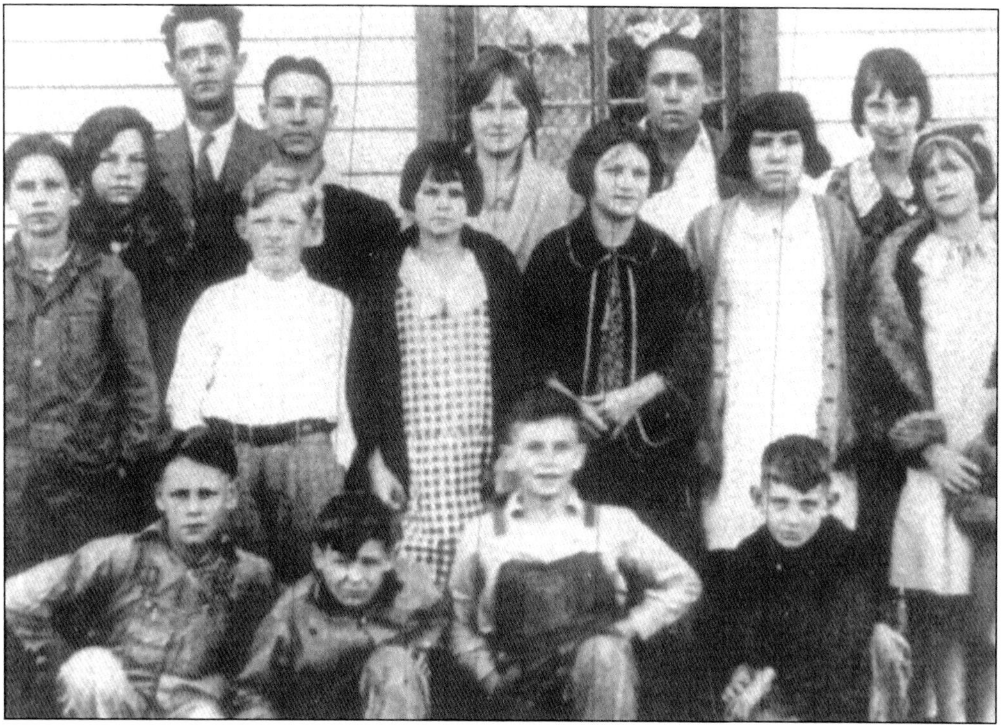

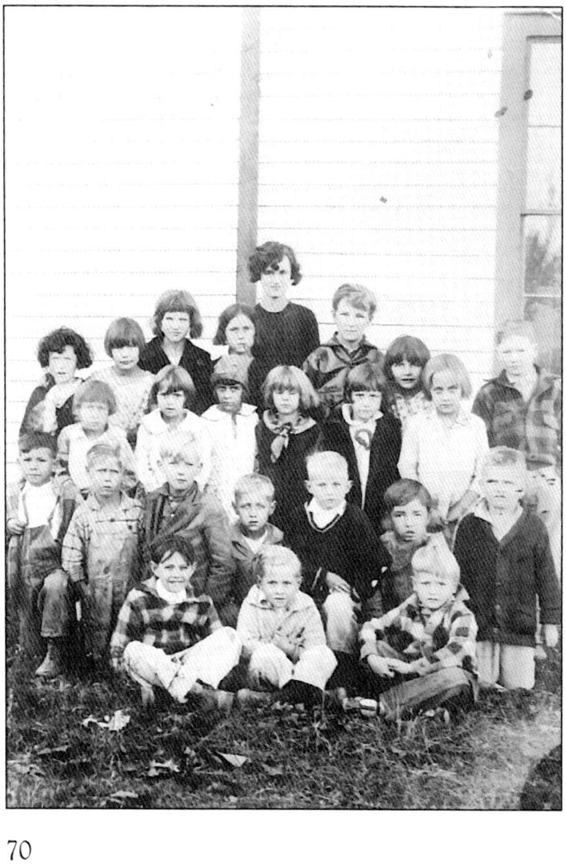

During the 1929–30 school year at Fair Oaks School in Cross County, Mr. L.D. Ball, standing in the back row of the photo, served as the teacher. Among the students in his upper elementary class that year, fifth through eighth grade, was his son Trafton, pictured kneeling third from the left. (Courtesy of Larry Ball Collection.)

While Mr. Ball was the teacher for the upper elementary at Fair Oaks School, Miss Jeanette Primm was placed in charge of the lower elementary students. This 1929 photograph illustrates both the young age at which individuals were called upon to teach as well as the tremendous challenge they faced teaching students at such a variety of grade levels, all in the same class. (Courtesy of Larry Ball Collection.)

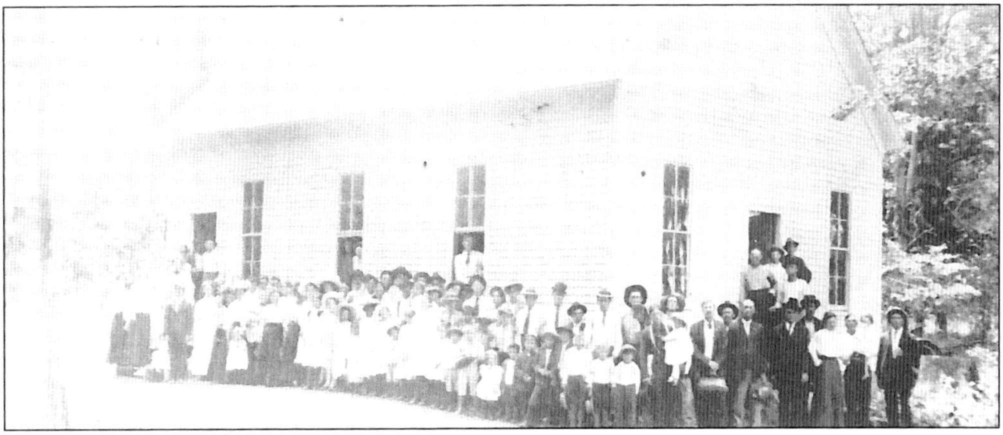

Goodluck was a short distance from Bay and represented one of 104 schools that existed in Craighead County during the early part of the twentieth century. It was not unusual for schools and churches to share buildings during the early development period. (Courtesy of Edgar Morrison Collection.)

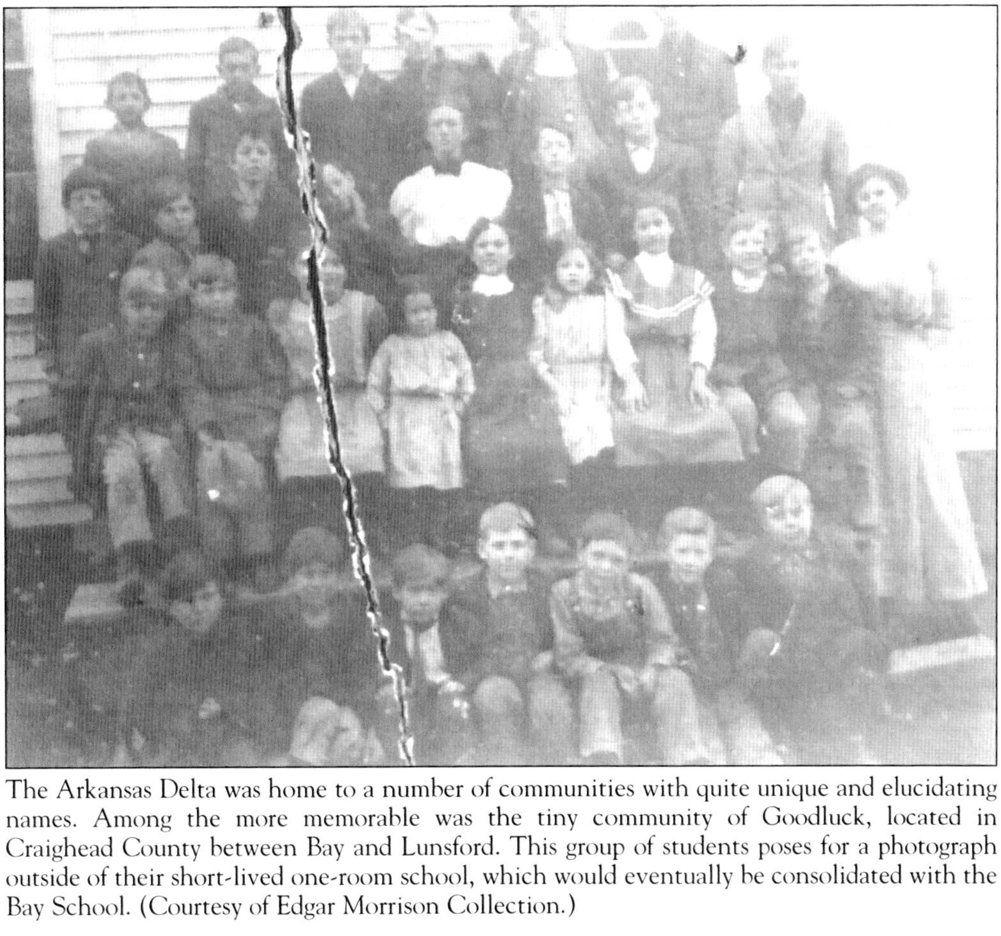

The Arkansas Delta was home to a number of communities with quite unique and elucidating names. Among the more memorable was the tiny community of Goodluck, located in Craighead County between Bay and Lunsford. This group of students poses for a photograph outside of their short-lived one-room school, which would eventually be consolidated with the Bay School. (Courtesy of Edgar Morrison Collection.)

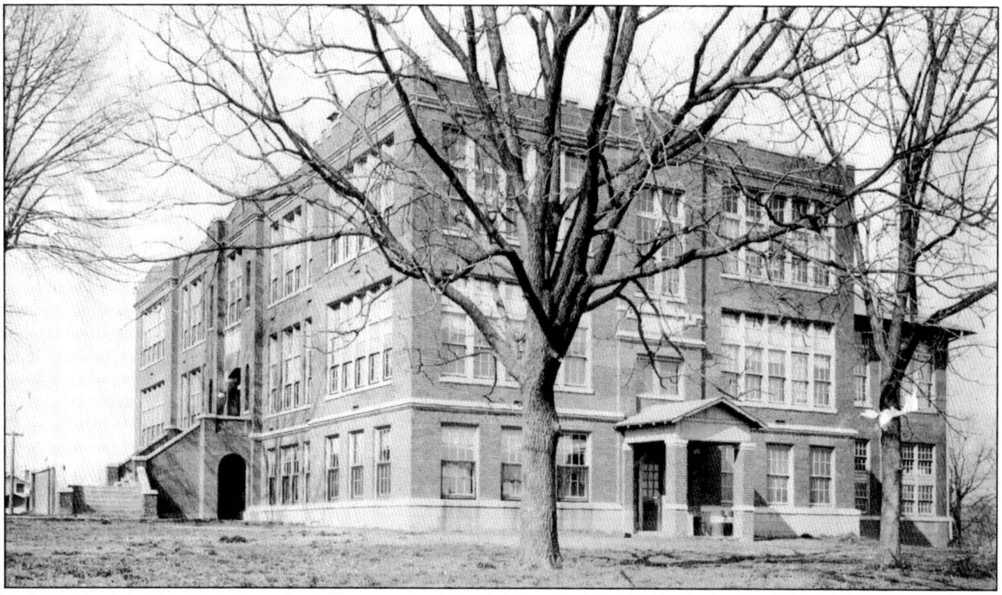

When the county of Craighead, originally scheduled to be named Crowley and then temporarily changed to Buchanan in honor of the president, was formed in 1859, Greensboro was the largest community within its borders. After a short period of time, however, the newly established community of Jonesboro, named after Senator William A. Jones of St. Francis County, eclipsed all others. Within a few decades, the most modern educational facilities in the Delta, such as Jonesboro High School pictured above, were being constructed in this growing community. In addition, some of the wealthiest residents of northeast Arkansas were also flocking to the city in order to send their sons and daughters, such as those pictured below in their JHS class composite, to the progressive schools it had established. (Courtesy of Arkansas State University Museum.)

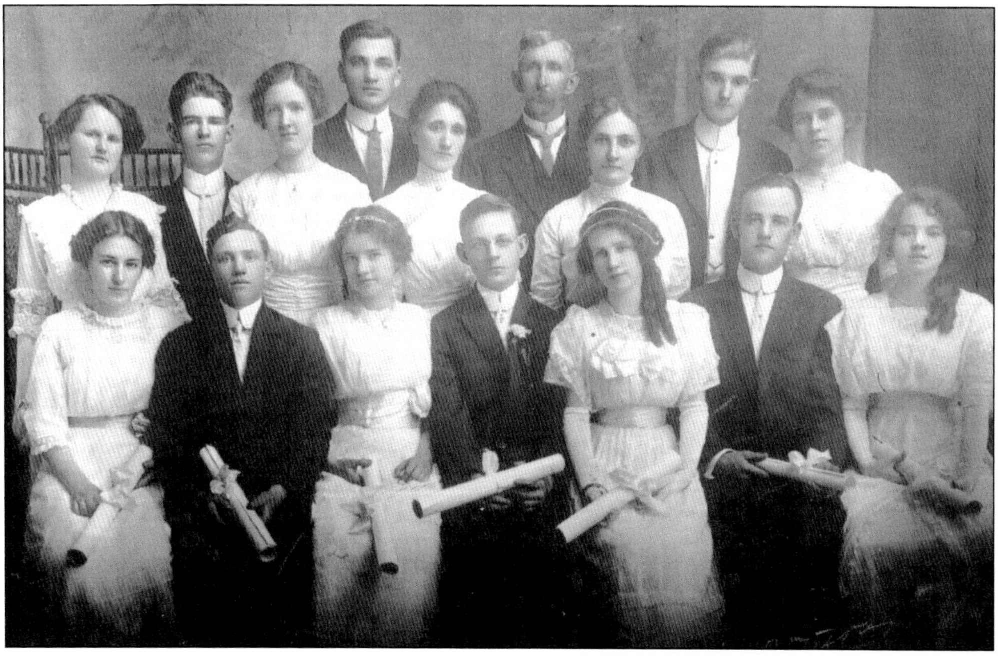

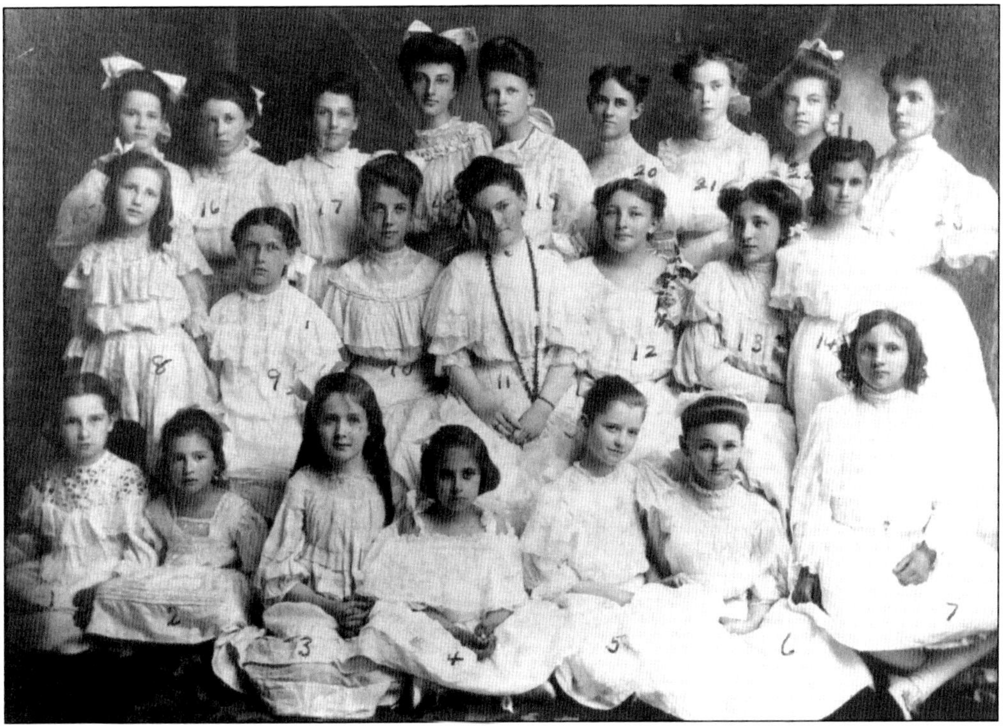

In addition to modern facilities and a progressive curriculum, Jonesboro schools during the 1920s also offered students opportunities to engage in culturally rich activities once found only in cities the size of Little Rock and Memphis. A perfect example is Miss Emily Babcock and her music students who pose for this *c.* 1920 photograph. (Courtesy of Arkansas State University Museum.)

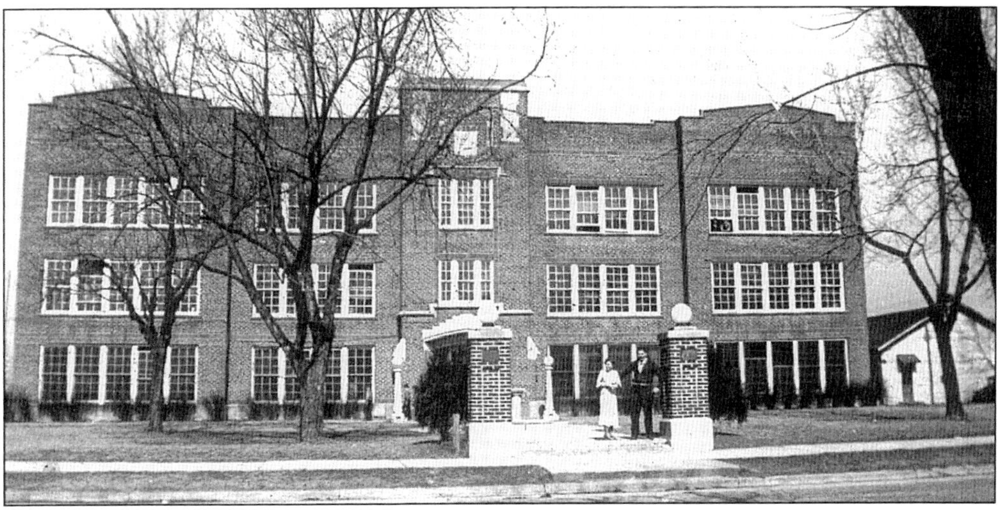

Blytheville High School is located in Mississippi County. This photograph is from the late 1920s–early 1930s. Blytheville is the largest Delta community in the northern part of the Arkansas Delta, just a few short miles from the Mississippi River. With the major north-south highway, Interstate 55, also running through the city, Blytheville quickly became a major Delta transportation and economic center. (Courtesy of Arkansas History Commission.)

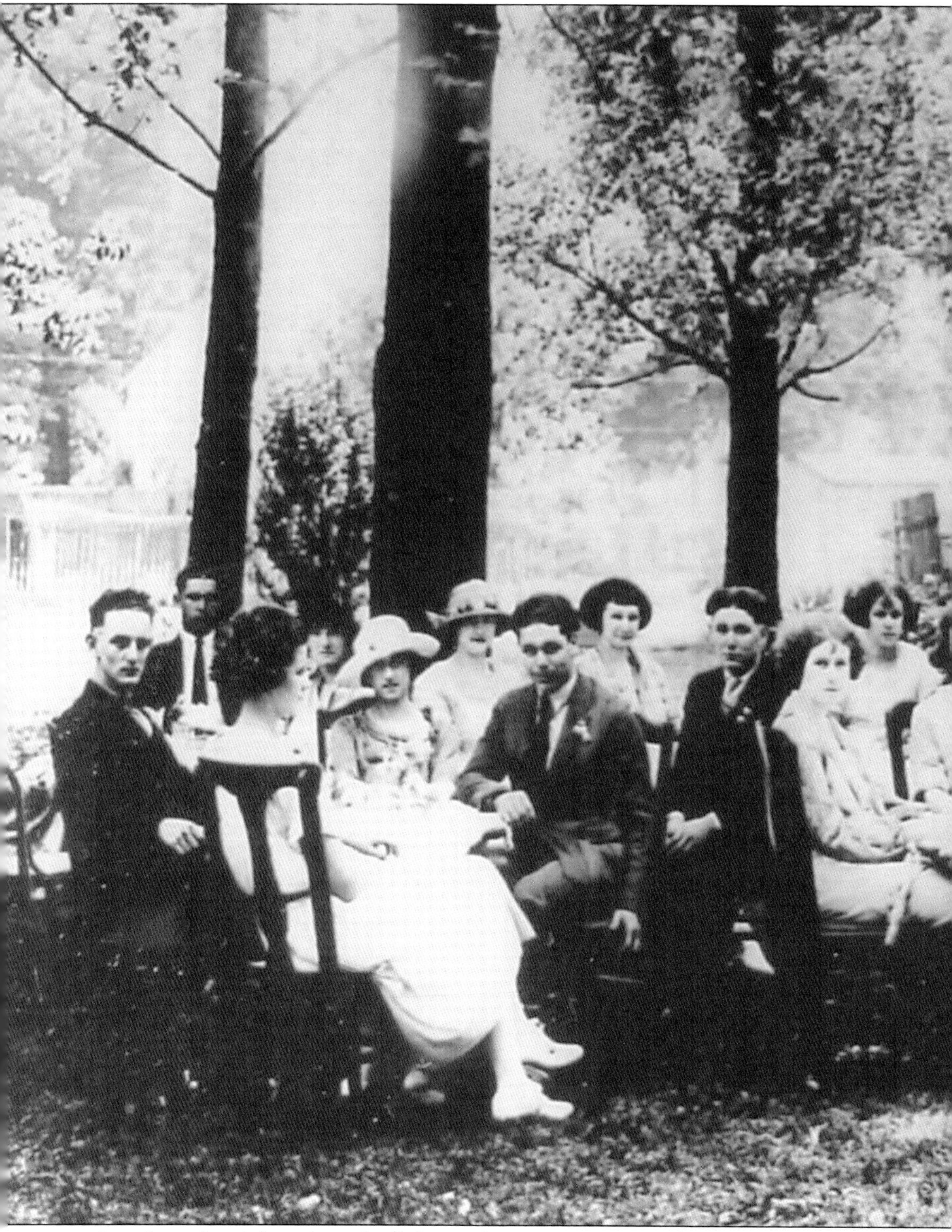

A tradition found throughout the Delta, graduating seniors were often honored at a breakfast held the day before or the day of graduation. In this case, the honorees are members of the 1923

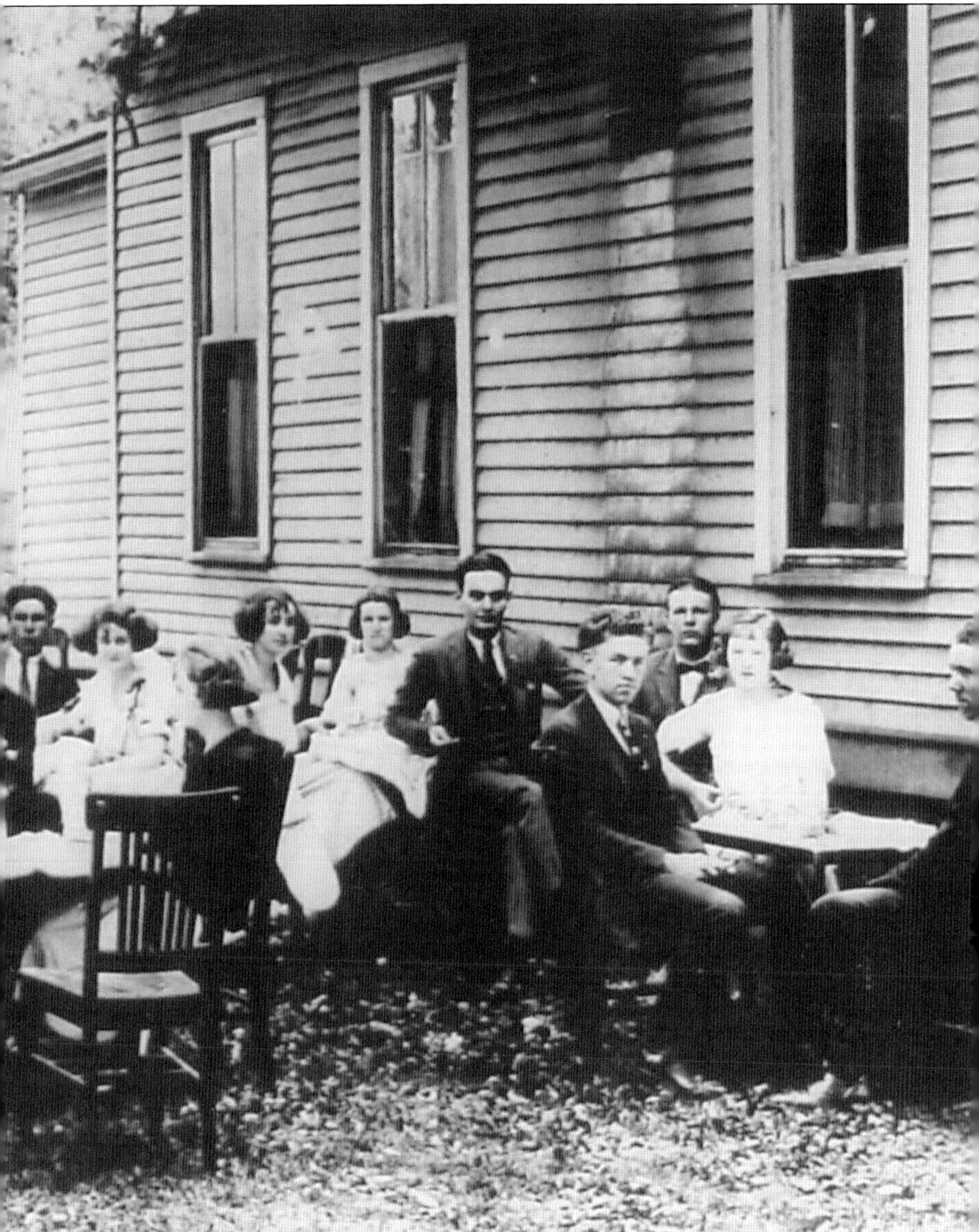

graduating class at Wynne High School. Wynne is the county seat of Cross County, located on the banks of the L'Anguille River. (Courtesy of Arkansas History Commission.)

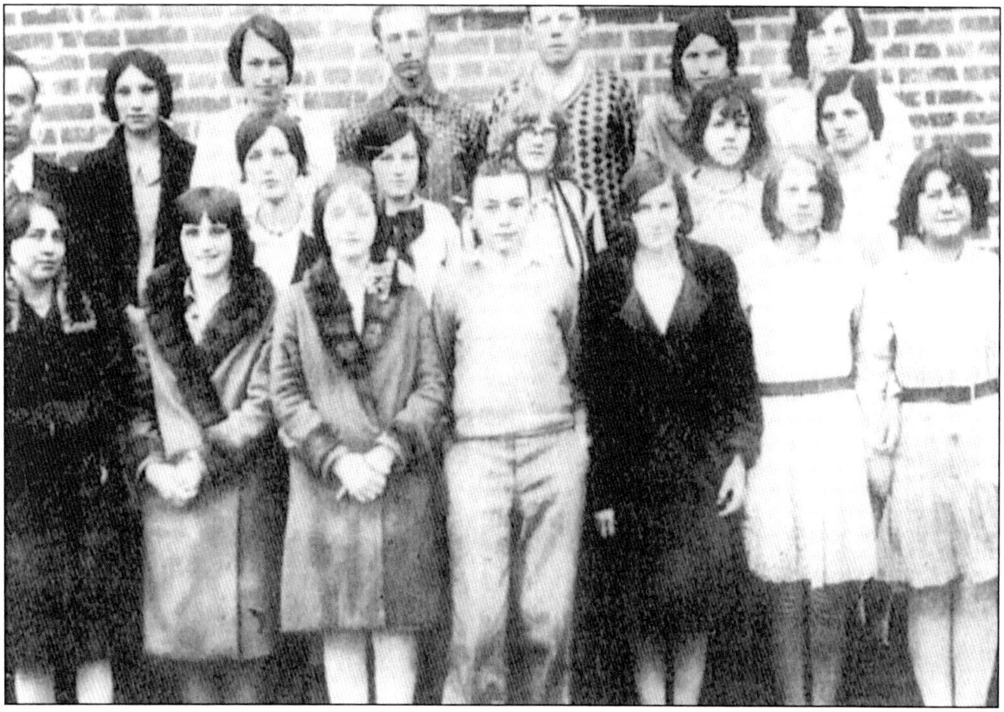

The first Bay High School freshman class posed for this photograph. Upon the establishment of the high school, students were offered English, math, science, and social studies classes. By 1932, however, enough classes were offered for students to get the 16 credits needed for graduation. (Courtesy of Edgar Morrison Collection.)

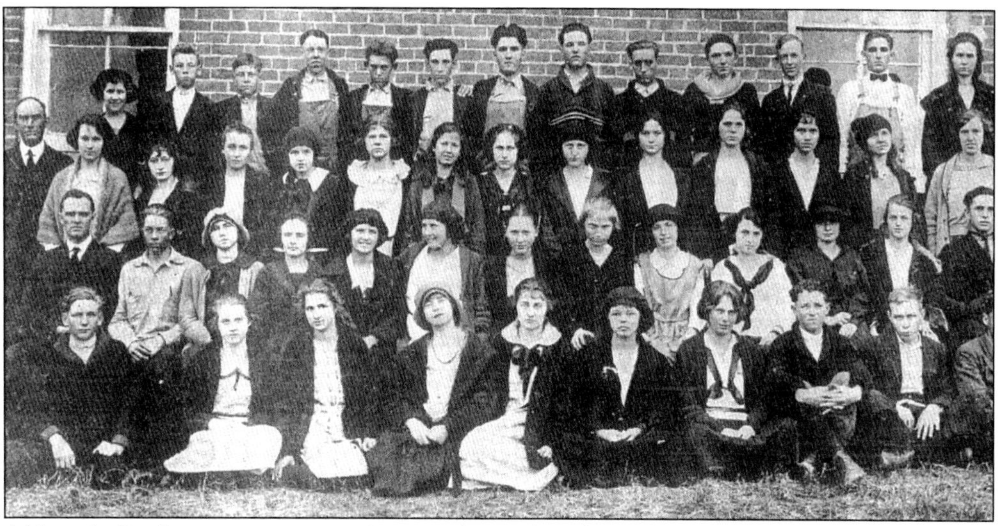

Although Ozark is, as its name infers, not located in the Delta, this photograph of the 1921 high school freshman class illustrates two major points. First, one will note the common style of hair and dress shared by both Delta and Ozark students. One is quick to note, however, the greater amount of wealth in this region, as reflected in the students clothing. Ozark was a smaller community, yet the clothing worn by the students is more analogous with that of the students in only the largest Delta cities. (Courtesy of Larry Ball Collection.)

Five

1930s and 1940s
Fighting a Depression and World War

Arkansas suffered from natural as well as economic disasters in the 1930s. Drought struck hard in 1930 and again in 1934. The floods of 1937 served to illustrate yet another destructive tool in Mother Nature's arsenal which she chose to unleash on the Delta. These natural disasters only added to the national economic problems of the Great Depression, greatly limiting the ability of residents to improve their educational institutions.

Historian Neal Buffaloe described the situation for Delta schools in the 1930s by stating, "In those days, the small town and country schools in eastern Arkansas operated on a split term basis. There would be six weeks of school from about the first of July until the middle of August when the cotton started to open. They stayed closed until around the first of November then started up again and ran until about the middle of May, when it was time to start hoeing cotton. Only after the cotton was 'laid by' did the new term commence. Thus, in one way or another, cotton dominated just about every phase of rural and small town life."

Another problem was the negative attitude some residents still held toward formal education. The father of a student in one subscription school, for example, berated a particular schoolteacher who sought to teach his wife: "Lemme tell you sumpthin," Ike interrupted. " My ol'lady thinks she's better'n me, and if that is what book-learnin' does for a woman, then I say to hell with it and the same thing goes for my kid, my mama and daddy ain't got no book-learn'n, I ain't got none, and we've did all right. I'm gonna take my kid outta school, and I don't mean for you to be sneakin around tryin to learn my woman to be uppity."

By 1940, there were over three thousand school districts in Arkansas. With teacher salaries averaging $750 a year, half the average salary of a wartime factory worker or of a neighboring state teacher, a shortage of teachers developed. Only 70,000 Arkansas students, out of a total of 170,000 eligible, attended high school. By 1950, however, the state reduced the total number of school districts to five hundred, and a constitutional amendment was passed mandating the creation of high schools available to all. These events form the backdrop for this chapter.

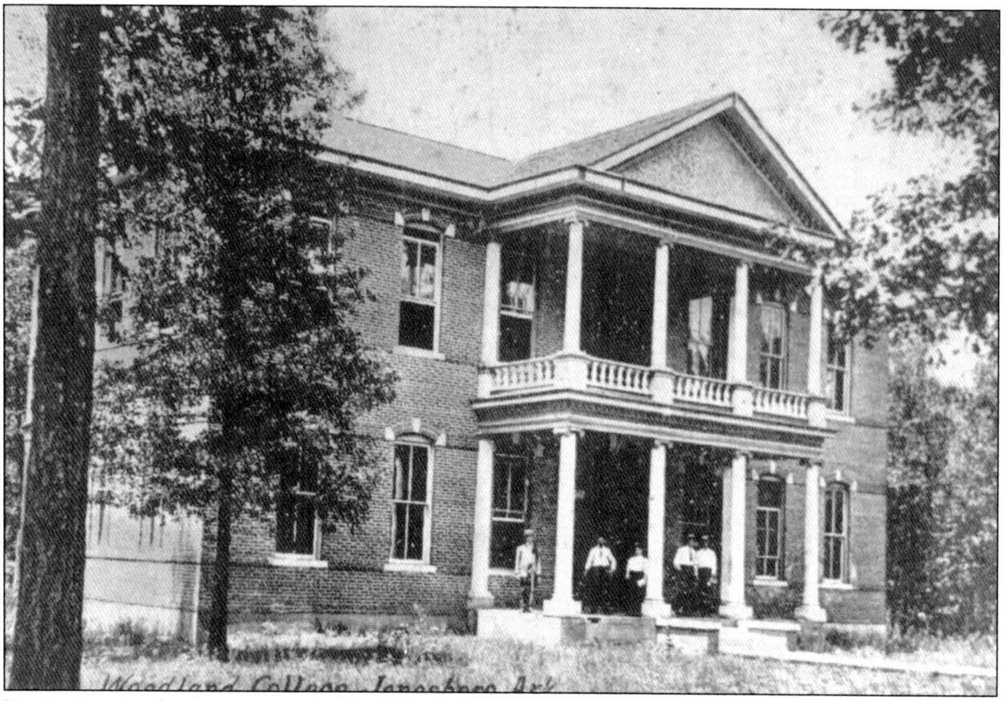

Beginning in the late nineteenth century, a number of colleges would make Jonesboro their home. Among the earliest institutions of higher learning to locate there was Woodland College, founded by Baptists. For this reason, the short-lived institution is often referred to in historical records as Woodland Baptist College. (Courtesy of Arkansas State University Archives.)

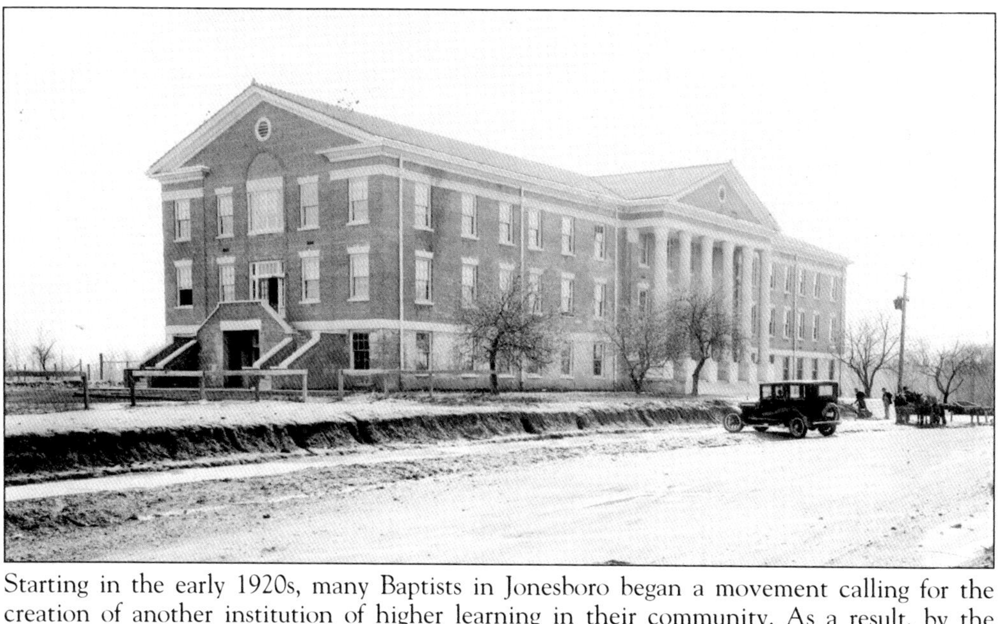

Starting in the early 1920s, many Baptists in Jonesboro began a movement calling for the creation of another institution of higher learning in their community. As a result, by the end of the decade, Jonesboro Baptist College was created. Despite the name, it was to be a non-sectarian institution. Plagued by money problems during the Great Depression, the college closed down by the late 1930s. (Courtesy of Arkansas State University Museum.)

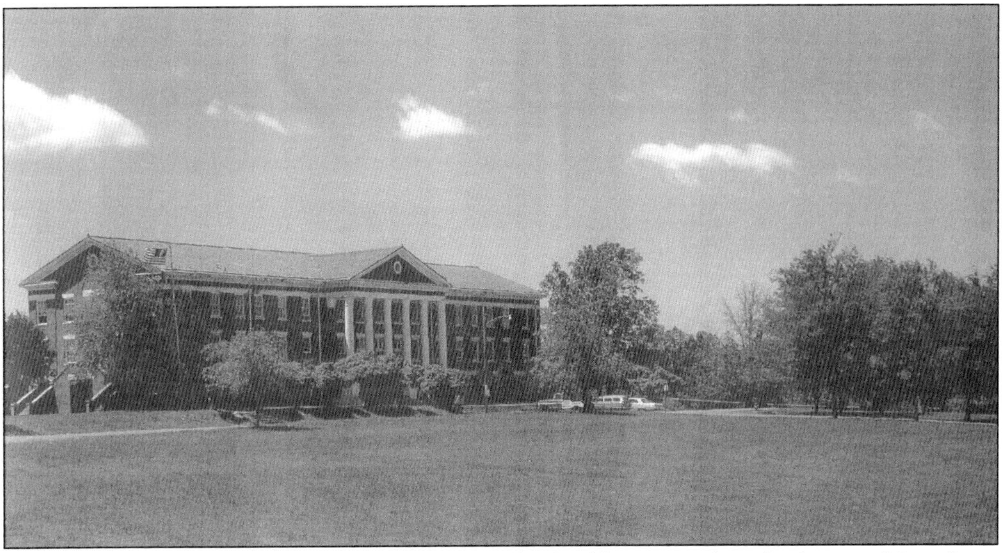

After its construction was completed in 1934, this building served as the home of Jonesboro College, founded by the Home Mission Board of the Southern Baptist Church. After the building sat vacant for several years, the Jonesboro Public Schools acquired the property in 1939. It was the home of Jonesboro High School between 1939 and 1973, when it was destroyed by a tornado on May 27 of that year. (Courtesy of Roselyn Horner Collection.)

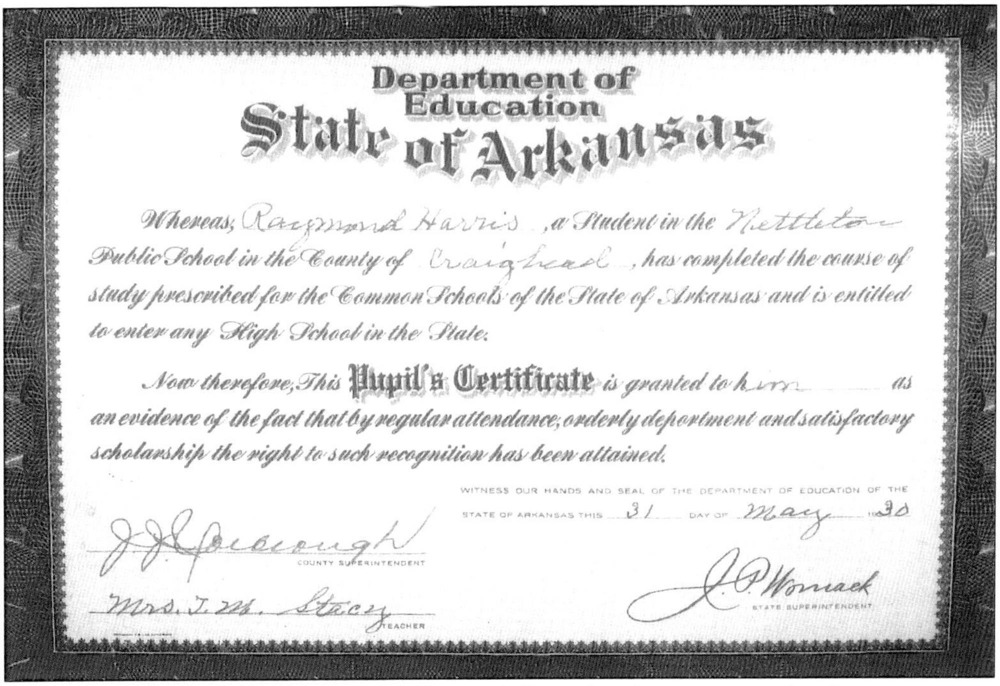

Department of Education
State of Arkansas

Whereas, Raymond Harris, a Student in the Nettleton Public School in the County of Craighead, has completed the course of study prescribed for the Common Schools of the State of Arkansas and is entitled to enter any High School in the State.

Now therefore, This Pupil's Certificate is granted to him as an evidence of the fact that by regular attendance, orderly deportment and satisfactory scholarship the right to such recognition has been attained.

WITNESS OUR HANDS AND SEAL OF THE DEPARTMENT OF EDUCATION OF THE STATE OF ARKANSAS THIS 31 DAY OF May 1930

COUNTY SUPERINTENDENT

Mrs. T. M. Stacy
TEACHER

J. P. Womack
STATE SUPERINTENDENT

For many Delta students in the 1930s, an eighth grade education was, for the most part, a terminal degree. Even today, nearly four out of ten Arkansans still do not possess a high school diploma. In this c. 1930 eighth grade certificate, awarded to Raymond Harris at Nettleton Public School, you can find reference to using this certificate as admission into "any High School in the State." (Courtesy of Nettleton Pubic Schools.)

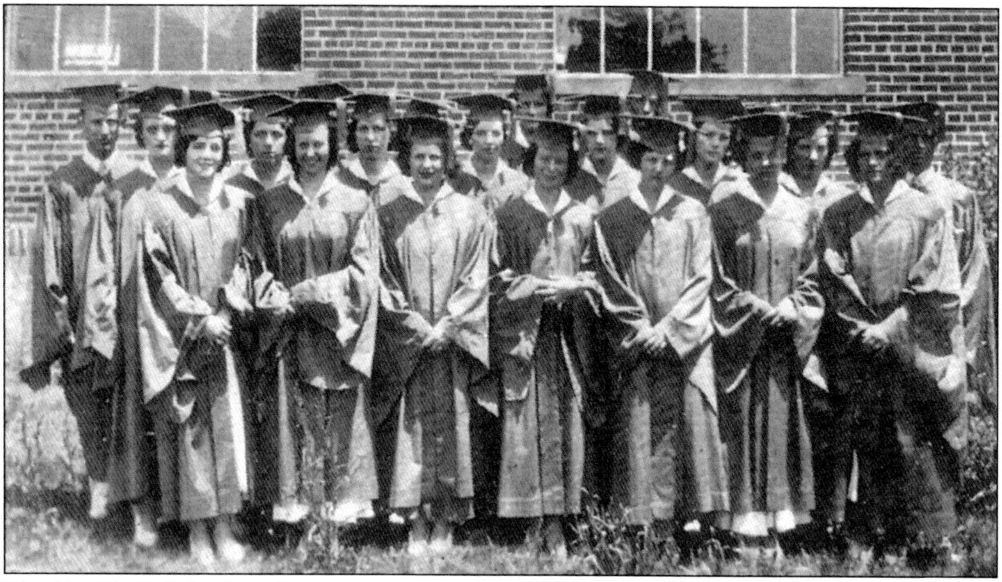

The Bay High School graduating class of 1934 posed for this photo dressed in the traditional regalia. Bay did not start offering high school courses until the new building was constructed in 1928–29. These students, therefore, are among the first to graduate from the new facility. (Courtesy of Edgar Morrison Collection.)

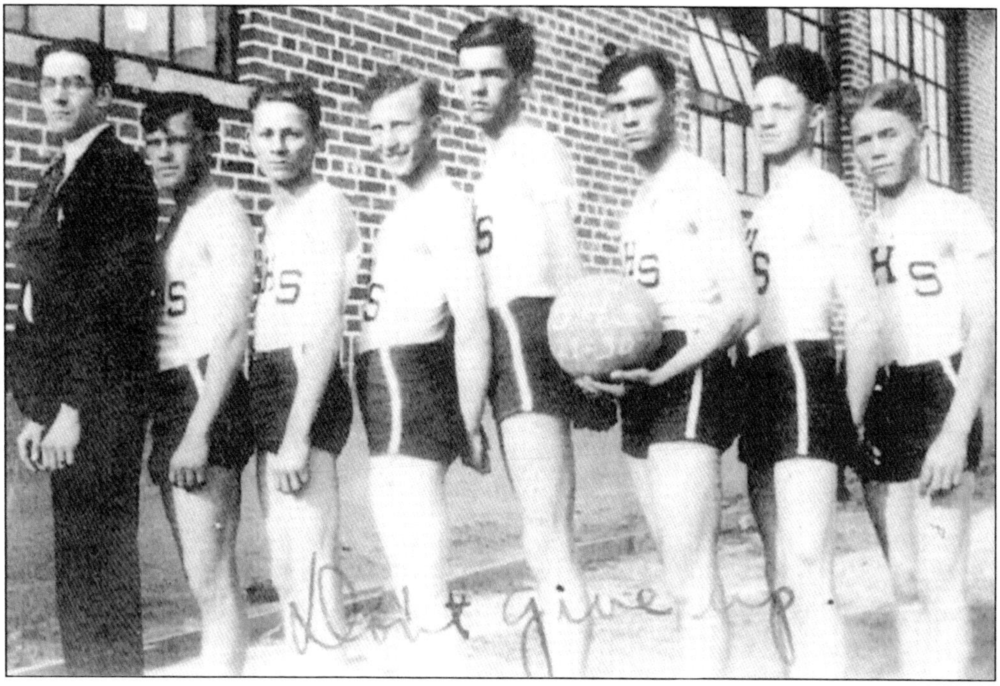

The Bay High School basketball team is pictured above in the 1930s. Although the team had few substitutes available and lacked the height and size of modern teams, their spirit was not diminished. This is evident in the inscription at the bottom of the photo, which reads, "Don't give up." (Courtesy of Edgar Morrison Collection.)

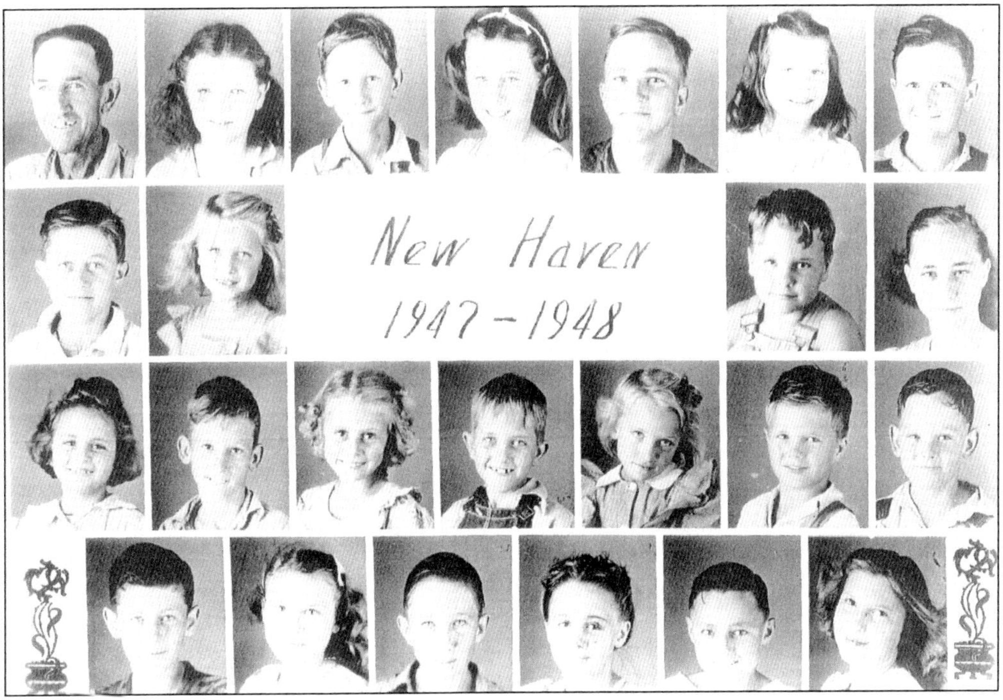

This class composite from the late 1940s reflects the traditional, rural culture of the Delta at that time. Although bib overalls of many male students are evident, the attempt to look their "Sunday School Best" is quite successful. New Haven, a small community north of Jonesboro in Craighead County, still consisted of a one-room schoolhouse at this time. (Courtesy of Elsie Dawson Collection.)

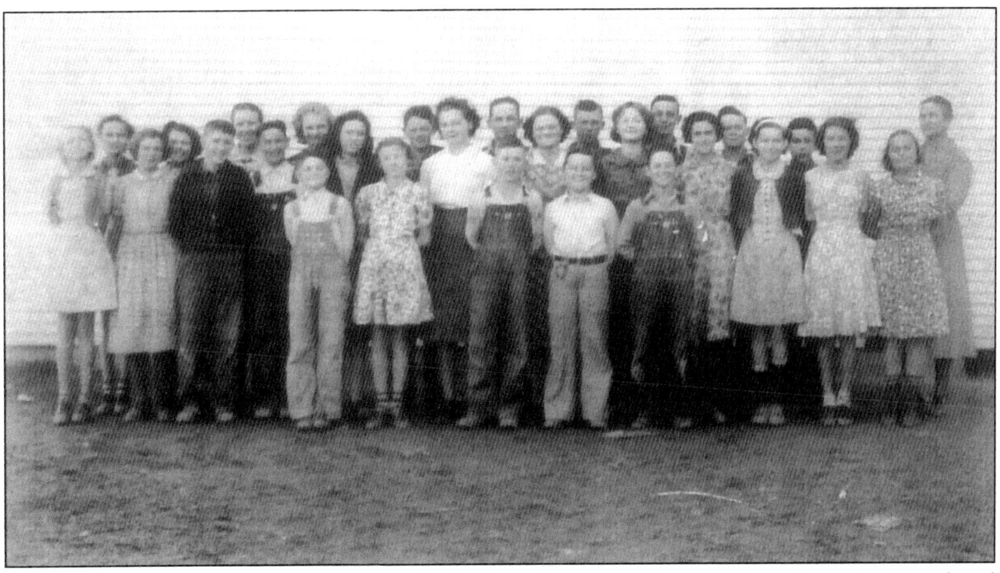

New Hope, a community approximately halfway between Bay and Jonesboro in Craighead County, had a thriving elementary school in the 1930s and '40s. Mrs. Ela Cantrell's fifth through eighth grade students took time out of their daily routine to pose for this 1937 photo. (Courtesy of Nettleton Public Schools.)

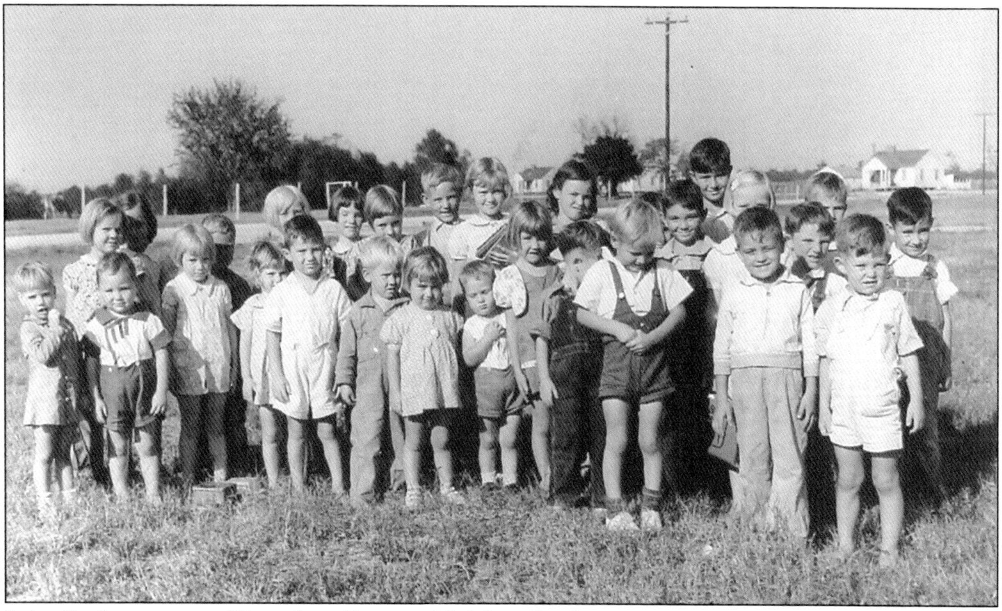

Lake Dick was one of President Roosevelt's New Deal projects to provide jobless and landless Arkansans with land. It was located in eastern Jefferson County close to Altheimer. Snow Lake was a similar project for Black Arkansans. Part of the effort was to buy up land, divide it into 40-acre plots, and distribute it. (Courtesy of Arkansas History Commission.)

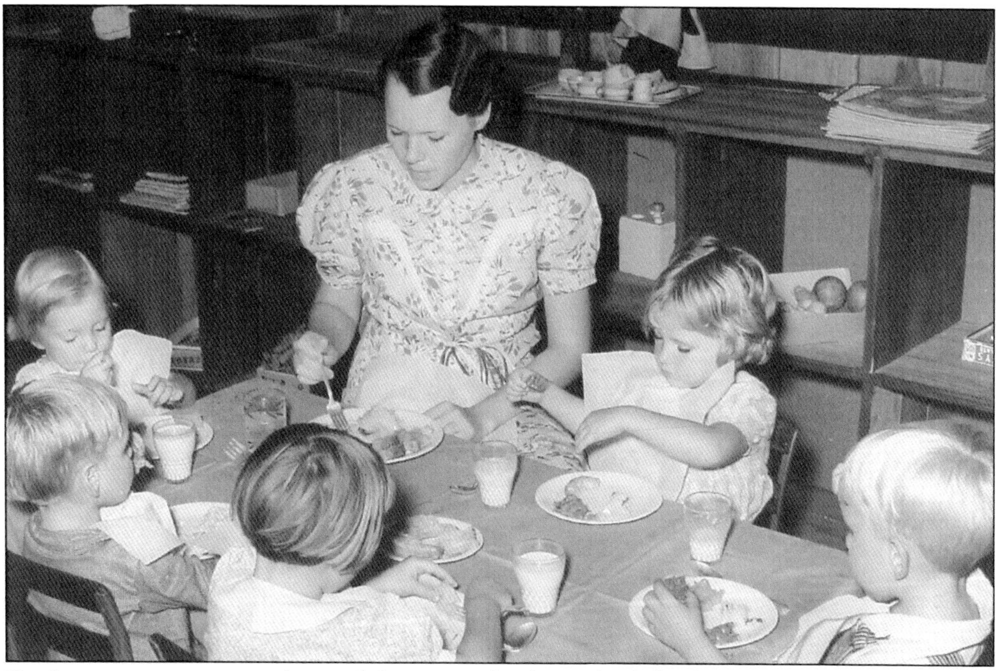

Kindergartens were not widespread; however, thanks to the federal government, the Lake Dick children were indeed fortunate to have both a kindergarten and a school lunch provided. The federal government began to support school lunches in the late 1930s by distributing surplus commodities to schools throughout the country. (Courtesy of Arkansas History Commission.)

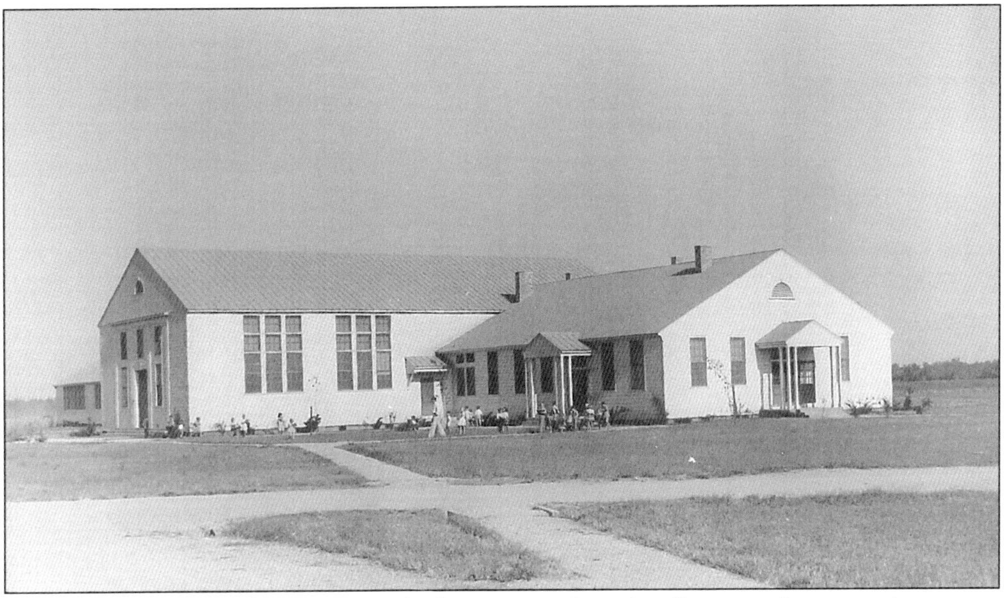

By 1938, the Lake Dick community had constructed a schoolhouse and community center. One of the aims of the federal program was to develop a new, more optimistic spirit among the residents of these communities. Better schools, earlier education, and community centers were provided as a way of doing this. (Courtesy of Arkansas History Commission.)

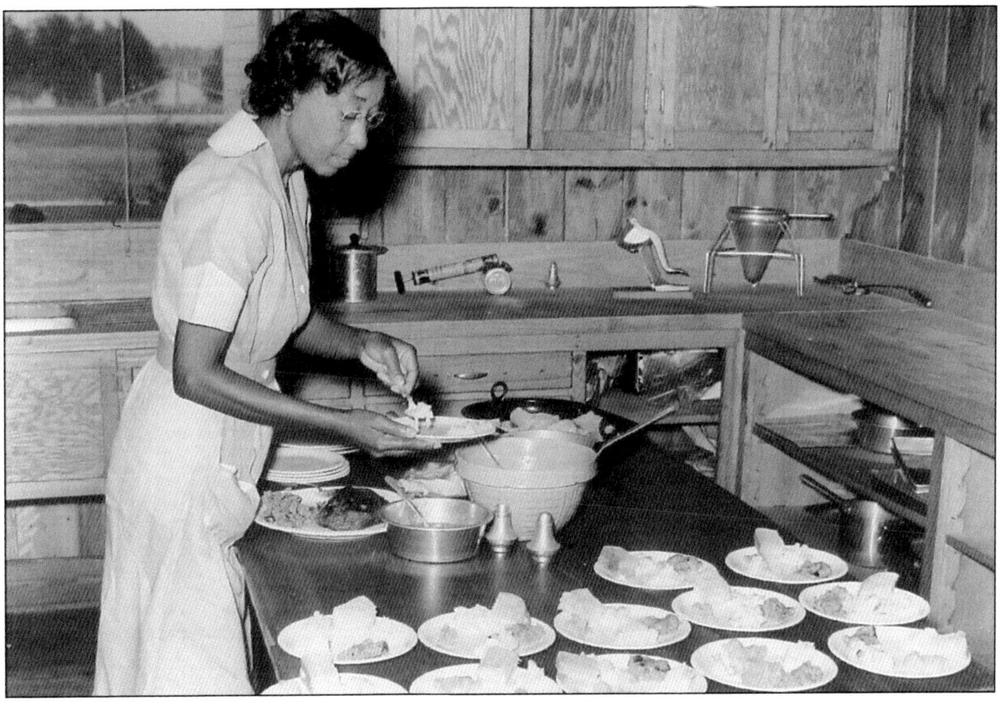

The kitchen area located at Lake Dick is shown above. Lunches were often prepared from fresh food—vegetables, fruit, and meat, some of which was provided by the commodities program. Children were provided with foods, such as citrus fruit from Florida, that many of them had never seen before. (Courtesy of Arkansas History Commission.)

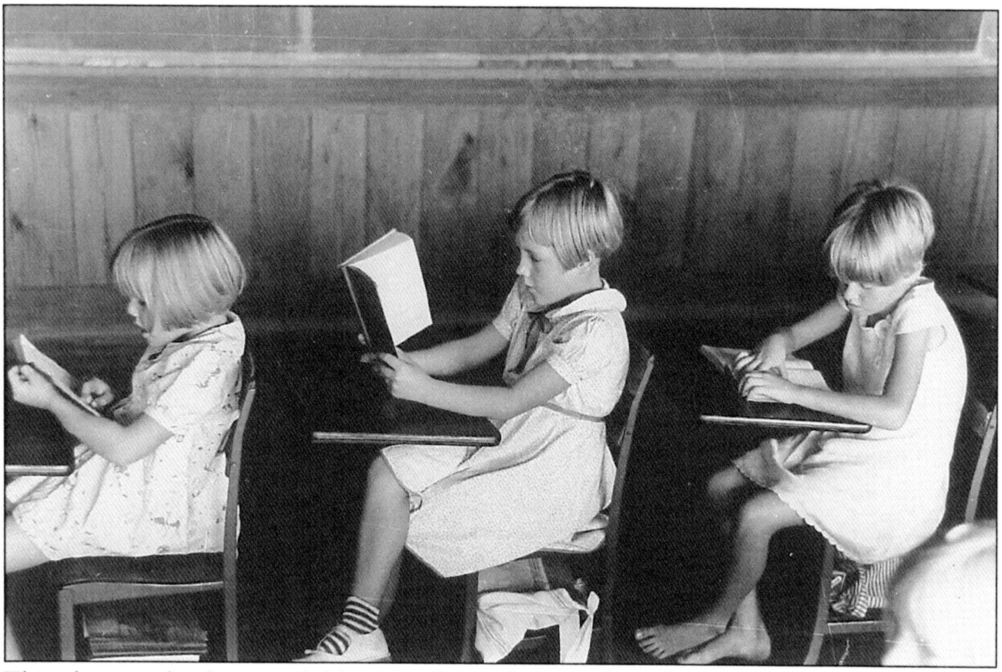

This photograph of young children in class at Lake Dick evokes considerable emotions. All three girls are wearing similar dresses; however, it is obvious that the one on the far right has no shoes. One might argue that children often prefer to go without shoes, but many Delta children could not afford shoes, and this would have been particularly true of those in the resettlement programs. Even among the poor, there was a degree of economic disparity. (Courtesy of Arkansas History Commission.)

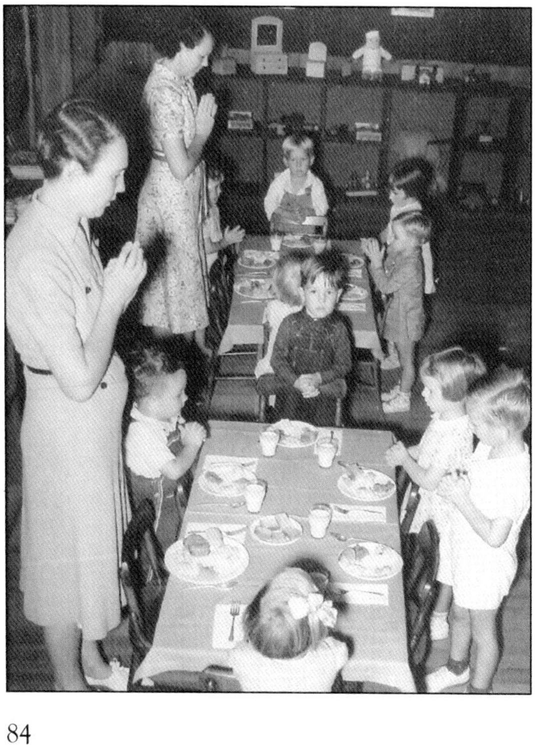

Before every lunchtime meal, Lake Dick schoolchildren and teachers in the 1930s would give thanks for their lunch. Although the school was constructed with public funds and operated by the federal government, no one thought twice about giving grace before school lunches were served. In the "Bible Belt" of the Delta during the 1930s, to raise the issue of "separation of church and state" was quite unpopular. (Courtesy of Arkansas History Commission.)

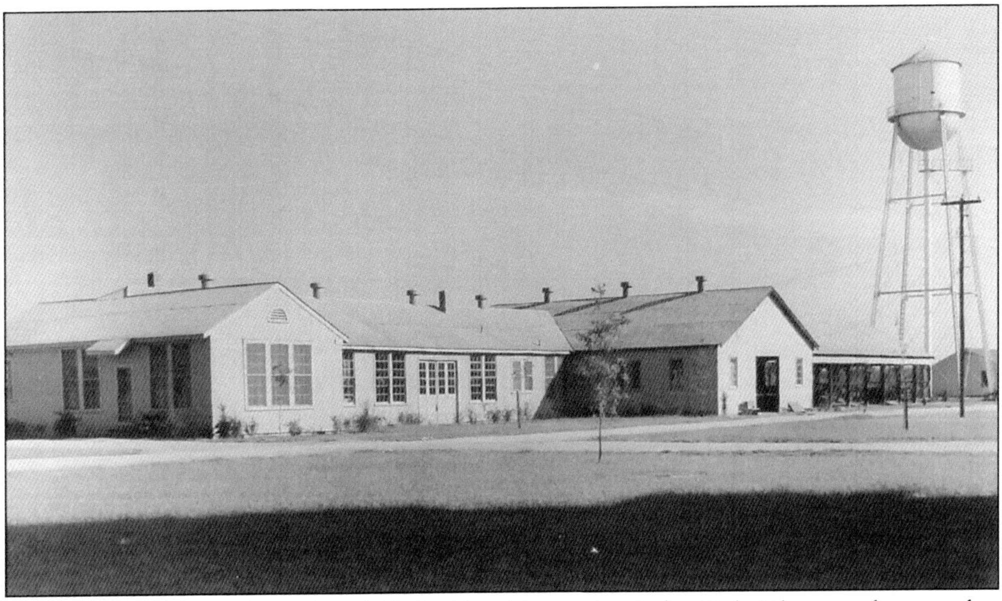

Pictured above is the Agricultural High School located at Lake Dick. The resettlement plan assumed that the farmers brought in would remain on the land, and thus training the young men in better techniques of farming seemed realistic. In many cases, it did not work out because the amount of land was too limited, and the nature of Delta agriculture was changing drastically. (Courtesy of Arkansas History Commission.)

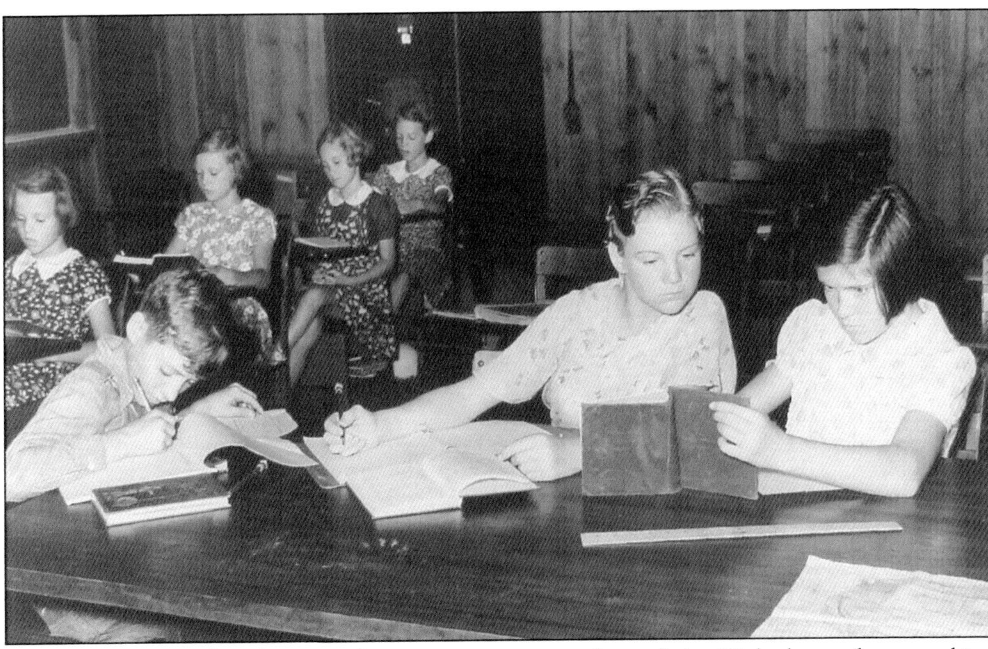

This photograph of students in the upper primary grades at Lake Dick shows them working together, building a cooperative spirit that would serve them well later in life. In addition, one will note that the majority of the girls are wearing homemade flour or feed sack dresses, a very common method of providing clothing among the rural poor of this era. (Courtesy of Arkansas History Commission.)

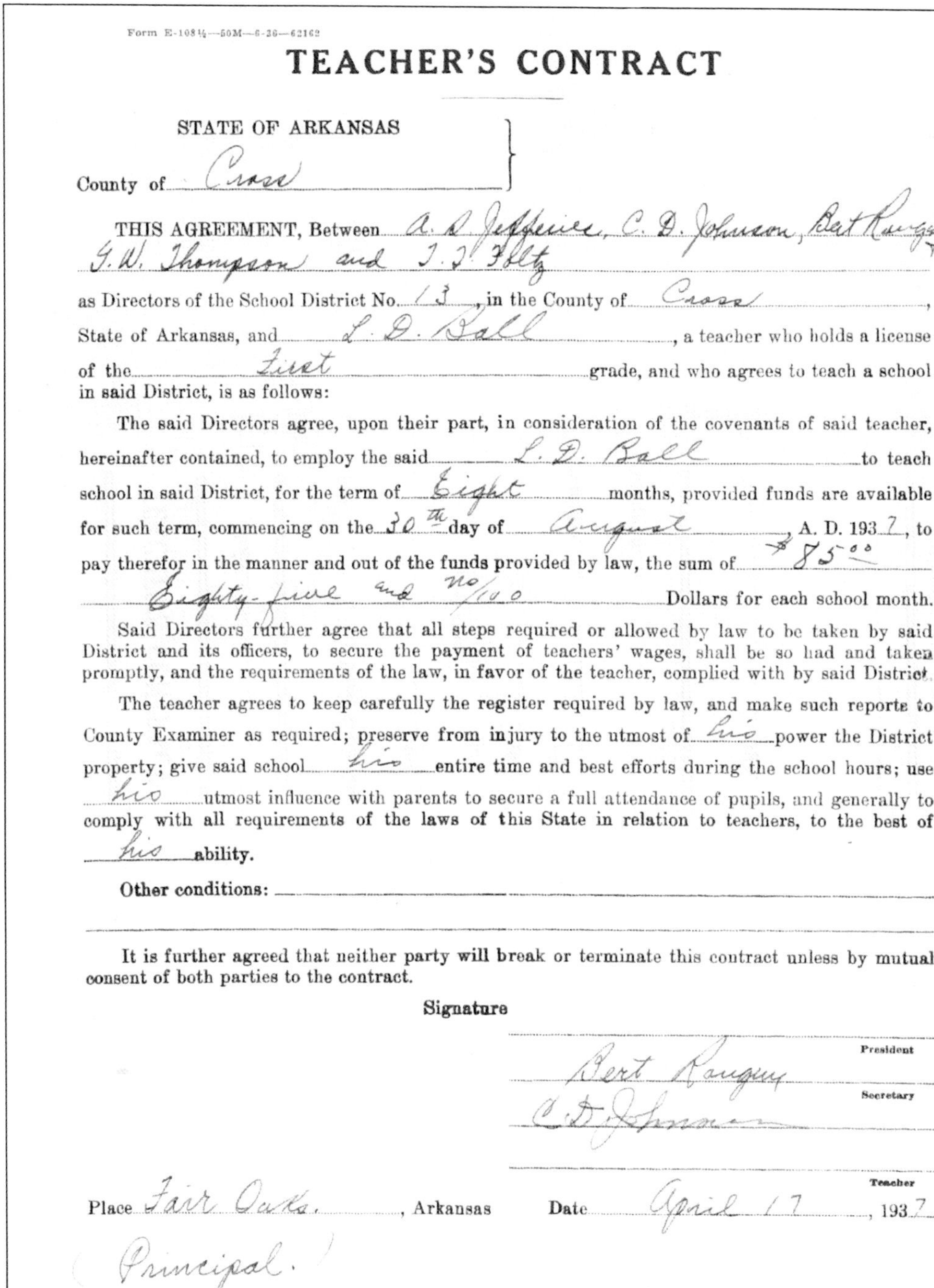

Form E-108¼—50M—6-36—62162

TEACHER'S CONTRACT

STATE OF ARKANSAS
County of Cross

THIS AGREEMENT, Between A. A. Jeffries, C. D. Johnson, Bert Rangey, G. W. Thompson and J. J. Feltz as Directors of the School District No. 13, in the County of Cross, State of Arkansas, and L. D. Ball, a teacher who holds a license of the First grade, and who agrees to teach a school in said District, is as follows:

The said Directors agree, upon their part, in consideration of the covenants of said teacher, hereinafter contained, to employ the said L. D. Ball to teach school in said District, for the term of Eight months, provided funds are available for such term, commencing on the 30th day of August, A. D. 1937, to pay therefor in the manner and out of the funds provided by law, the sum of $85.00 Eighty-five and no/100 Dollars for each school month.

Said Directors further agree that all steps required or allowed by law to be taken by said District and its officers, to secure the payment of teachers' wages, shall be so had and taken promptly, and the requirements of the law, in favor of the teacher, complied with by said District.

The teacher agrees to keep carefully the register required by law, and make such reports to County Examiner as required; preserve from injury to the utmost of his power the District property; give said school his entire time and best efforts during the school hours; use his utmost influence with parents to secure a full attendance of pupils, and generally to comply with all requirements of the laws of this State in relation to teachers, to the best of his ability.

Other conditions:

It is further agreed that neither party will break or terminate this contract unless by mutual consent of both parties to the contract.

Signature

President: Bert Rangey

Secretary: C. D. Johnson

Teacher

Place Fair Oaks, Arkansas Date April 17, 1937

Principal.

Despite the fact that Delta residents found themselves in the midst of the Great Depression, nearly all schools operated as usual. This teacher's contract for the 1937 school year illustrates that teachers' salaries in the Delta remained constant for nearly a decade, and also ranked among the lowest in the state during this period. It is also interesting to note the blank spaces within the contract to denote the gender specific pronoun (i.e., his, her) to accommodate the high percentage of females in the profession. (Courtesy of Larry Ball Collection.)

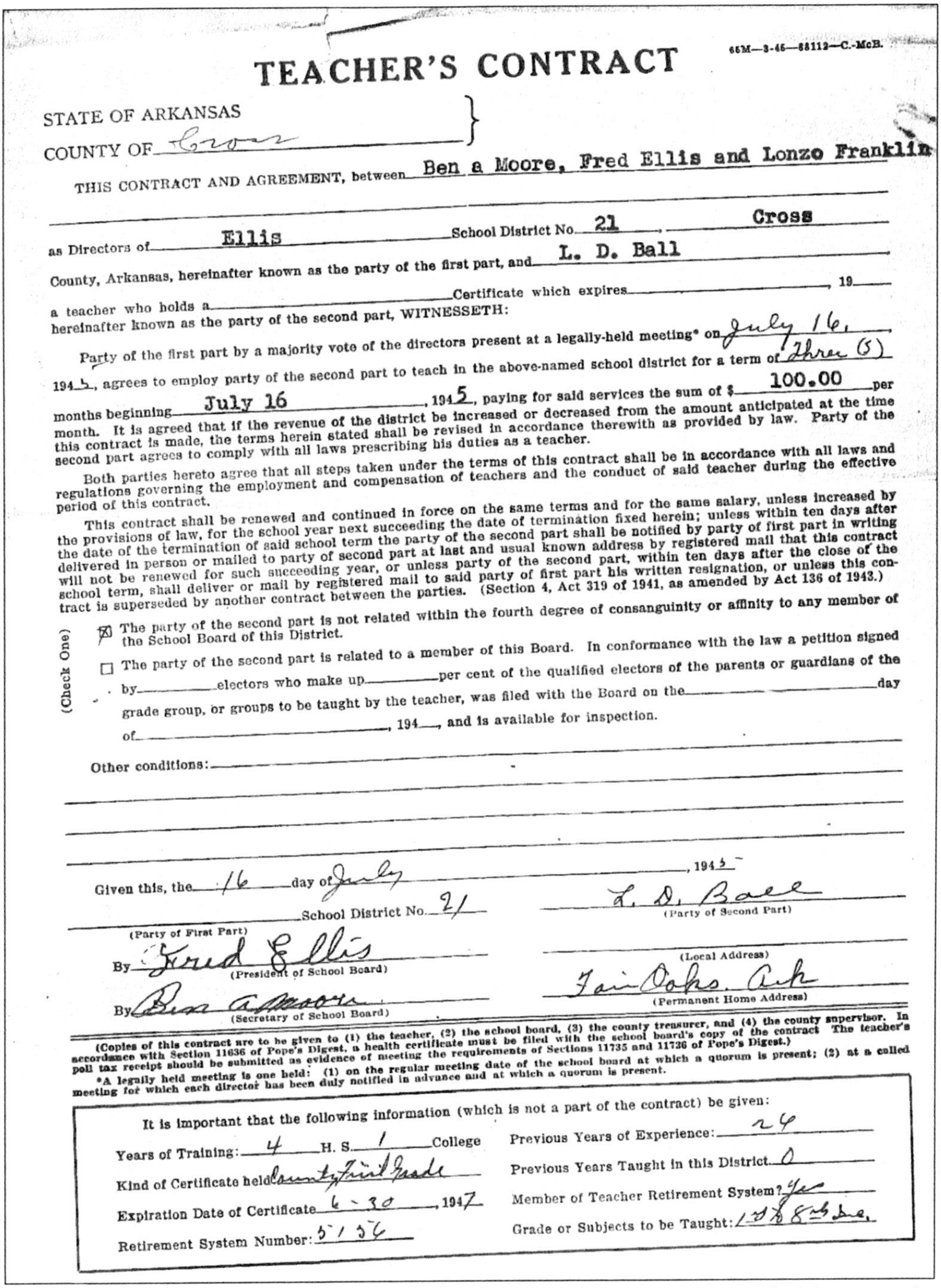
65M—3-46—65112—C.-McB.

TEACHER'S CONTRACT

STATE OF ARKANSAS
COUNTY OF Cross

THIS CONTRACT AND AGREEMENT, between Ben a Moore, Fred Ellis and Lonzo Franklin as Directors of Ellis School District No. 21, Cross County, Arkansas, hereinafter known as the party of the first part, and L. D. Ball a teacher who holds a ______ Certificate which expires ______, 19__ hereinafter known as the party of the second part, WITNESSETH:

Party of the first part by a majority vote of the directors present at a legally-held meeting* on July 16, 1945, agrees to employ party of the second part to teach in the above-named school district for a term of Three (3) months beginning July 16, 1945, paying for said services the sum of $100.00 per month. It is agreed that if the revenue of the district be increased or decreased from the amount anticipated at the time this contract is made, the terms herein stated shall be revised in accordance therewith as provided by law. Party of the second part agrees to comply with all laws prescribing his duties as a teacher.

Both parties hereto agree that all steps taken under the terms of this contract shall be in accordance with all laws and regulations governing the employment and compensation of teachers and the conduct of said teacher during the effective period of this contract.

This contract shall be renewed and continued in force on the same terms and for the same salary, unless increased by the provisions of law, for the school year next succeeding the date of termination fixed herein; unless within ten days after the date of the termination of said school term the party of the second part shall be notified by party of first part in writing delivered in person or mailed to party of second part at last and usual known address by registered mail that this contract will not be renewed for such succeeding year, or unless party of the second part, within ten days after the close of the school term, shall deliver or mail by registered mail to said party of first part his written resignation, or unless this contract is superseded by another contract between the parties. (Section 4, Act 319 of 1941, as amended by Act 136 of 1943.)

(Check One)

☒ The party of the second part is not related within the fourth degree of consanguinity or affinity to any member of the School Board of this District.

☐ The party of the second part is related to a member of this Board. In conformance with the law a petition signed by ______ electors who make up ______ per cent of the qualified electors of the parents or guardians of the grade group, or groups to be taught by the teacher, was filed with the Board on the ______ day of ______, 194__, and is available for inspection.

Other conditions: ______

Given this, the 16 day of July, 1945

School District No. 21 (Party of First Part)

By Fred Ellis (President of School Board)

By Ben a Moore (Secretary of School Board)

L. D. Ball (Party of Second Part)

(Local Address)

Fair Oaks, Ark (Permanent Home Address)

(Copies of this contract are to be given to (1) the teacher, (2) the school board, (3) the county treasurer, and (4) the county supervisor. In accordance with Section 11636 of Pope's Digest, a health certificate must be filed with the school board's copy of the contract. The teacher's poll tax receipt should be submitted as evidence of meeting the requirements of Sections 11735 and 11736 of Pope's Digest.)

*A legally held meeting is one held: (1) on the regular meeting date of the school board at which a quorum is present; (2) at a called meeting for which each director has been duly notified in advance and at which a quorum is present.

It is important that the following information (which is not a part of the contract) be given:

Years of Training: 4 H. S. 1 College
Kind of Certificate held County First Grade
Expiration Date of Certificate 6-30, 1947
Retirement System Number: 5156
Previous Years of Experience: 26
Previous Years Taught in this District 0
Member of Teacher Retirement System? Yes
Grade or Subjects to be Taught: 1st to 8th Grs.

L.D. Ball signed a 1945 contract to teach at Ellis, in Cross County, for a period of three months for $100 a month. The three-month term illustrates the development of the split term system, which permitted the break in October to allow for the cotton harvest. By this point, Ball had accumulated 26 years of teaching experience and was certified to teach first grade. (Courtesy of Larry Ball Collection.)

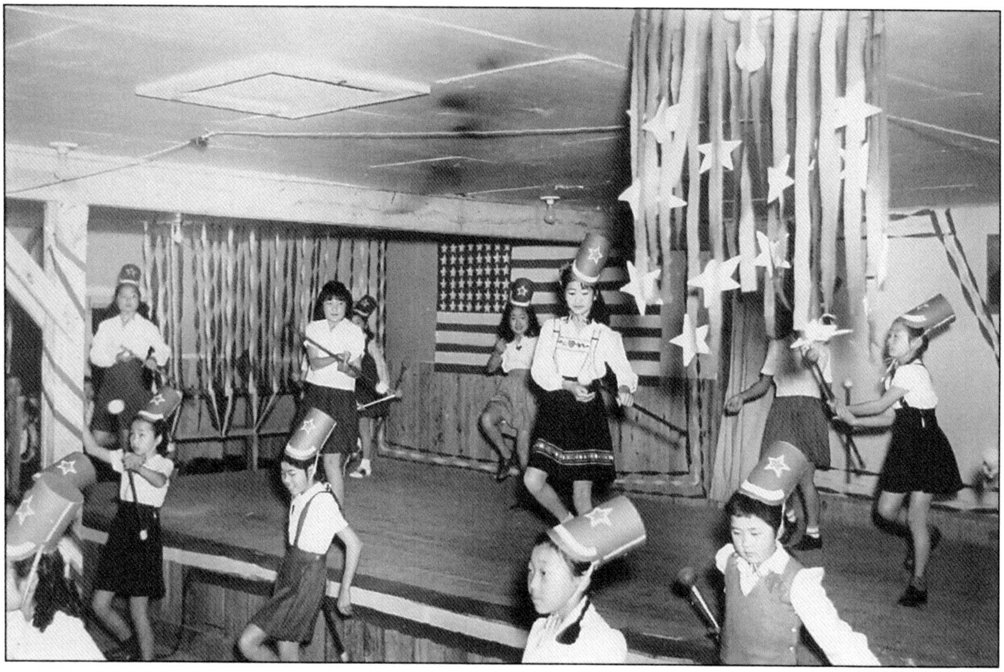

Jerome Relocation Center, located in southeastern Arkansas at Denson, was constructed during World War II to house Japanese-Americans during World War II, under Executive Order 9066. Even though they were forced from their homes and their civil rights were denied, these students still participated in all of the patriotic ceremonies, such as the baton routine above, and educational activities they were provided with at Jerome, such as participating in morning exercises, pictured below. (Courtesy of Arkansas History Commission.)

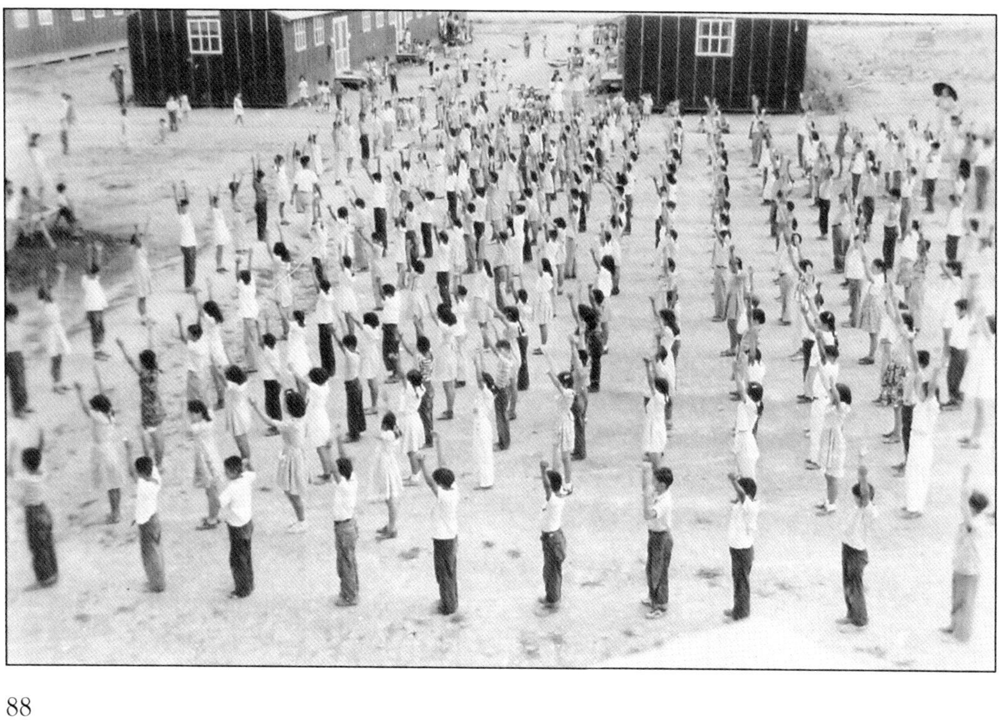

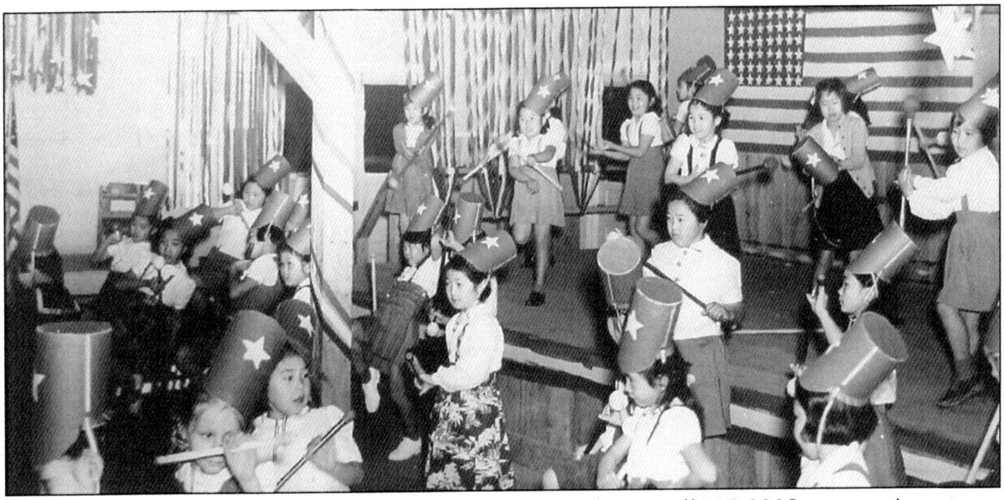

These students at Jerome Relocation Center were among the overall 110,000 Japanese-Americans who were evacuated from the West Coast during World War II. Decades later, President Ronald Regan would sign HR442 into law, issuing reparations, $20,000 each, and a letter of apology to all surviving Japanese-Americans who were interned during the war. (Courtesy of Arkansas History Commission.)

STATE DEPARTMENT OF EDUCATION
DIVISION OF FREE TEXT BOOKS
LITTLE ROCK, ARKANSAS

(Duplicate)

Form TexB-7—200M
8-37—65402—C.-McB.

ASSIGNMENT CARD FOR FREE TEXT BOOKS

SESSION 1939, 1940 Card No. 4

Pupil Fletcher McGhee — New Hope School

Parent H F McGhee — District No. 30

Address R 3 Jonesboro — County Craighead

Date Books Issued 11-17-39 — Grade 9 Teacher Mrs G E Jones

List of Books	Grade	Book No.	Years Used	Condition of Book	Date Returned	List of Books	Grade	Book No.	Years Used	Condition of Book	Date Returned
Readers (Pre-P.)						History (U.S.)	8	29	1	N	4-19-40
Reader (Pr.)						Civics	8	4	1	N	" " "
Reader						Agriculture					
Arithmetic	8	4	1	G	4-19-40	Phy.-Hygiene					
Spelling	8	2	2	GM	" " "	Home Eco. Sci	9	3	0	N	" " "
Language	8	3	1	N	" " "	Writing					
Geography											
History (Ark.)											

Duplicate card must be filed with the teacher. The pupil must return all books at the close of the school term or upon moving to another school and receive this duplicate card fully receipted. Without it he will not be granted free text books for the next session. When the pupil has completed any book assigned to him during the term, that book must be taken up and receipted for on this card.

I hereby certify that the pupil's record listed above is clear.

Mrs G E Jones
Teacher

In the 1939–40 school year, Fletcher McGhee received free textbooks. The textbooks were listed on a Department of Education assignment card. The teacher was required to list each book handed out and to record the date upon which the book was returned. The provision of free books was important and, for the students, the red tape a necessary but valuable exchange.

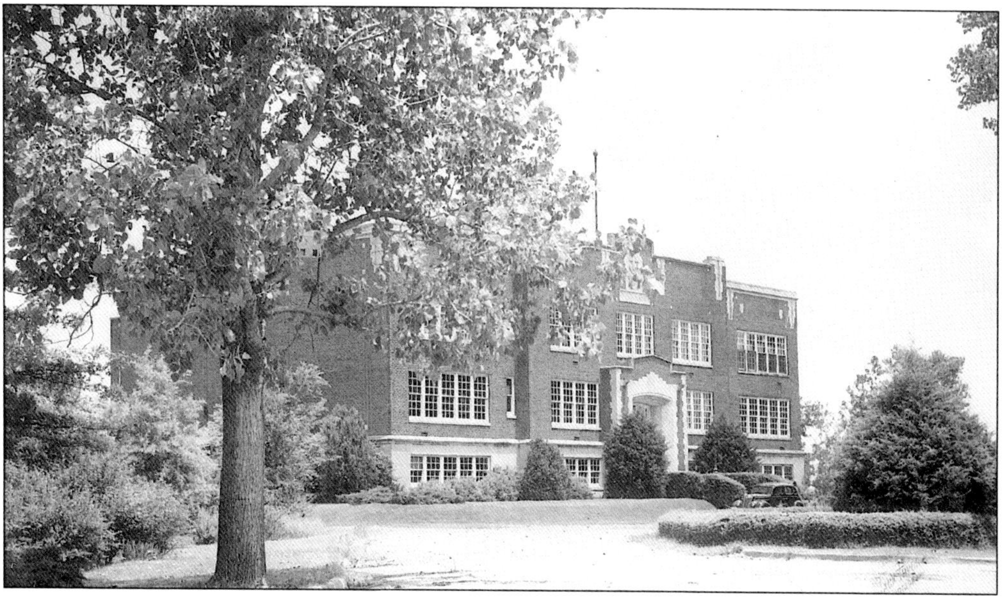

R.E. Lee Wilson, whose portrait is visible in the photograph below, was instrumental in bringing economic development and settlement to northeast Arkansas. A lumber industry entrepreneur, Wilson owned thousands of forested acres in the Delta during the early 1900s. Wilson and his descendants would donate vast amounts of money to ensure the success of what is now Arkansas State University, serving as a member of the board of trustees from 1917 to 1933. In addition, he founded an educational institution, Wilson School, pictured above, for elementary and secondary students who lived in the Mississippi County community that also bore his name. The school at Wilson Farm provided students with one of the most modern educational facilities in the state. Many graduates went on to college and successful careers thanks in part to Wilson School. (Courtesy of Arkansas History Commission.)

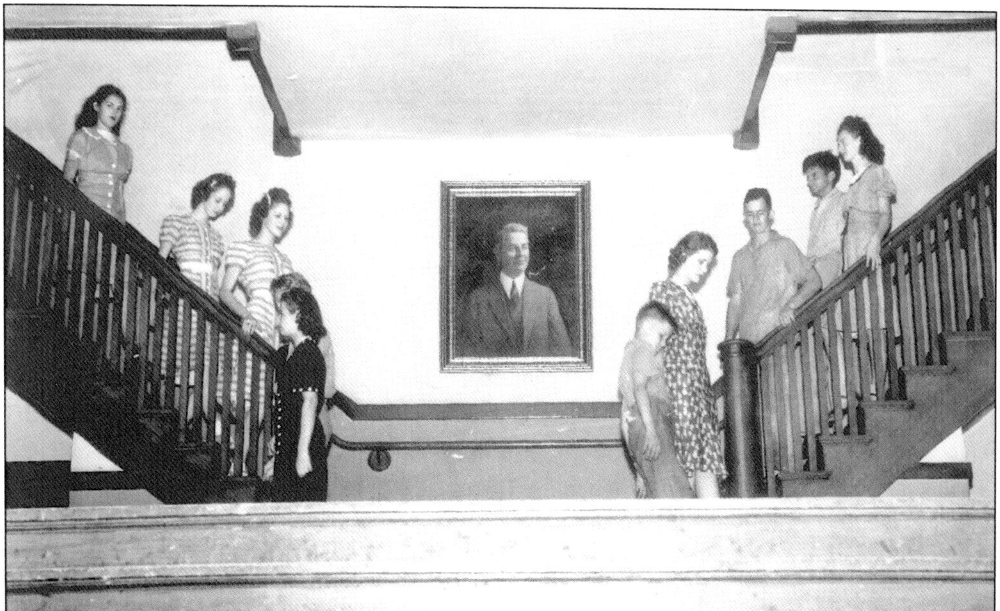

Six

1950s–1970s
Surviving the Storm

In an era when national unrest was rampant, the Delta appeared relatively immune. Traditions, customs, as well as social prescriptions and proscriptions, remained relatively untouched for most of the period.

The major educational focus for much of the 1950s was on desegregation. Despite the fact that Arkansas was one of only two states in the South, Texas being the other one, to have any integrated schools prior to the 1954 *Brown v. Board of Education* decision, the image many have of Arkansas during the 1950s is that of the "Little Rock Nine" and federal troops on the steps of Central High School in 1957. As many communities sought to integrate voluntarily, however, the emergence of opposition groups and events under Governor Orval Faubus' tenure brought reliance and intervention by federal power. Therefore, change invariably came to the Delta, although much later than in the rest of the country.

The 1960s ushered in a certain degree of change in the educational landscape of the Arkansas Delta, although not near as much as that witnessed by residents in other states and regions. Although there was some evidence of a change in dress and hairstyle on Arkansas Delta high school and college campuses during the late 1960s and early 1970s, it was often late in coming and short in duration. Other examples that the Delta was not immune to outside forces included an increase in drug use among youth and a growing number of protest movements visible across the region. Once again, however, these protests were by far the exception, in large part due to the paternalistic leadership that fought to resist such activity and change from occurring under their watch. Indeed, it seems that the major turmoil or change that 1960s and '70s Delta residents witnessed was once again at the hands of Mother Nature.

In 1968, a large tornado destroyed numerous buildings in the Nettleton school district, forcing students to meet in makeshift quarters for a period of time. In 1973, disaster struck the Delta yet again. This time, several tornados struck the city of Jonesboro, demolishing the high school building. For some time thereafter, while a new building was being constructed, Jonesboro students met in a variety of facilities, including the county fairgrounds. The social and natural storm that struck the Arkansas Delta and the impact it had on education in the region constitute the focus of this chapter.

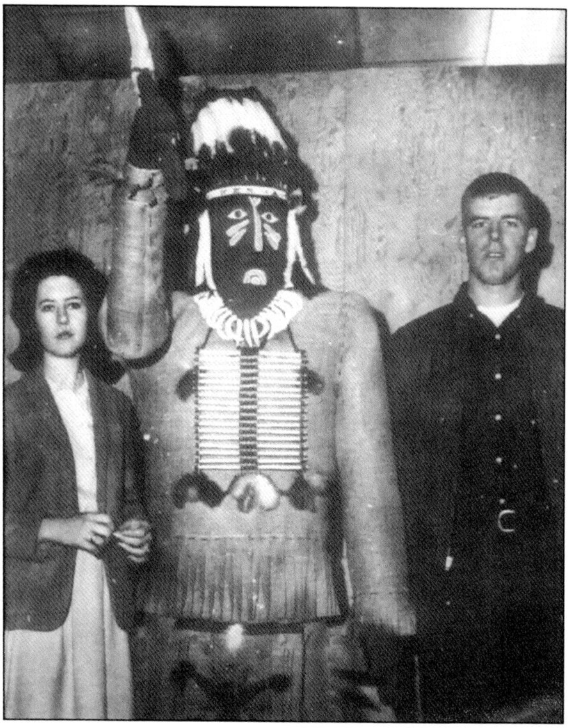

Symbols of special events are important to most Arkansas Delta students. The Raider mascot of Nettleton, Craighead County, may be one of the most ferocious of all. This display was constructed for the first homecoming event in 1965. Although such mascots have been questioned in recent years, they remain popular. (Courtesy of Nettleton Public Schools.)

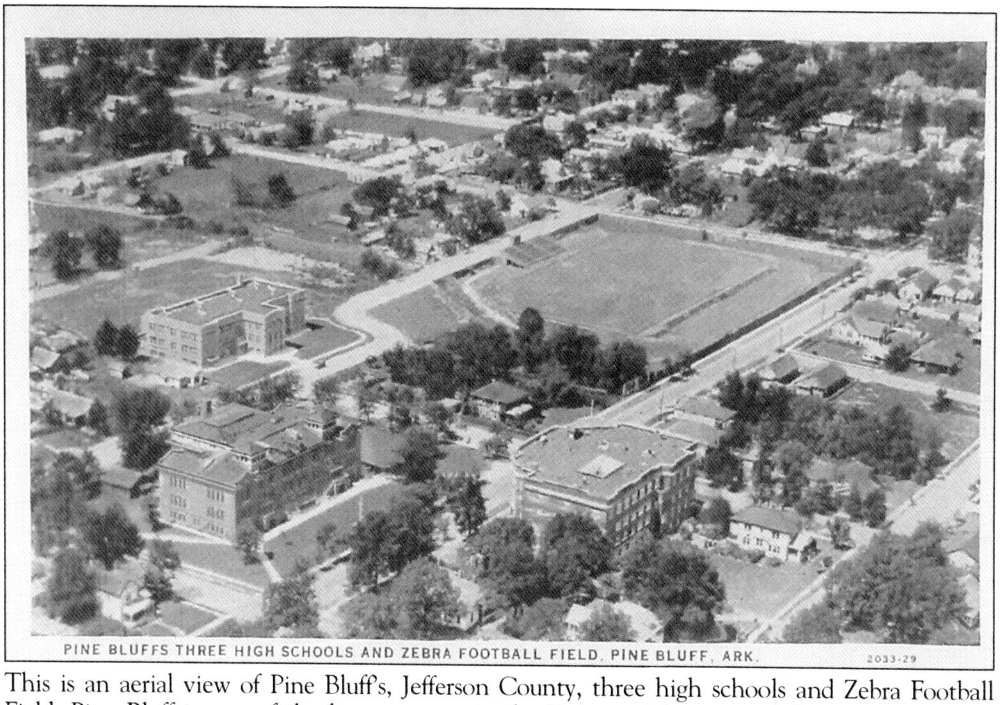

This is an aerial view of Pine Bluff's, Jefferson County, three high schools and Zebra Football Field. Pine Bluff is one of the largest towns in the Delta and has one of the most significant African-American populations as well. It is highly unusual to find three high schools located at the same site anywhere else in the Delta, or the nation for that matter. (Courtesy of Arkansas History Commission.)

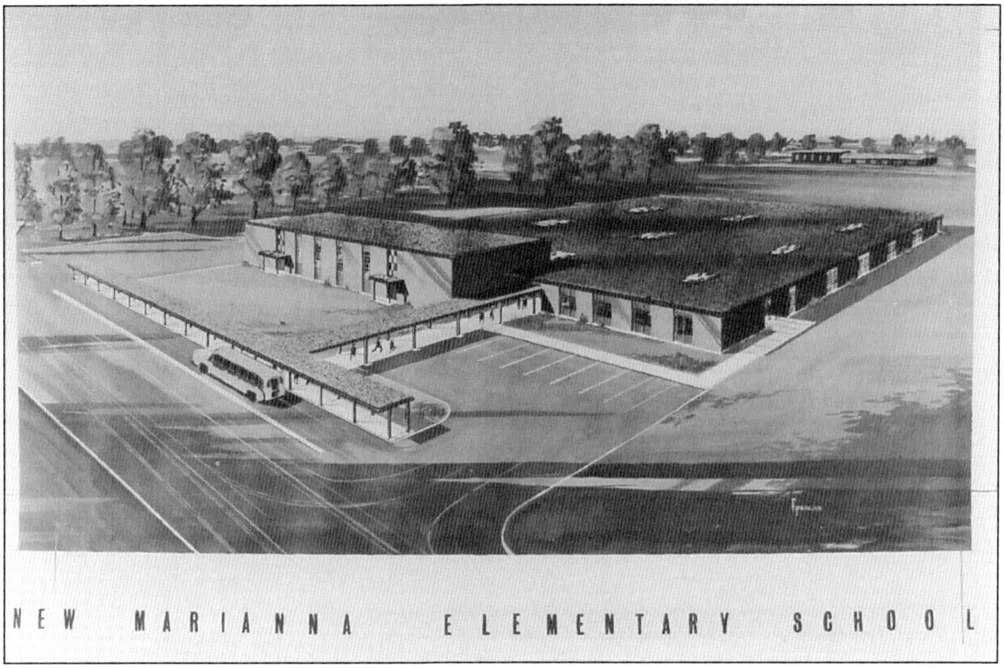

The architectural plans for A.L. Whitten Elementary School in Marianna, Lee County, reflect the modern design movement that was evident in numerous Delta schools' construction in the late 1950s and 1960s. This also serves to illustrate something about the growth experienced at the elementary, secondary, and university levels during this same period, especially in the larger Delta communities. (Courtesy of Arkansas History Commission.)

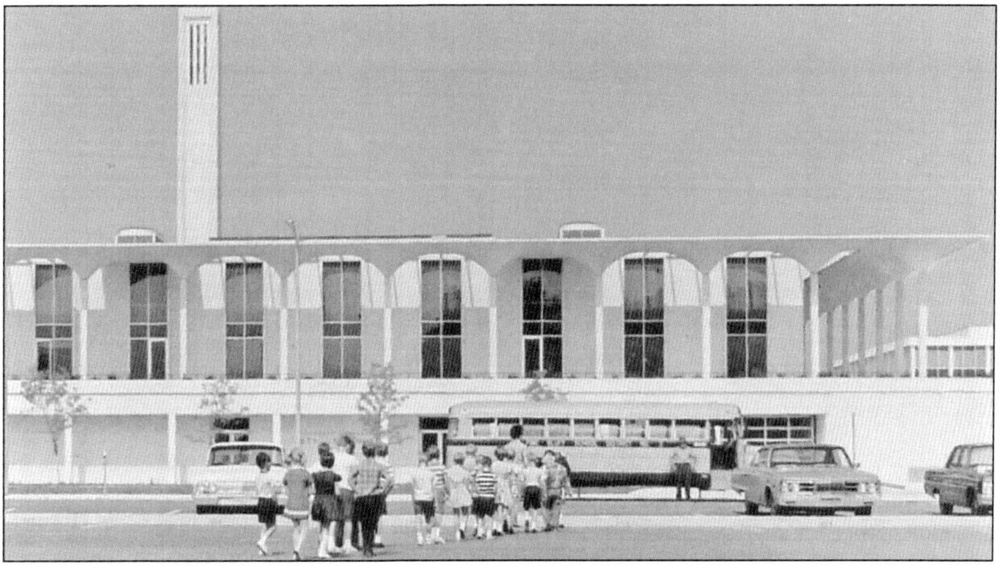

The Pine Bluff Civic and Cultural Center suggests that the same investment residents made in education did not end with the construction of school buildings. Numerous Delta communities also invested a tremendous amount of time and money in the development of other educational forums such as civic centers, museums, theaters, and libraries. (Courtesy of Arkansas History Commission.)

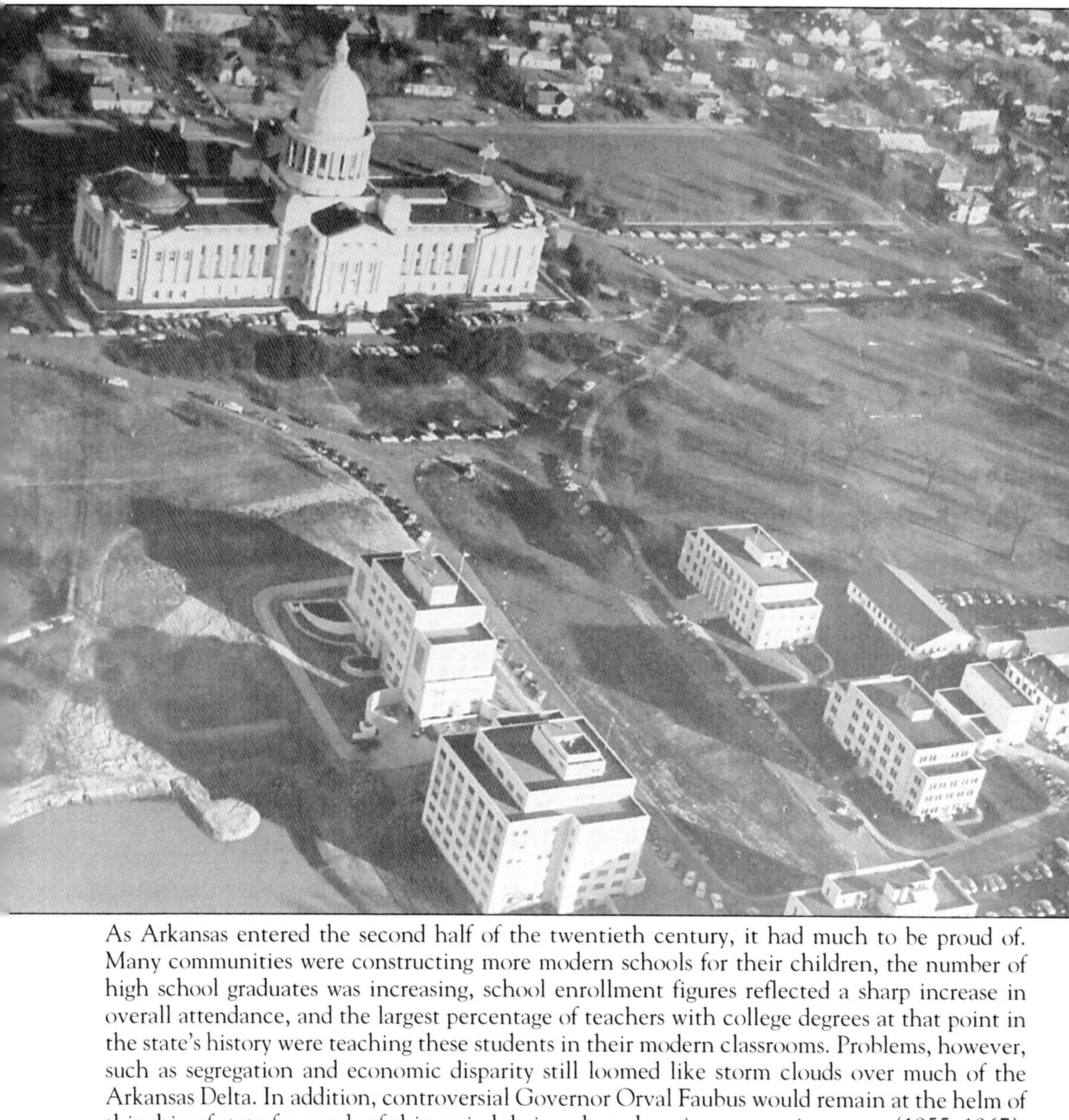

As Arkansas entered the second half of the twentieth century, it had much to be proud of. Many communities were constructing more modern schools for their children, the number of high school graduates was increasing, school enrollment figures reflected a sharp increase in overall attendance, and the largest percentage of teachers with college degrees at that point in the state's history were teaching these students in their modern classrooms. Problems, however, such as segregation and economic disparity still loomed like storm clouds over much of the Arkansas Delta. In addition, controversial Governor Orval Faubus would remain at the helm of this ship of state for much of this period, being elected to six consecutive terms (1955–1967). (Courtesy of Arkansas History Commission.)

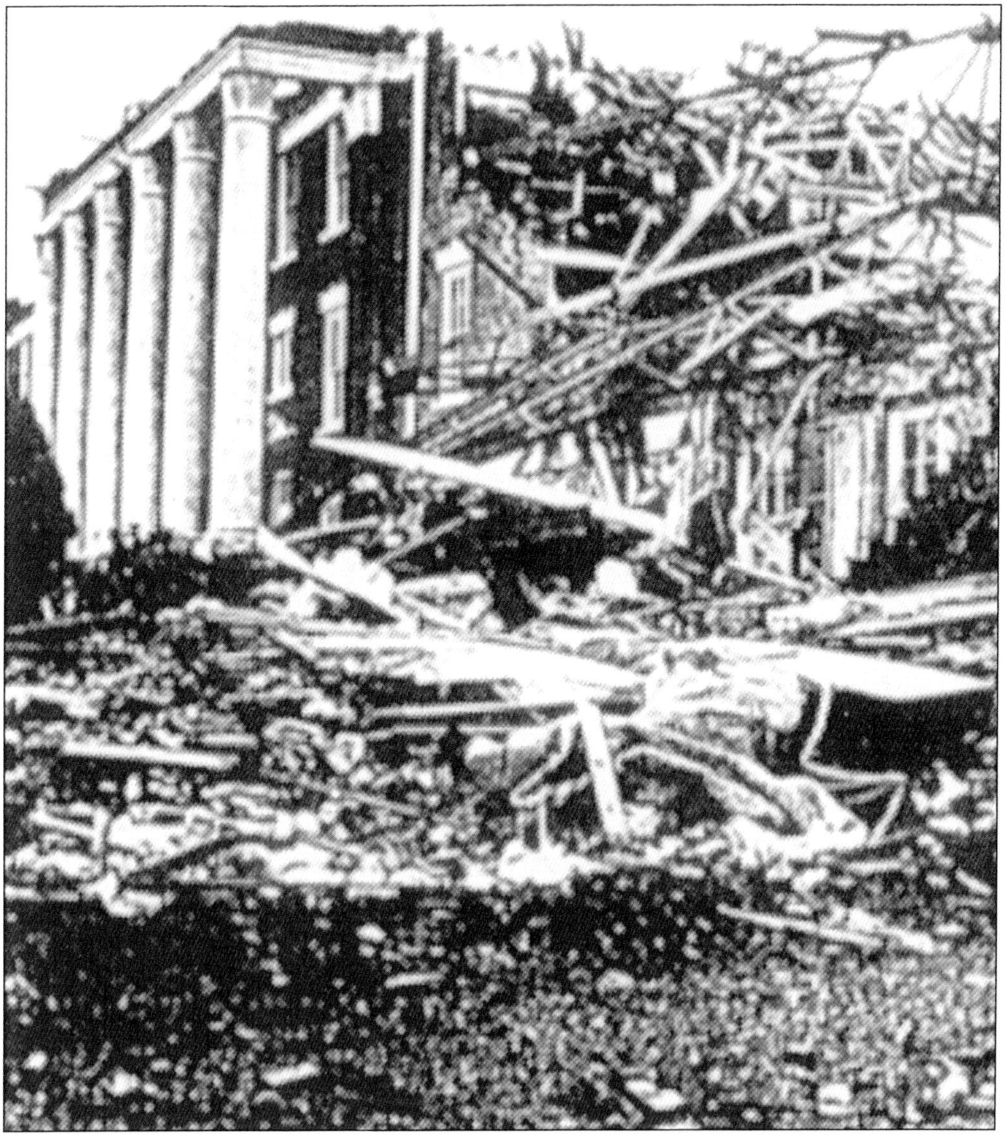

In the spring of 1973, a devastating set of tornados hit Jonesboro. Numerous buildings were destroyed that day, including Jonesboro High School. The event had such an impact on the community that a book was written that same year, *The Jonesboro Tornado, May, 27 1973*, chronicling the events that took place that day and the subsequent clean-up and rebuilding that followed. Even today, many of Jonesboro High School alumni still lament the loss of the old building. (Courtesy of Arkansas State University Archives.)

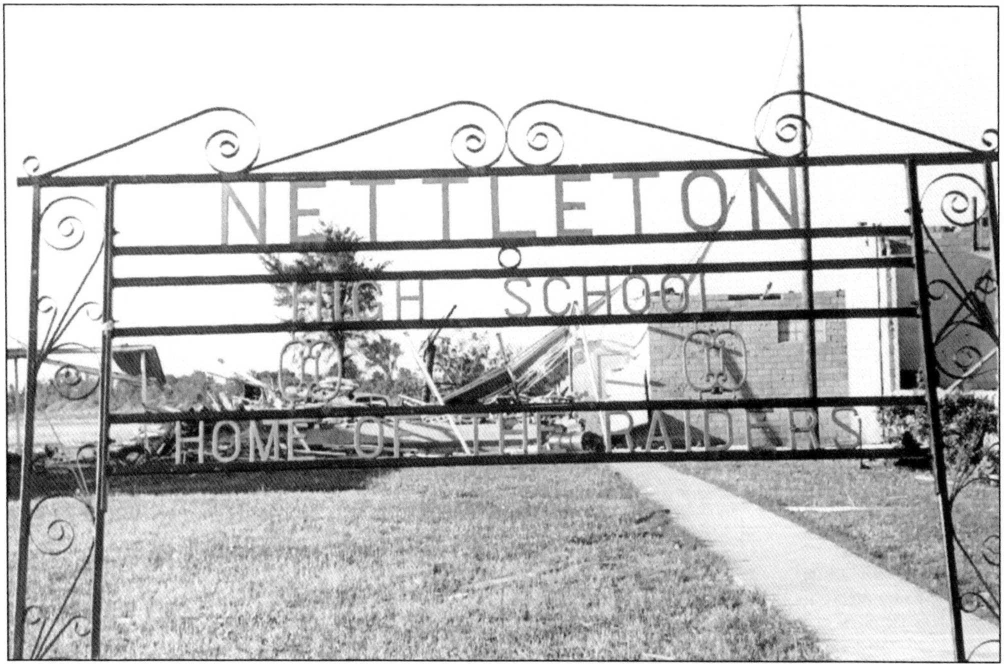

In 1968, a massive tornado hit the area of Nettleton and all but totally destroyed a major part of the physical facilities. Through the gate pictured above, which was amazingly left standing, and in the classroom below, one can see the extent of the damage and devastation left in the path of the tornado. The tornado not only destroyed physical facilities but took a score of lives as well. (Courtesy of Nettleton Public Schools.)

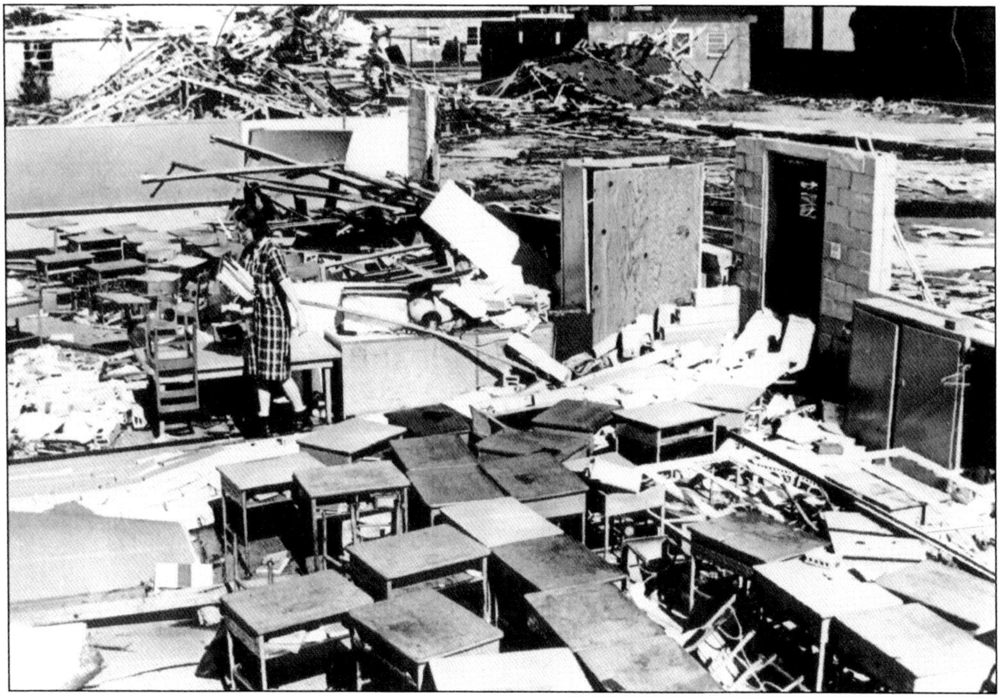

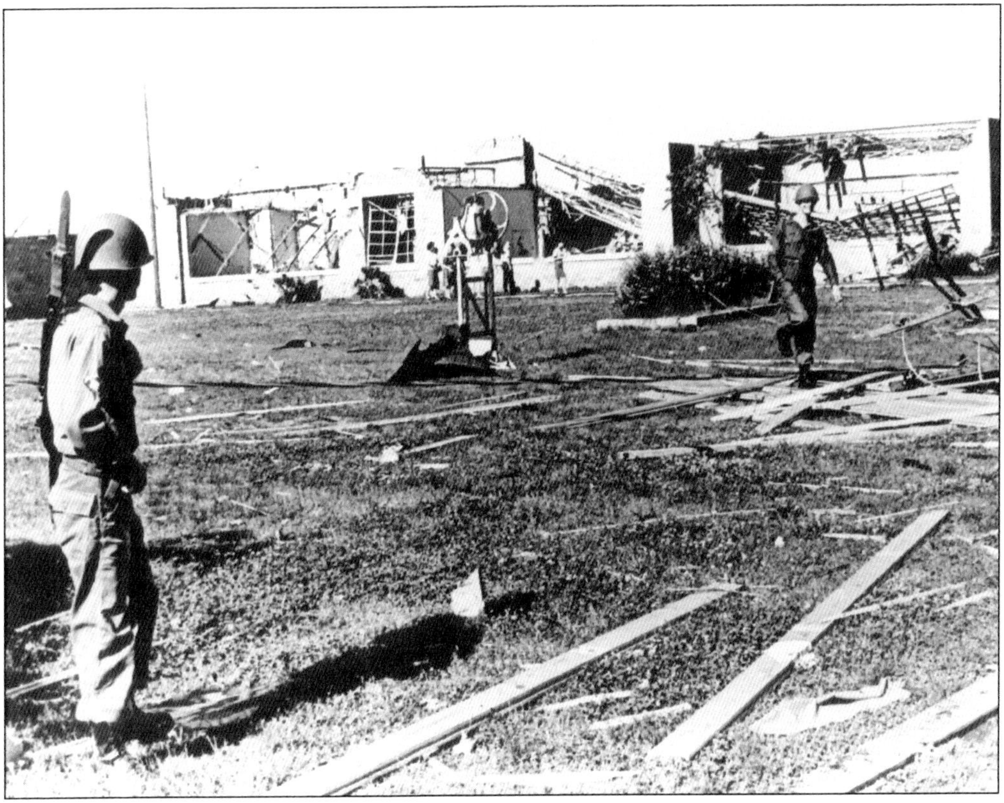

A national guardsman, pictured above, stands watch over what remained of Nettleton Schools following the tornado. Despite the destruction, many valuable items (student desks, tables, books) remained relatively intact. Although residents from throughout Craighead County pulled together during the crisis, there was still a need for such a presence to deter potential looters. While decades have passed since the disaster, it remains a topic of discussion even today. (Courtesy of Nettleton Public Schools.)

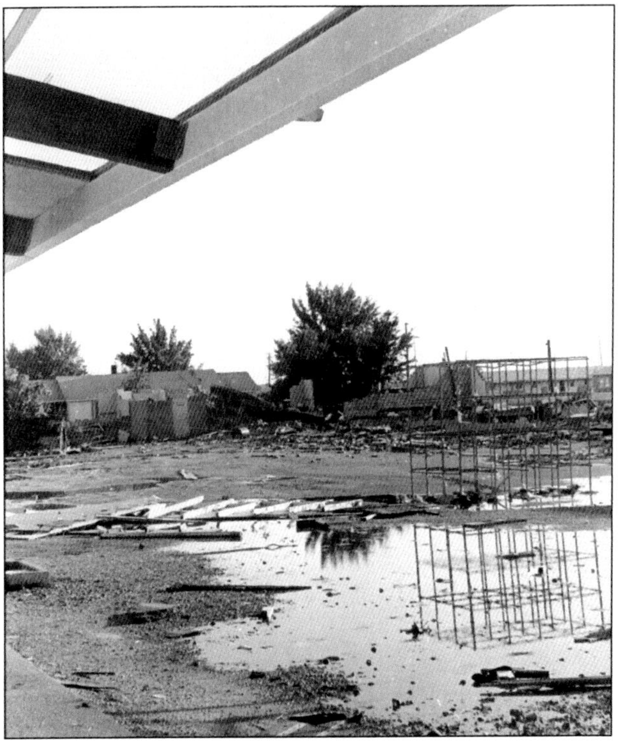

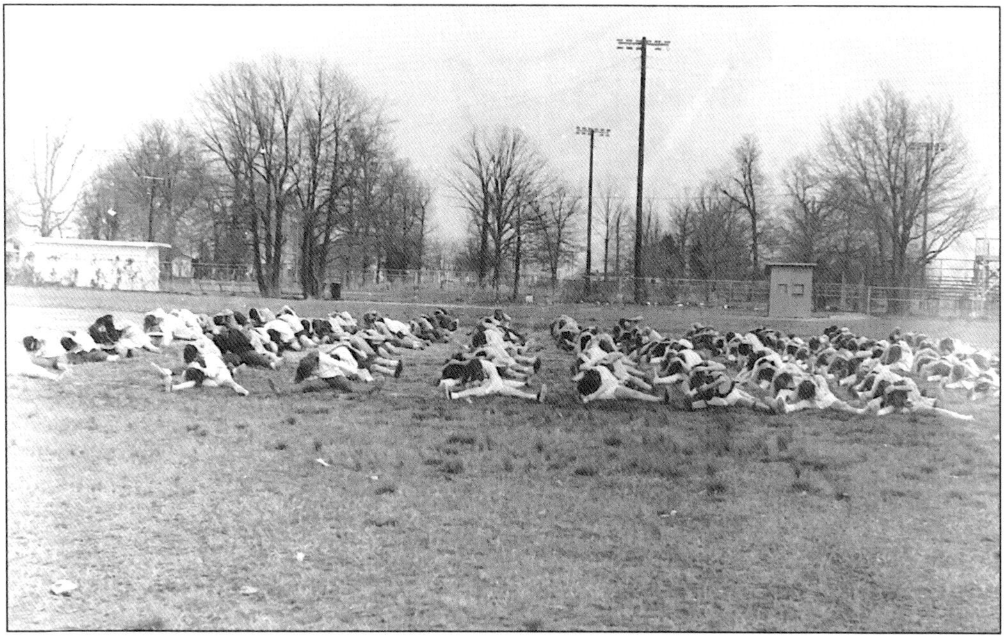

The tornado destroyed the gymnasium and other physical education facilities. This forced the physical education classes, pictured above, to find another way to perform their activities during the interim building period. This usually meant going outside for many classes and using the provision of nature, except during periods of rain or extreme temperatures. Construction soon commenced on the new buildings, such as the one below, that Nettleton students would once again call home. (Courtesy of Nettleton Public Schools.)

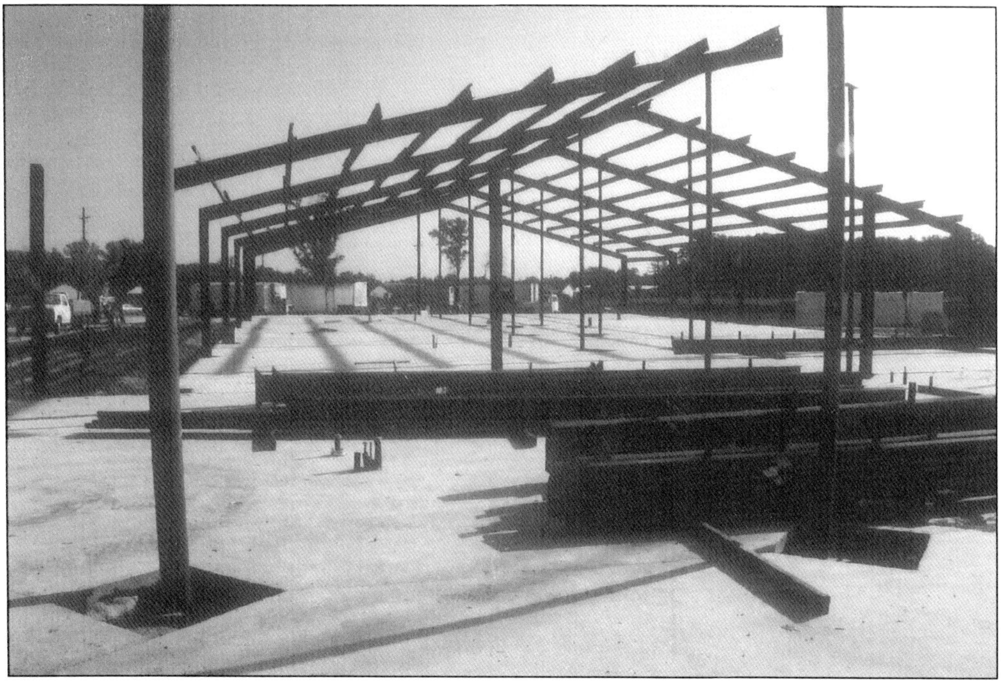

Seven

African-American Education

Arkansas Governor Mike Huckabee was recently quoted as saying that, "people in east Arkansas have a strong sense of continuity, a sense of place. Now, we must build on those strengths. We can't alter the past." Certainly no group in the Delta better epitomizes the strength and courage Governor Huckabee alluded to that is requisite to overcoming the hurdles that have been placed in their paths than the African-Americans who live in the Arkansas Delta. Historically, this group of Delta residents have risen from an antebellum period in which they were denied any form of education access whatsoever, to the "inherently unequal" form of segregated public schooling that evolved out of the Reconstruction period and did not change, for the most part, until the *Brown v. Board of Education* decision in 1954. Even then, African-Americans had to endure the opposition of some to desegregation, perhaps best illustrated by the events surrounding desegregation attempts at Little Rock Central High School in 1957. Out of this educational evolutionary process, African-Americans have persevered, and their triumphs over the past century serve as testimony to their dedication and belief in the value of education for their children.

Numerous individuals and events have played roles in helping to shape education in the Delta for African-American students. As mentioned previously, Arkansas was one of the first states in the South to even have desegregated schools prior to the 1954 *Brown* decision. The roots of African-American education in the Delta actually date back to 1864, to the establishment of the first school in the state for freed slaves in Helena. Despite these events, by 1920, black schools remained disproportionately poor, with only nine counties providing any form of education beyond the eighth grade for African-American students. In 1921, the Rev. J.H. King, a priest in the Protestant Episcopal Church, came to Forest City to begin missionary work. Concerned with the lack of quality in black public schools and the split sessions, King founded Christ Church School, a private school for African-American students that, in King's words, "enlightened the mind and trained the hands— Christian school, a training school." The school remained a viable option for African-American students for nearly a half-century after its founding. Triumphs such as this, as well as hurdles along the way, serve as the focus of this chapter.

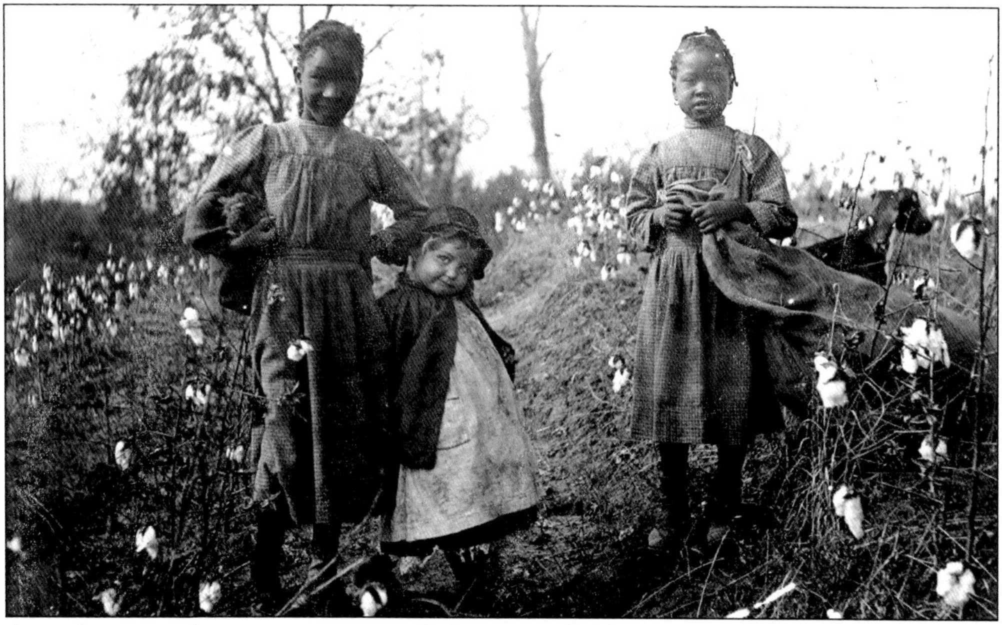

An early twentieth-century scene in a Delta cotton field is depicted above. This photograph shows two young black girls with cotton sacks and a younger white girl, more elegantly dressed, leaning against one of the black girls. Cotton harvest usually began in October, and this appears to be late in the harvest season. Some Arkansas schools followed a split session as late as the 1940s, to accommodate such harvesting. (Courtesy of Arkansas State University Museum.)

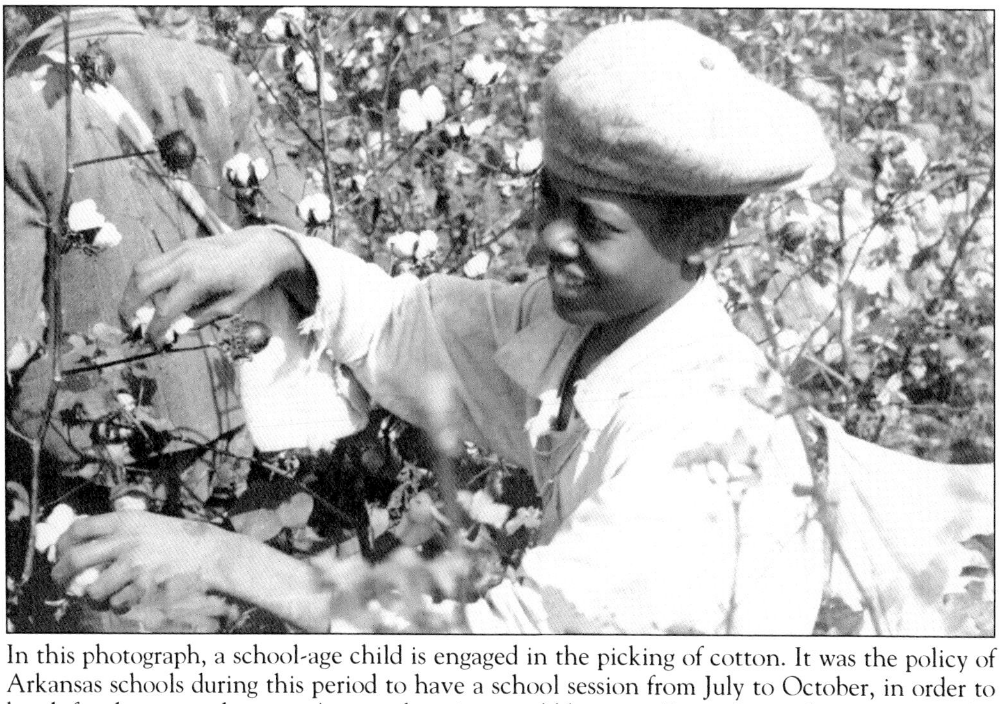

In this photograph, a school-age child is engaged in the picking of cotton. It was the policy of Arkansas schools during this period to have a school session from July to October, in order to break for the cotton harvest. A second session would begin in December and continue until it was time to hoe the young cotton plants. (Courtesy of Arkansas State University Museum.)

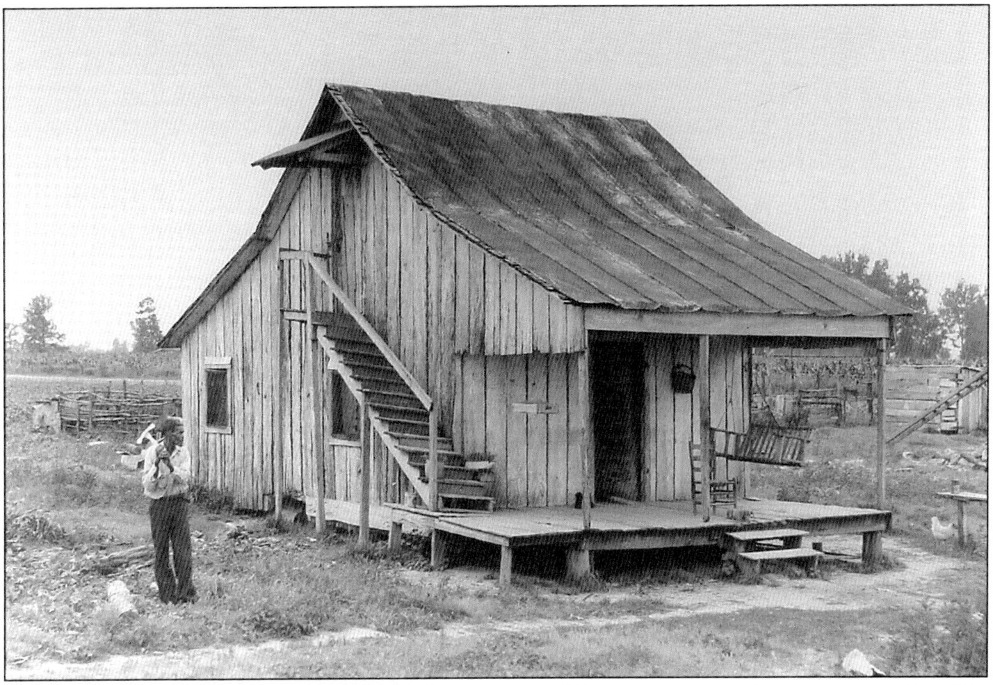

The cotton crop seemed to define the Delta economy. Here a cotton worker poses outside of his Blytheville, Mississippi County, home in 1937. An Arkansas historian once wrote, "Arkansas' fortunes rose and fell with the price of cotton." During the late nineteenth and early twentieth centuries, only three Delta counties had fewer than 1,000 acres in cotton production. Both extreme wealth and poverty, however, were byproducts of King Cotton. (Courtesy of Arkansas History Commission.)

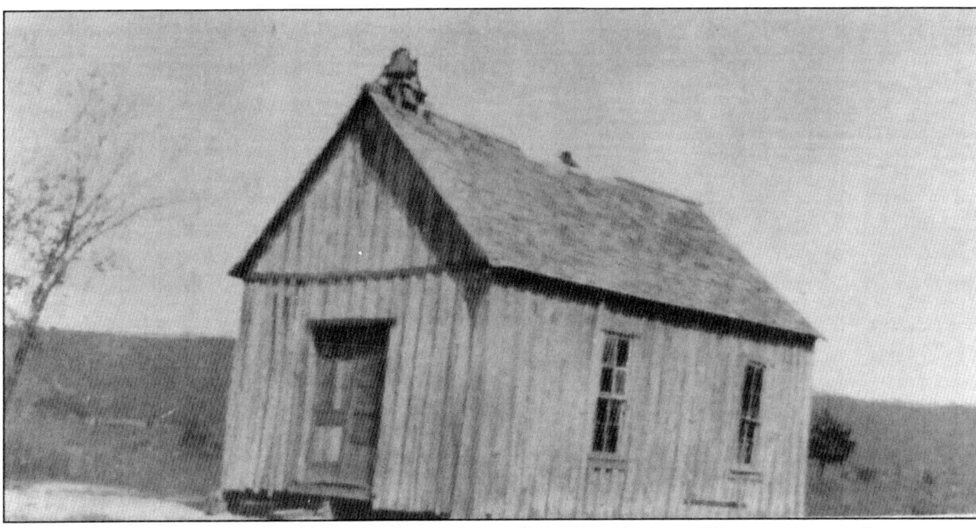

The old Negro School Building at Round Pond in St. Francis County raises the issue of financial support. The amount of money that went to black schools was significantly less than that which white schools received. While many communities erected large brick structures for white students, most blacks in rural Arkansas attended this type of school building. (Courtesy of Arkansas History Commission.)

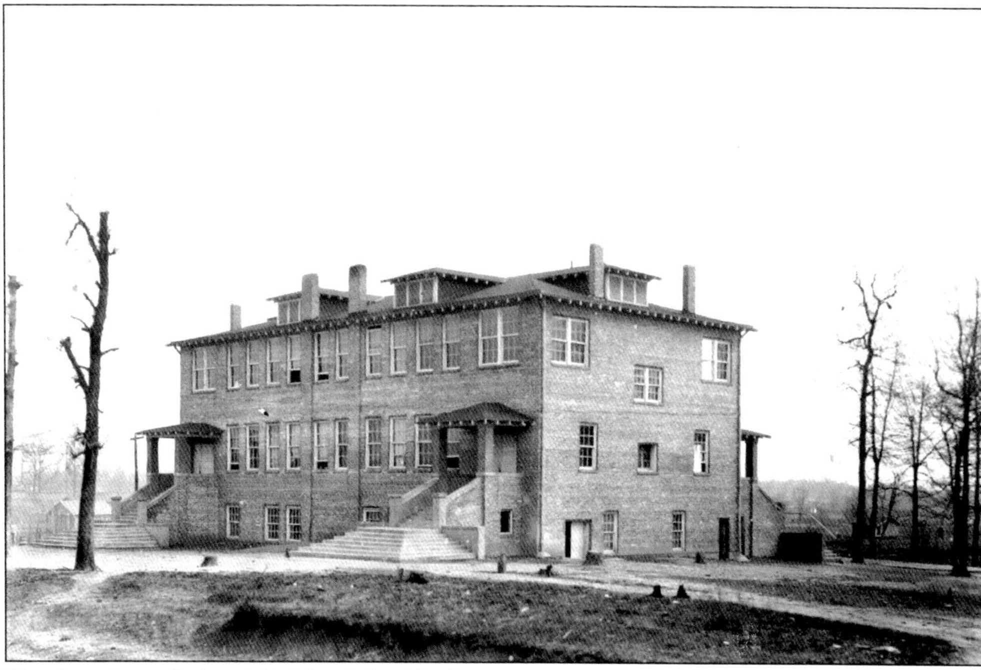

The Jonesboro Industrial School for blacks was an impressive structure, a large three-story brick building. The Industrial School was built in the early 1920s by leaders of Jonesboro's African-American community. They cleaned old bricks after the end of the workday and on weekends. The school offered education through high school, replacing the Cherry Street School, which was a one-room school, and accepted students throughout the Delta. (Courtesy of Arkansas State University Museum.)

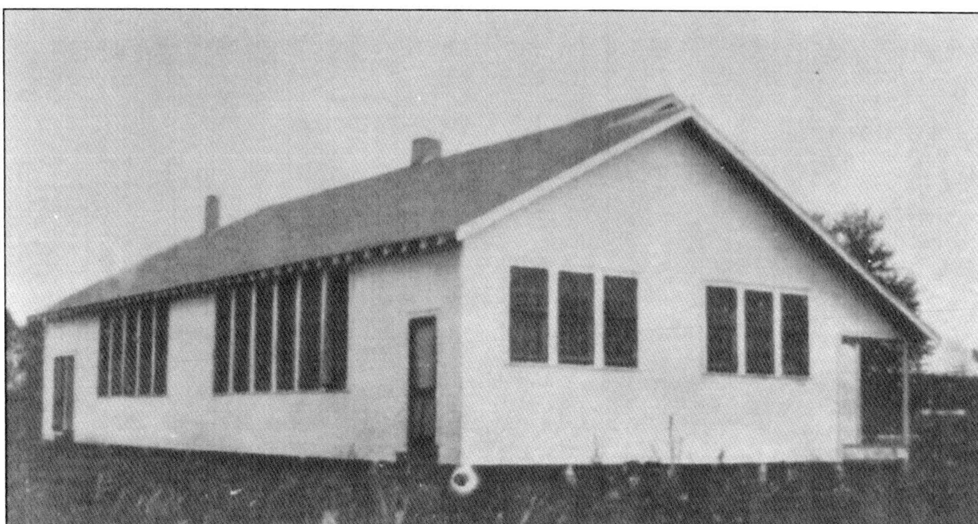

The new Negro School Building at Round Pond, St. Francis County, illustrates a change in many state's approaches to African-American education. As the movement emerged in the mid-twentieth century, many southern states began to develop more equitable formulas to divide the money for education between whites and blacks, and although disparity still existed, this was viewed as a concession. (Courtesy of Arkansas History Commission.)

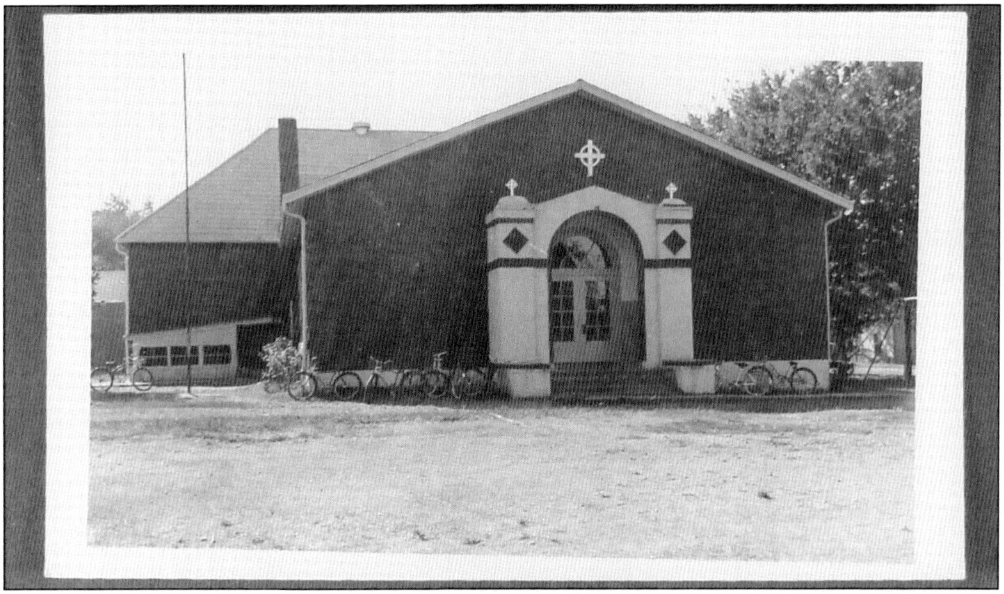

Jonesboro built the Booker T. Washington Colored High School in the early 1950s for African-American residents. Some believe it was perhaps the first school building in Jonesboro to be constructed in the 1950s. This was an attractive building, which may have represented as much the desire to continue the separate system as to improve facilities for black students. (Courtesy of Arkansas History Commission.)

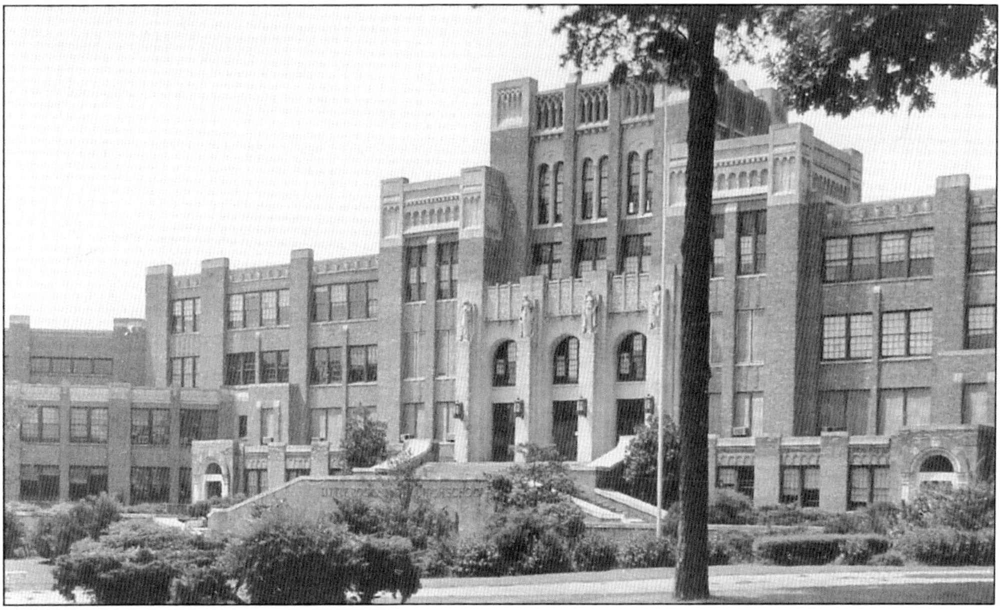

Pictured above is the now famous Little Rock Central High School building, located just west of the Delta. As the Supreme Court's *Brown* decision was weighed, some major Arkansas spokesmen indicated that Arkansas would obey the law. Hoxie, Arkansas even voluntarily moved to integrate. Some, however, including Governor Orval Faubus, began to move against integration. This culminated with President Dwight Eisenhower being forced to intervene with military force. (Courtesy of Arkansas History Commission.)

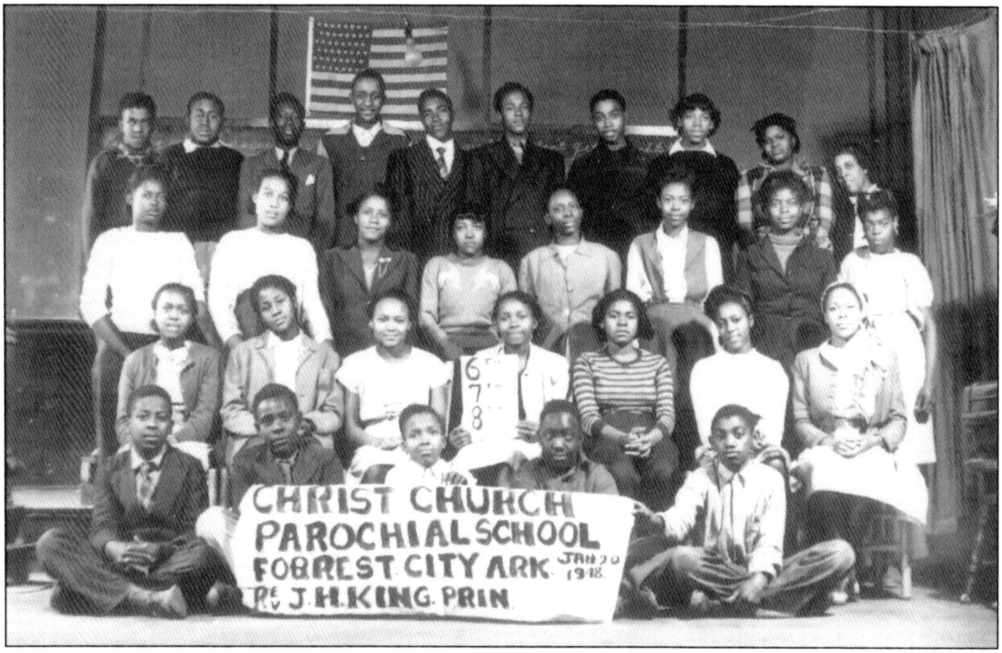

This composite of Christ Church Parochial students in Forrest City, St. Francis County, indicates how far the school had come since its founding in 1921. In that year, the Rev. J.H. King assumed a missionary duty in Forrest City among the blacks of the city for the Episcopal Church. (Courtesy of Arkansas History Commission.)

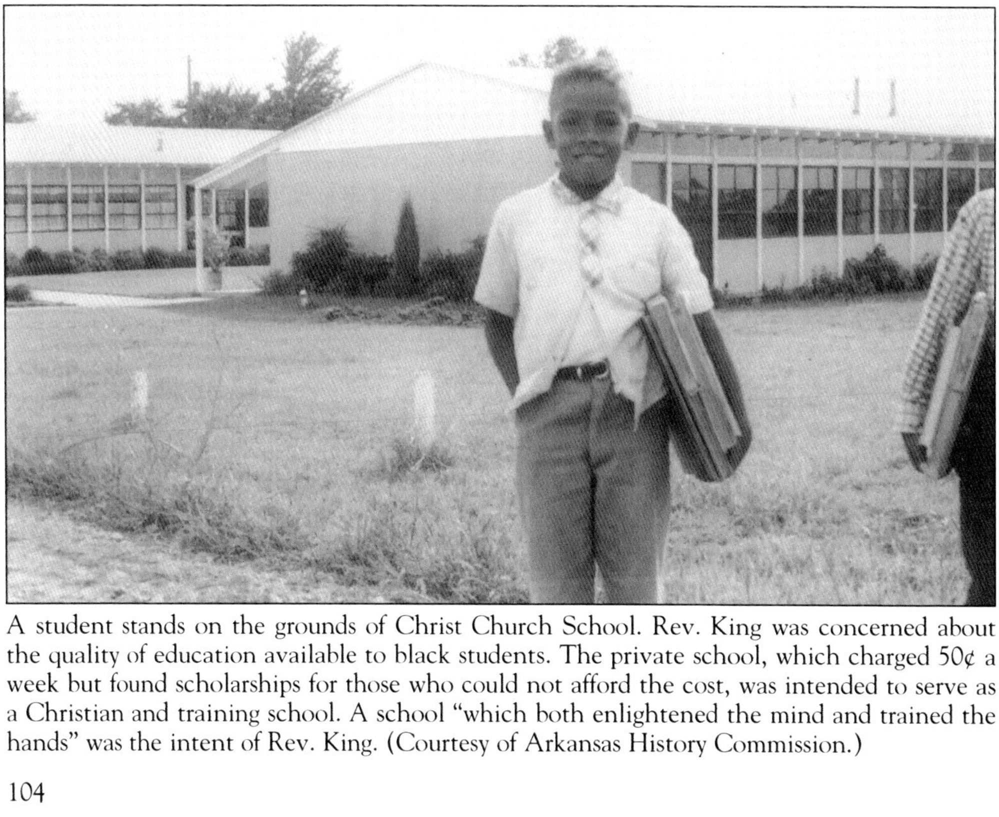

A student stands on the grounds of Christ Church School. Rev. King was concerned about the quality of education available to black students. The private school, which charged 50¢ a week but found scholarships for those who could not afford the cost, was intended to serve as a Christian and training school. A school "which both enlightened the mind and trained the hands" was the intent of Rev. King. (Courtesy of Arkansas History Commission.)

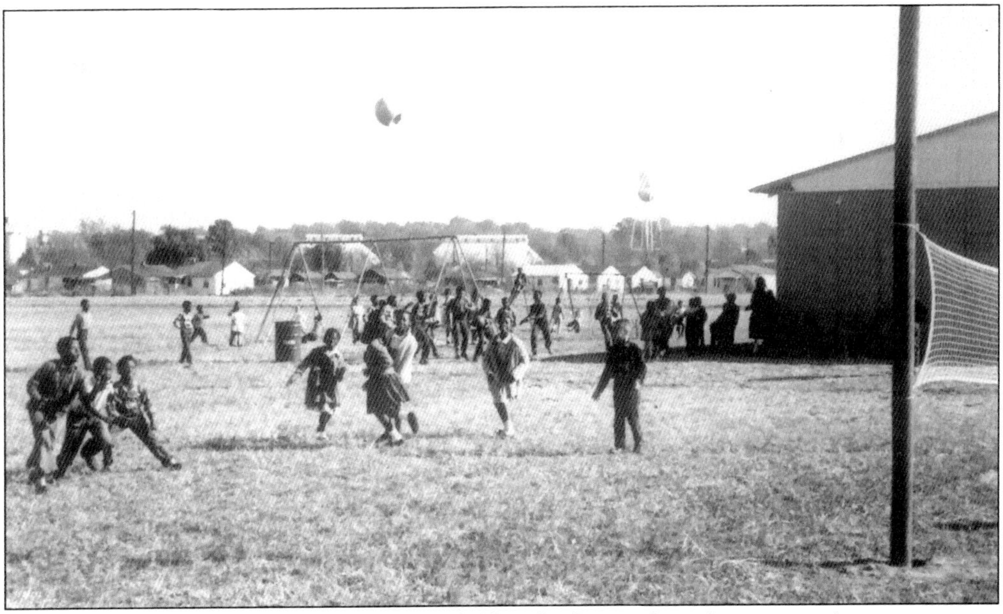

Christ Church Elementary School offered children both a quality education and an opportunity to build long-lasting friendships. The school began as a simple, two-story house with two classrooms, a shop, and living quarters for the King family. The girls were trained in domestic arts, while the boys received training in mechanics. (Courtesy of Arkansas History Commission.)

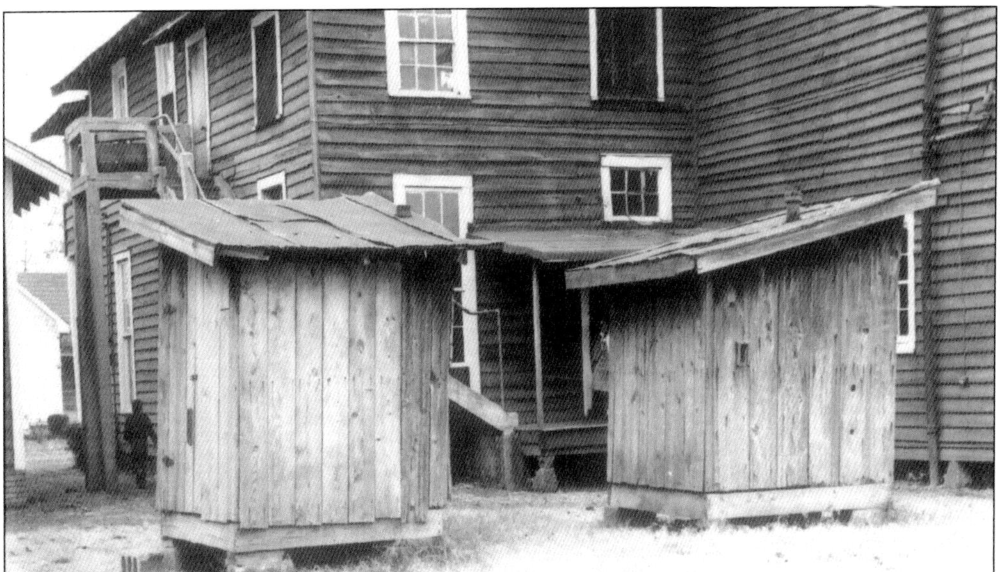

Although the facilities for the Christ Church School were not very palatial in those early years, founders would later acquire more funding to construct new buildings in 1948 and again in 1959. The aesthetics, however, did not diminish the quality of education received by thousands who attended the school, many of whom went on to college. One particular alumnus even went on to serve as president of the Forrest City School Board. (Courtesy of Arkansas History Commission.)

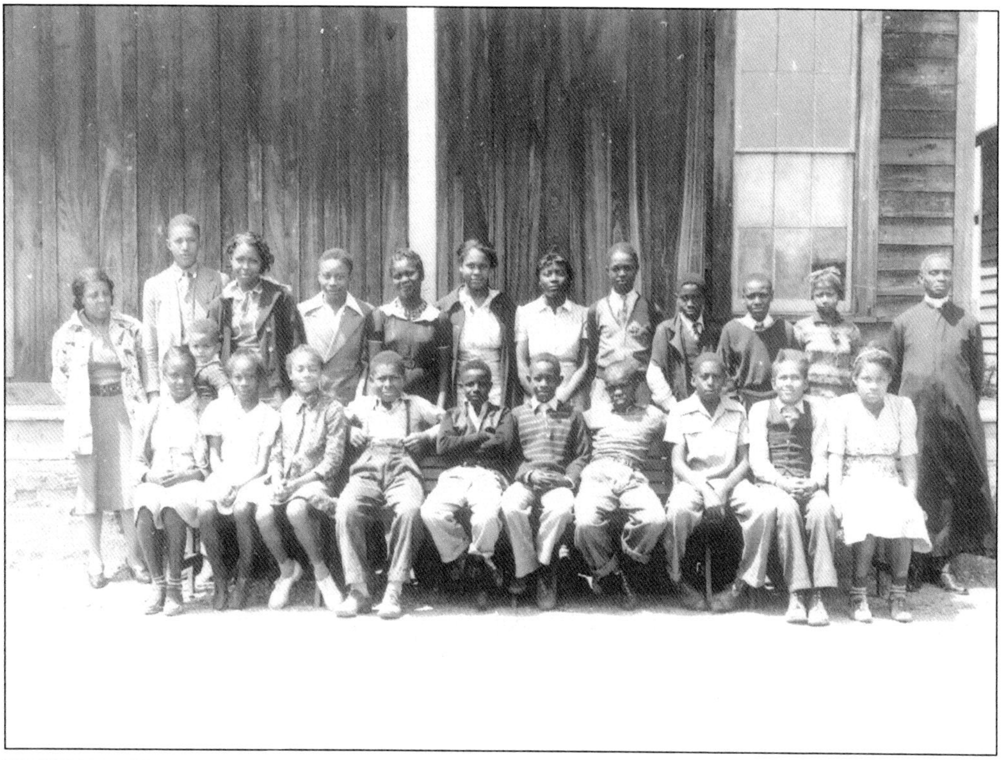

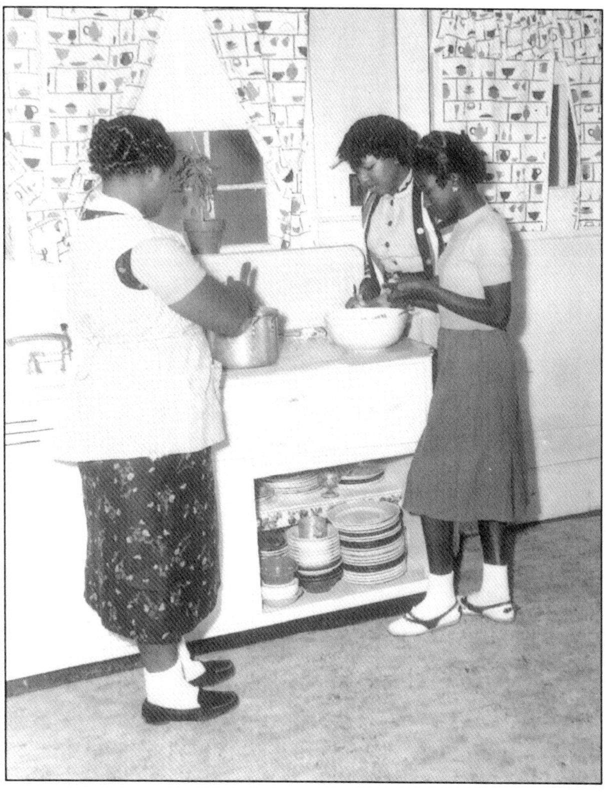

The student body of Christ Church School posed for this class composite. Most students who attended the school were from the Forrest City area. Others came from as far away as Detroit and Chicago. With smaller classes, more personal attention, and a strong PTA, many African-Americans were attracted to the school. (Courtesy of Arkansas History Commission.)

Older students often prepared the food for school lunches at the Christ Church School. The school faced serious challenges in the 1950s, with the passing of Rev. King in 1955, and a fire, which destroyed much of the school. The school was rebuilt and opened in 1959 under the leadership of headmaster Edward Norman. (Courtesy of Arkansas History Commission.)

Eight

Arkansas State University

Arkansas State University was established in 1909 as a result of one of two key education bills passed that session. The first education bill passed by the Arkansas legislature that spring called for compulsory school attendance. The other piece of education legislation passed that session, Act 100, called for the establishment of four public schools of agriculture to be established throughout the state, one in each of four districts established by this law. Jonesboro was chosen as the location in which to build the school for District One, serving twenty Arkansas Delta counties.

The institution, officially named the State Agricultural School, started as a vocational high school offering a curriculum consisting of agriculture, horticulture, and textile manufacturing. When the doors of "Aggie," as it was popularly referred to, opened on October 3, 1910, there were 189 students enrolled. The first president of the institution, at that time designated as principal, was V.C. Kays, a man who would have the longest tenure in that position, remaining at the helm for the next 34 years.

World War I ushered in a change for the young institution. The board of trustees reorganized Aggie into a junior college in 1918. Seven years later, while the Aggies maintained their junior college status, the state legislature changed the name to the "First District Agricultural and Mechanical College." The year 1930 marked another milestone in Aggie history, when the transition from a junior college to a four-year bachelor's degree program was finalized. This curricular change was followed three years later by a name change, whereby the Aggies officially became Arkansas State College. Governor Winthrop Rockefeller penned the final chapter in the story of Arkansas State on January 17, 1967, when he signed into law a bill that officially elevated the institution to university status. The decade-long political crusade launched by President Carl R. Reng and numerous other supporters had finally paid off.

Over the years, Arkansas State has expanded well beyond its Jonesboro campus. In 1955, it opened a branch campus at Beebe, and four decades later another campus was added in Mountain Home. In all, over 10,000 students are enrolled in the Arkansas State University system, and the university can boast of its nearly 50,000 alumni. This chapter focuses on the history of the university, the largest institution of higher learning in the Arkansas Delta.

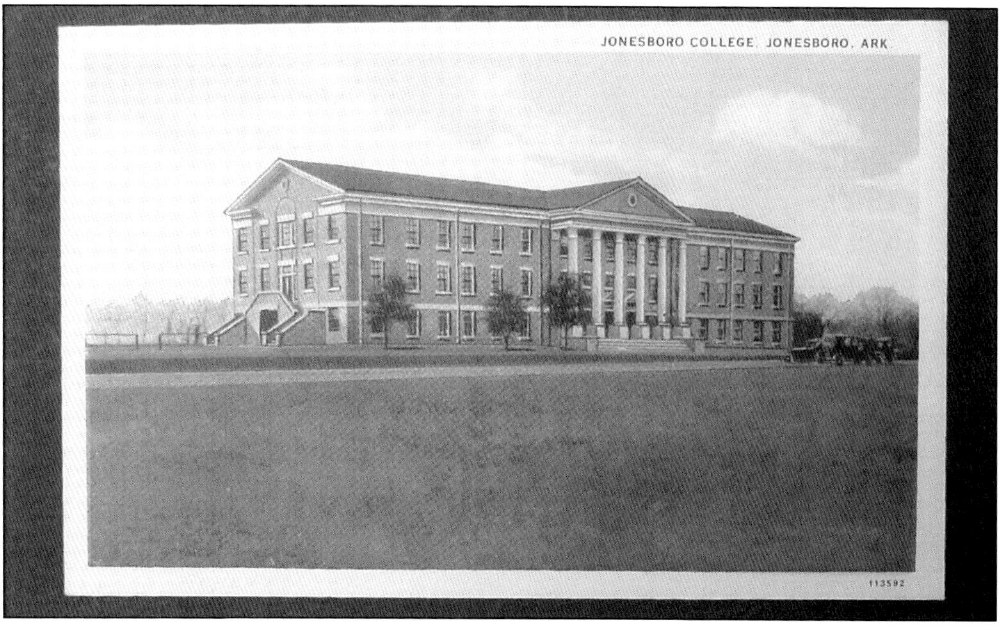

As part of the "Bible Belt," organized religion has a strong presence in the Delta. This is illustrated in the founding of Jonesboro College in 1934 by the Southern Baptists. Although the college would close within five years, the building would serve a new purpose, starting in 1939 and lasting until 1973, as part of the Jonesboro Public School system. (Courtesy of Arkansas History Commission.)

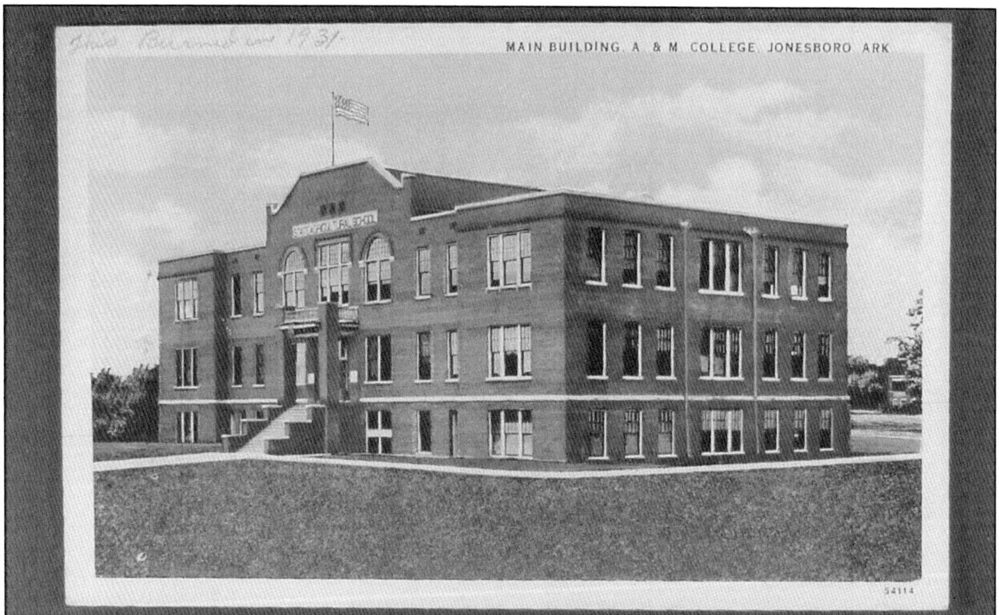

When the "State Agricultural School" in Jonesboro was designated as the "Agricultural and Mechanical (A&M) College" in 1925, this was one of the first buildings constructed. The Main Building, as it was designated, included administrative offices, classrooms, a gymnasium, and an auditorium. (Courtesy of Arkansas History Commission.)

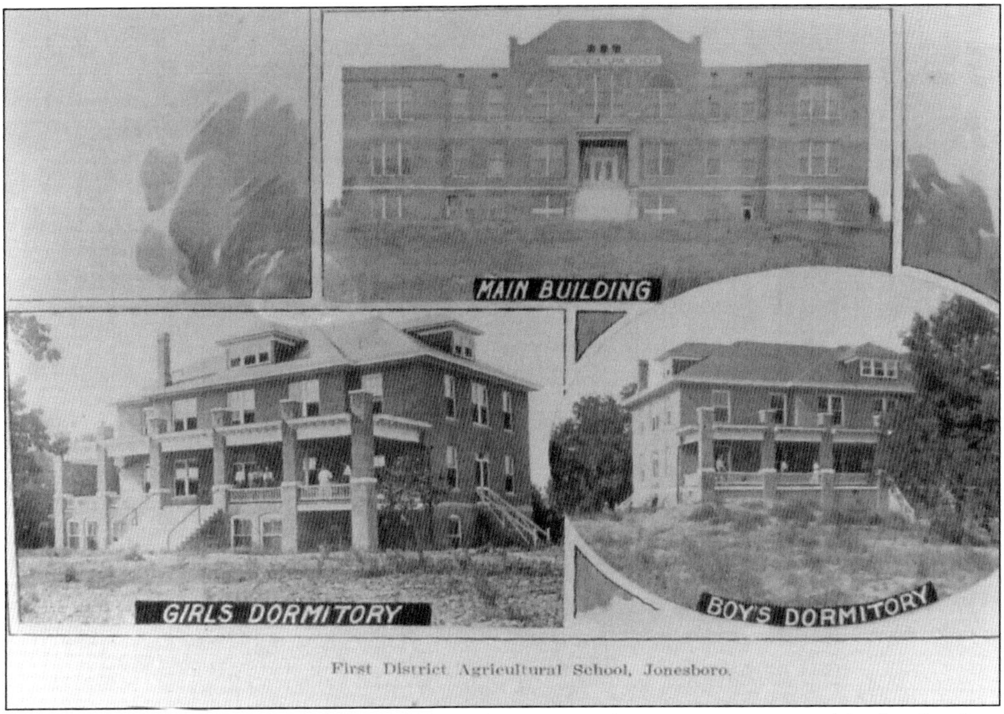

The First District Agricultural School, Jonesboro, started as a state-sponsored high school in 1910. In 1911, these three buildings were completed. V.C. Kays, principal, erected a very strict academic society in which all students worked, studied, and played. In less than a decade, the school would become a junior college. (Courtesy of Arkansas History Commission.)

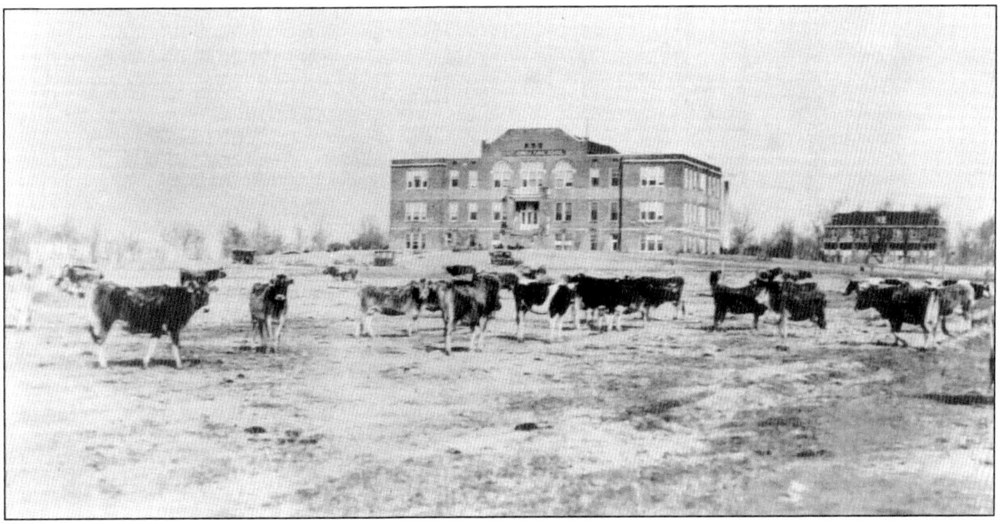

Although the official designation of the institution was changed in 1933 from Arkansas State A&M to Arkansas State College, there remained a number of reminders of the Aggie legacy. The south view of the first administration building shows cattle grazing where the old education building would be constructed. Leaders expected the practice farm to provide work for the students, food for the people on campus, and hopefully a profit for the institution. (Courtesy of Arkansas State University Archives.)

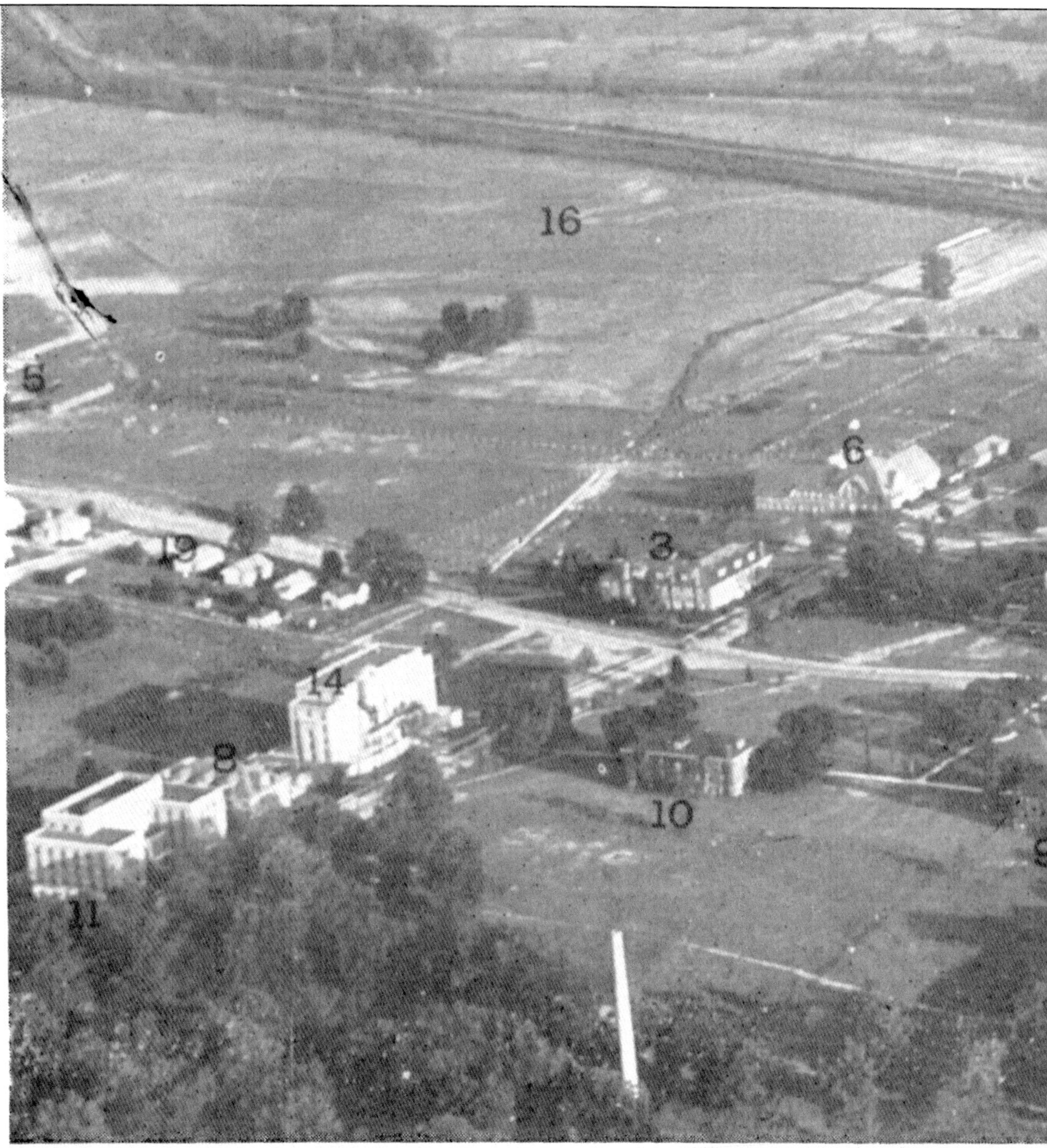

1. Administration Building
2. Health Hall
3. The Shop Building
4. Engineering Building and Heating Plant.
5. The Agricultural Unit

Airplane View of A

6. The Old Dairy Building and St
7. Science Hall and Armory Buil
8. The Col'ege Club
9. Barnhart Hall

An aerial view of Arkansas State College, the official name of the institution from 1933–1966, is provided in the above photograph. In the early 1930s, the growth of Arkansas State A&M was unparalleled. Students in some number even had to be turned away. Money, or the lack thereof,

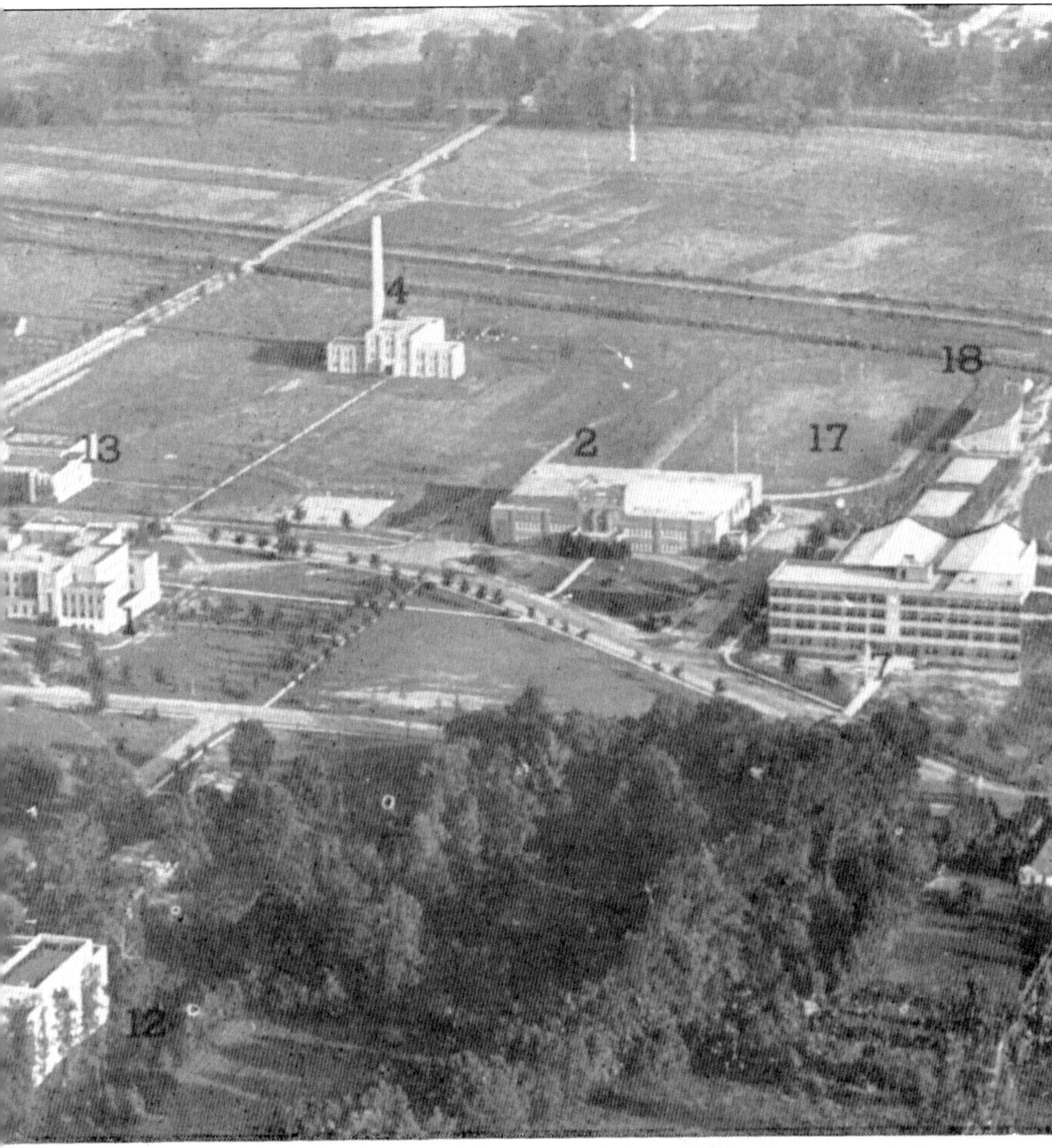

State College Campus

10. Lewis Hall
11. Danner Hall
12. Women's Residence Hall
13. The Training School Building
14. The Commons Building
15. Hanger Erected Here Since Picure
16. Airport
17. Kays Field
18. Stadium
19. Faculty Houses
20. Army Barracks

was the most critical problem. President Kays, along with Board of Trustees member R.E. Lee Wilson, a wealthy lumber industry entrepreneur, were successful in procuring the necessary funds to continue ASC's phenomenal growth. (Courtesy of Arkansas State University Archives.)

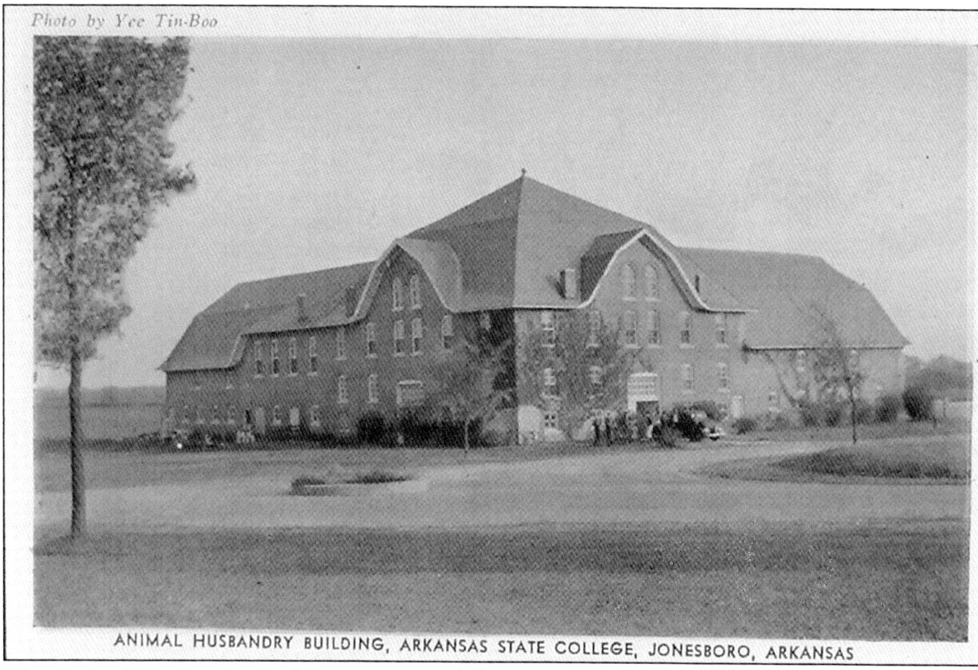

The Animal Husbandry Building was one of the more famous on campus in part because of the architectural style, which can be attributed to the northern origin of V.C. Kays. As the school became a junior college, and then in 1933 a four-year college, the emphasis on agriculture diminished; however, the agricultural studies tradition still continues. (Courtesy of Arkansas History Commission.)

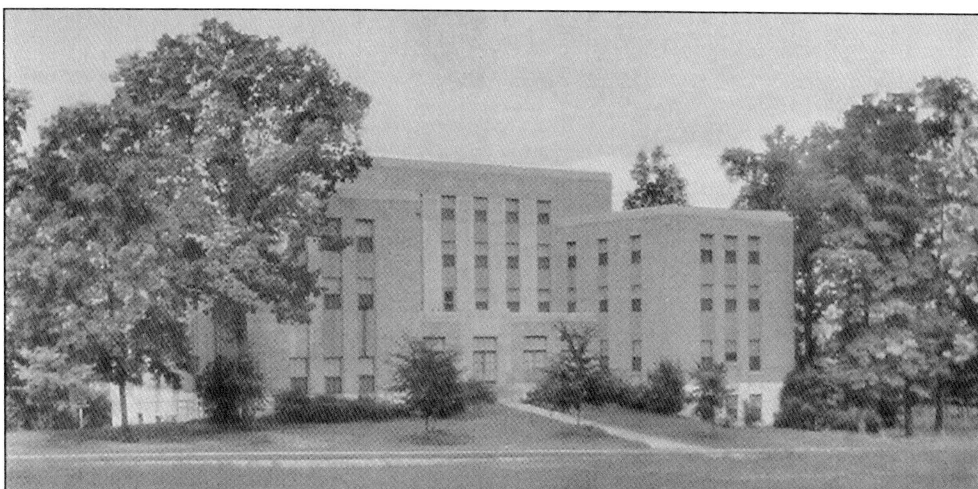

Only two dormitories originally existed at Arkansas State College, one for each gender of students. At various times, therefore, a number of students would be sent home because of the shortage of rooms. In 1932, 30 women were sent home, prior to the construction of a new women's dormitory in 1934. In 1961, the building was named Carraway Hall after Senator Hattie W. Carraway. (Courtesy of Arkansas History Commission.)

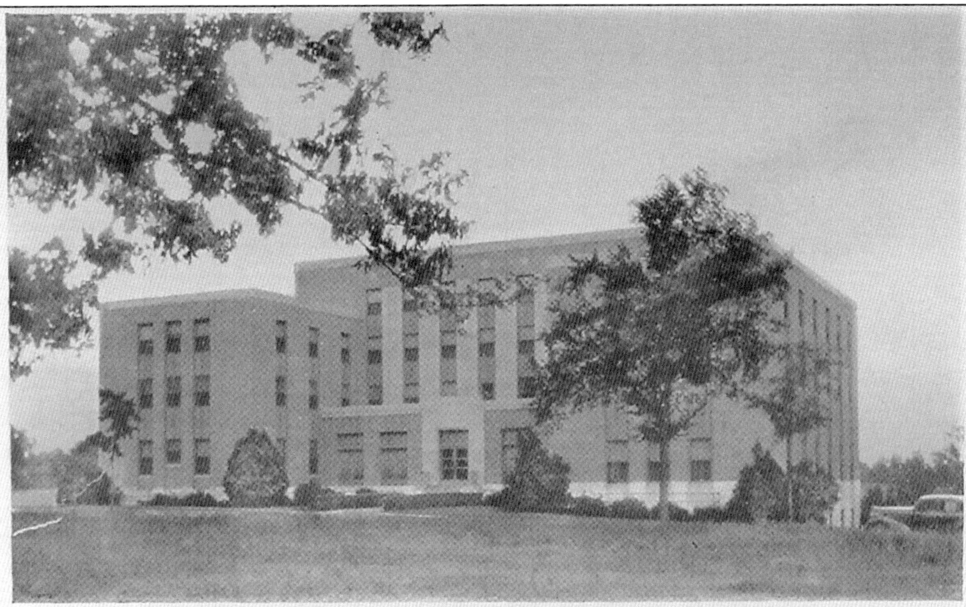

DANNER HALL, ARKANSAS STATE COLLEGE, JONESBORO, ARKANSAS

Danner Hall was the new men's dormitory, completed in 1934. There were 70 men staying in the original dormitory and nearly 150 living in private homes or rented quarters. Most students commuted, especially as roads were improved. With a rapidly increasing enrollment, additional housing was essential. (Courtesy of Arkansas History Commission.)

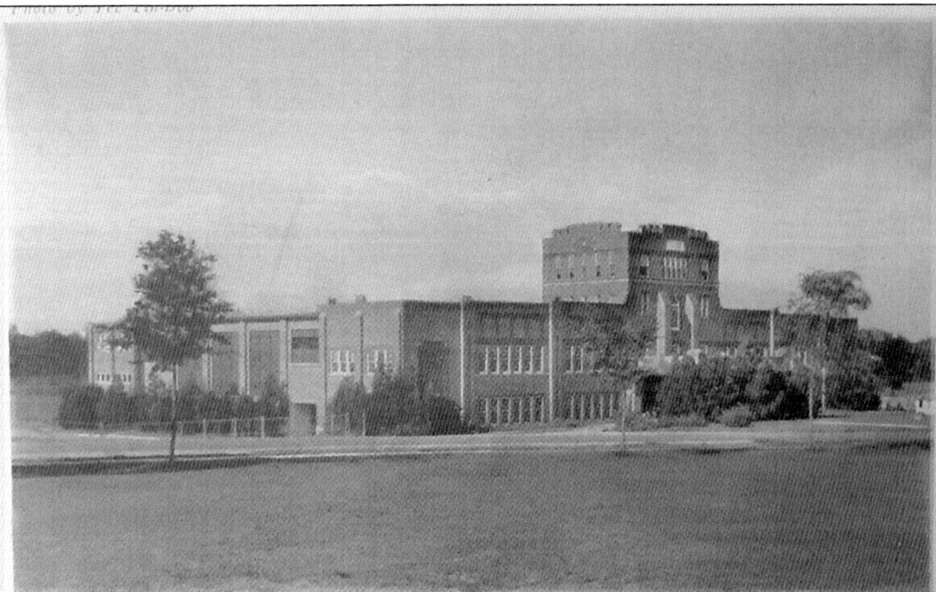

ARMORY, ARKANSAS STATE COLLEGE, JONESBORO, ARKANSAS

In 1923, a National Guard unit was assigned to the Arkansas State College campus. The armory building, completed in 1927, was described as the largest in the South. As usual, the building served multiple purposes. It had the largest "gymnasium" in the state to provide physical education, as well as a large basketball court and auditorium that could accommodate six thousand people. (Courtesy of Arkansas History Commission.)

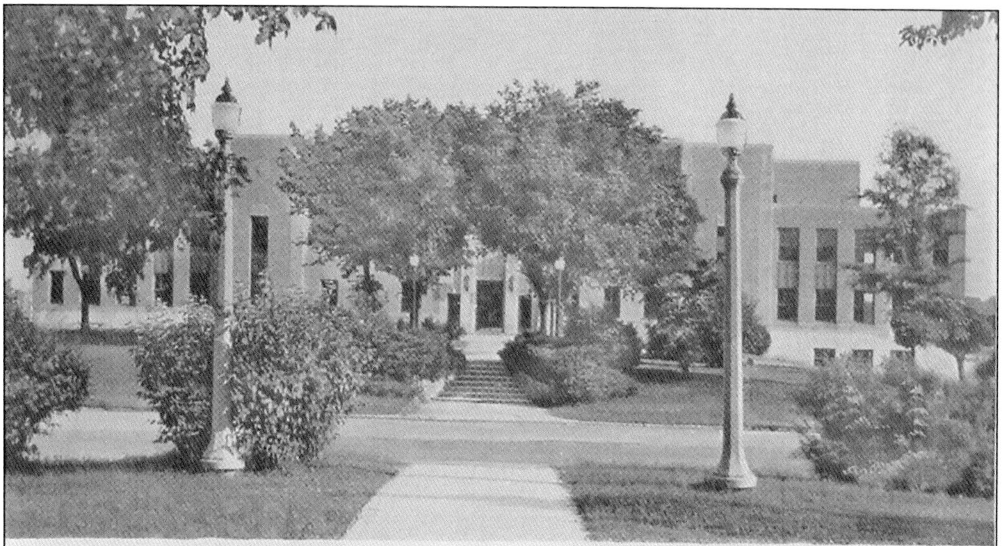

WILSON HALL, ADMINISTRATION BUILDING, ARKANSAS STATE COLLEGE, JONESBORO, ARKANSAS

Wilson Hall was constructed after the original administration building was destroyed by fire in January of 1931. The new building opened in late 1932, and was named Wilson Hall after the lumber, planting capitalist, R.E. Lee Wilson, who was on the board and had provided tremendous assistance through donations of lumber and money to other building projects. (Courtesy of Arkansas History Commission.)

Photo by Yee Tin-Boo

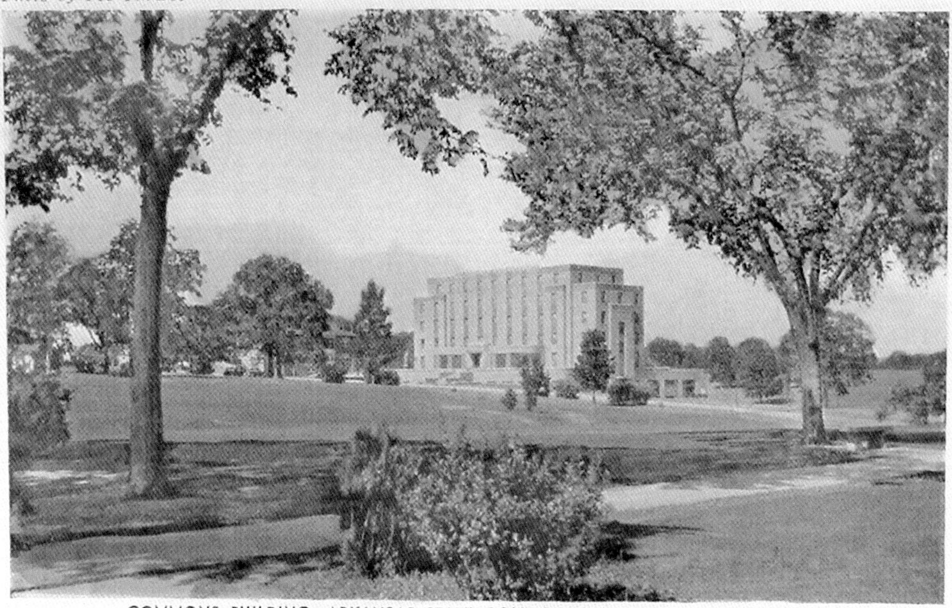

COMMONS BUILDING, ARKANSAS STATE COLLEGE, JONESBORO, ARKANSAS

Arkansas State College experienced tremendous growth in the 1930s, adding ten new buildings to its campus. One of the most magnificent of these new structures was the Commons building, which provided students a new air-conditioned dining hall, cafeteria, and kitchen. The second floor of the building included an apartment for the Dean of Men, lounges, and guest rooms. The top three floors consisted of a dormitory for 150 men. (Courtesy of Arkansas History Commission.)

Standards for Rooming Houses

I Standards for the House Itself

1. There shall not be more than eight (8) to use one bathroom or one complete set of facilities. This number of persons includes students and other members of the household.

2. Adequate parlor space shall be provided for women students and their guests.

3. No basement rooms will be approved for women students.

4. Women students shall not live in the same house with men (excepting those members of the immediate family of the householder who live with the householder) unless the men are near relatives.

5. Apartments will not be approved unless an approved chaperone is living with, and as one of, the group.

6. A house shall be subject to inspection by the Dean of Women or her representative at any time.

7. The premises surrounding the house shall be kept hygienically clean.

8. A sufficient supply of hot water will be provided for the lavatory night and morning and for daily baths.

9. Each window of the house must be well screened.

II Standards for Student Rooms

1. No student room shall have an outside entrance or serve as a passage between other rooms of the house.

2. Not more than two students shall occupy one room.

3. Study tables and clean comfortable beds shall be provided. Other furnishings shall include: adequate closet space, dresser with one good mirror and adequate drawer space, a workable shade on each window, curtains and one straight chair for each occupant.

4. Sufficient heat, and light must be provided for students to study in their own rooms.

5. There shall be no cooking and eating in students' bedroom.

6. Student cooking privileges cannot be allowed where there is no separate sink and provision for garbage disposal.

One of the prevalent problems for growing educational institutions is provision of adequate living space for students. With only two original dormitories, Arkansas State A&M as well as Arkansas State College often did not have enough rooms to accommodate the student population. Many students were forced to seek housing in the nearby town of Jonesboro. Naturally, the institution provided student guidelines, such as the one above, for these private rooming houses. (Courtesy of Arkansas State University Archives.)

The Institute will be held in cooperation with the Home Missions Council, which represents 23 denominations, Dr. Mark A. Dawber, Secretary.

Classes will begin at 4 P. M. on Monday, January 19th

The last class will close at noon on Saturday, January 24th

All classes will be held in Room 302 of the Administration Building Rooms will be provided for the pastors on the third floor of the Commons Building. (Bring your own towels and soap)

Meals will be provided in the college cafeteria. The pastors will eat together in the private dining room.

Expenses: There will be no tuition fee. Rooms for the five nights will cost $2.50. Meals will cost approximately 60 cents per day, or three dollars for the five days.

Scholarships amounting to $5.50 will be provided for the first thirty pastors who apply. Applications should be sent to T. N. Threlkeld, Jonesboro, Arkansas.

On Friday evening January 23, a banquet will be held for the pastors with speakers from the College.

FACULTY AND LECTURE TOPICS

Dr. V. C. Kays, President of Arkansas State College and host to the Rural Pastors Institute.

D. F. Showalter, Dean of Arkansas State College.
"Better Country Life in Eastern Arkansas"
"How to Train Up a Child in the Way He Should Go"
"How to Keep Our Boys from Going to the Devil"

Mrs. Mary Rogers Brown, Prof. of Home Economics.
"Nutrition and National Defense"

The Rural Pastors Institute was held at Arkansas State College in the late 1930s. This program reflects that 23 denominations were represented at the institute. President V.C. Kays welcomed the participants. Dean D.F. Showalter presented a session on improving country life in eastern Arkansas, while a professor of home economics spoke about nutrition and national defense.

Dr. H. E. White, Prof. of Agricultural Economics.

"How to Own a Farm and Why"

"The Home Poultry Flock"

Dr. G. B. Grant, Prof. of Vegetable Gardening.

"The Home Garden"

"Landscaping the Grounds of the Home, the School and the Church"

Miss Aline McDonald, Representative of the Farm Security Administration.

"Better Farm Homes for Low-Income Families"

Miss Mary Britzman, Home Demonstration Agent for Craighead County.

"Better Housing"

Dr. Hewitt, Prof. of Sociology.

"Better Family Life"

Raybon Sullivant, Agricultural Agent of Craighead County.

"Improved Farm Practices Needed in Northeastern Arkansas"

Dr. Felton.

"The Program of the Rural Church" (three lectures)

H. W. Hollard.

"How to Teach a Sunday School Class" (two lectures)

A. W. Martin, Pastor of the Jonesboro Methodist Church.

"The Preparation and Delivery of a Sermon" (five lectures)

Ralph A. Felton, Head of the Rural Church Department, Drew Theological Seminary, Madison, New Jersey.

"Rural Church Methods" (five lectures)

T. N. Threlkeld, Presbyterian Field Worker, will preside at the Institute and make all arrangements regarding scholarship

Miss Mary Woolsey, County Director of Child Welfare.

"The Bad Boy or Girl"

Other sessions focused on a myriad of topics, to include the New Deal, morality, family, and poultry. This serves to illustrate the union between religion, agriculture, and education during this period. (Courtesy of Arkansas State University Archives.)

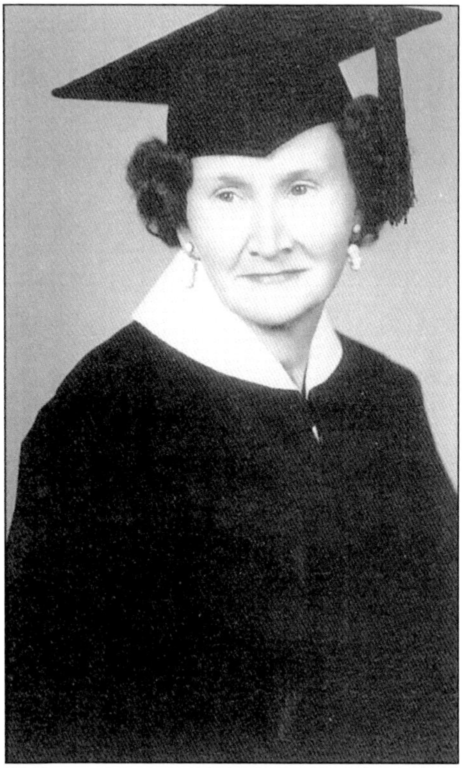

Throughout its nearly a century of existence, Arkansas State University has served two major purposes, first as an agricultural school, and second as a teacher training institution. Pictured here is one of the thousands of Delta teachers who received their degree from ASU. In this case, Elsie Dawson represents one of the countless teachers who began their teaching careers in a one-room schoolhouse and were required to go back to complete their degrees much later in life. ASU is still an institution where both traditional and non-traditional students can be found in every classroom, all with one common goal—to better themselves. (Courtesy of Elsie Dawson Collection.)

It is only fitting that Arkansas State University continue a large role for agricultural education, since the institution traces its origins to an agricultural high school. From the start, the institution has attempted to teach students the latest, most efficient methods of farming. The tradition of scholarly teaching and research continues today. (Courtesy of Arkansas State University—Communications Office.)

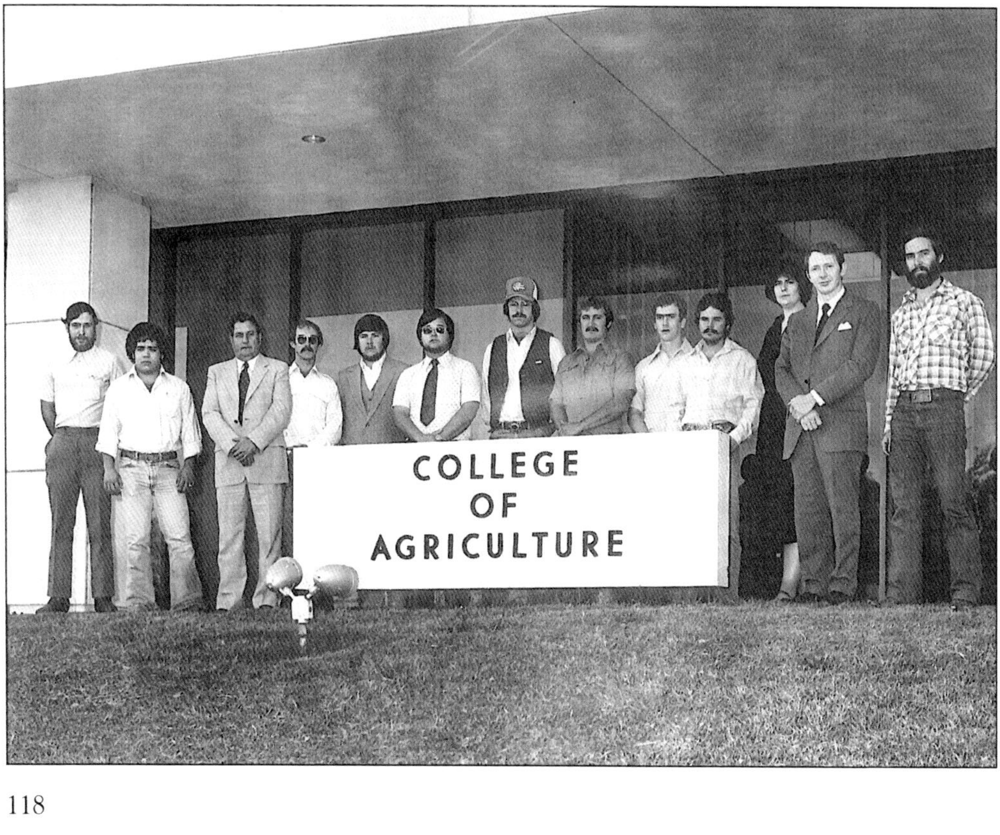

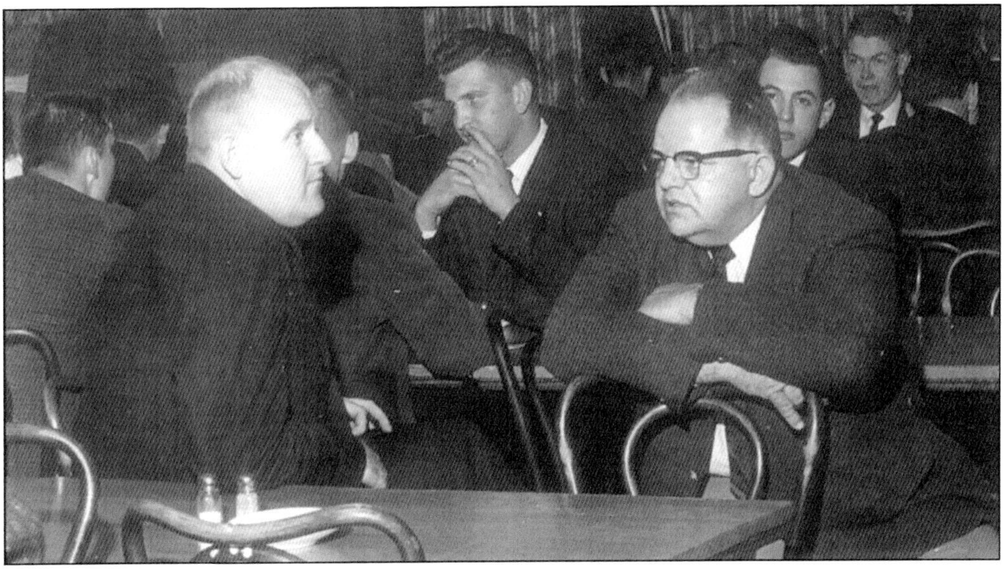

Pictured on the right is Dean Robert Moore (froggy), longtime Dean of Students at Arkansas State University. Moore was both well known and loved by many. During the late 1960s and 1970s, for example, when social and political unrest, Vietnam, dress, hairstyle, and drugs reached a volatile level, Moore seemed to be the only acceptable liaison or go-between to maintain peace on campus. (Courtesy of Arkansas State University—Communications Office.)

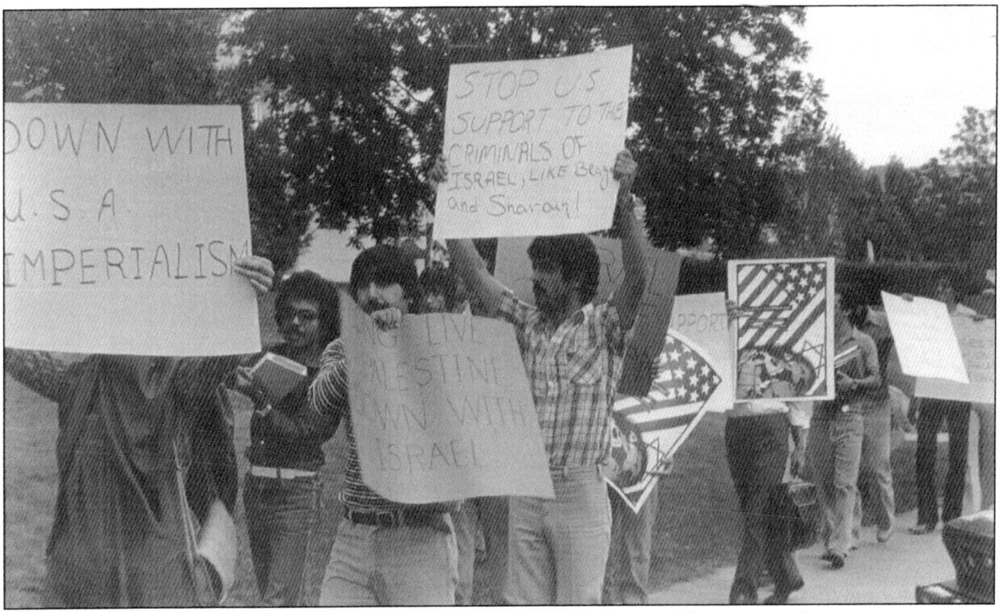

Over the years, Arkansas State University has attracted a host of foreign students to its campus. Hundreds of students have come to receive an advanced education, from regions of the world such as the Middle East and Asia. Others, who have come to participate in intercollegiate sports, are from various countries in South America, as well as South Africa and New Zealand. The above photograph illustrates that some of these students have been somewhat outspoken, at times, in voicing their opposition to certain U.S. foreign policies over the past few decades. (Arkansas State University—Communications Office.)

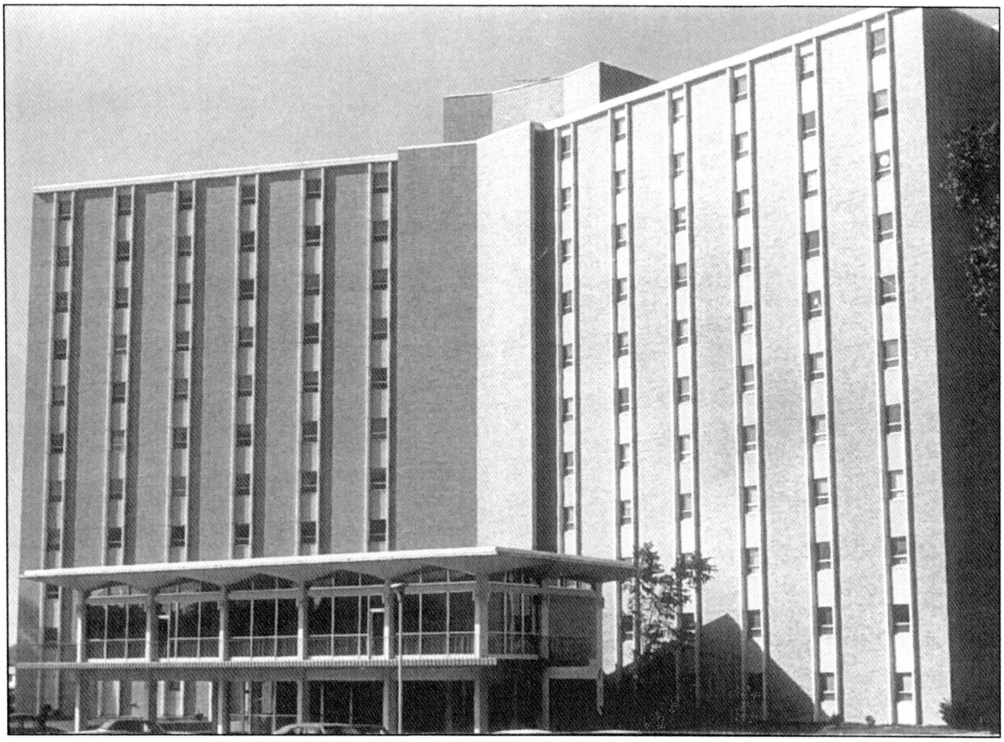

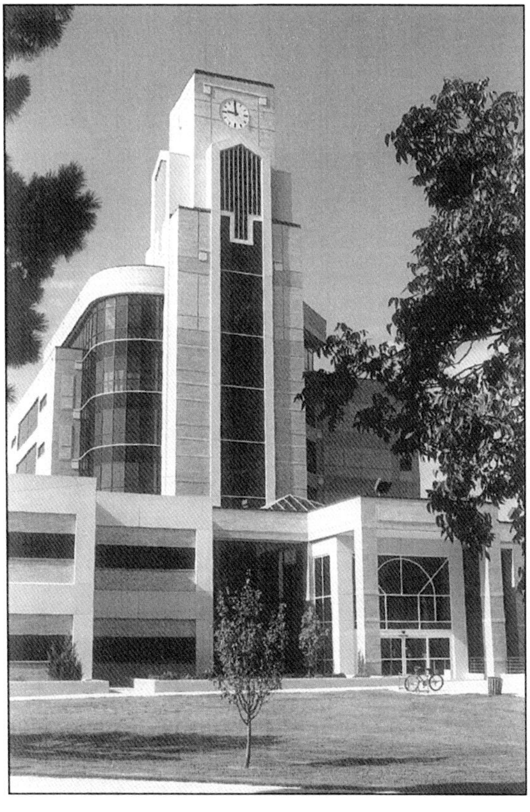

Kays Hall, a women's dormitory, was constructed in the mid-1960s at a cost of $2,250,000. Construction began at a time when Arkansas State College was experiencing an unprecedented increase in enrollment; in 1965 alone, enrollment jumped 20 percent. Today, Kays Hall remains the largest women's dormitory on campus, home to over five hundred students. (Courtesy of Arkansas State University—Communications Office.)

Arkansas State University has experienced tremendous growth over the past century. It has grown from a small public school of agriculture to a university with two branch campuses and over ten thousand students. Perhaps one of the most defining moments occurred in 1995 when President Bill Clinton, a native Arkansan, dedicated the new Dean B. Ellis Library, whose bell tower serves as a beacon of hope for countless Delta residents. (Courtesy of Arkansas State University—Communications Office.)

Nine

1980s–2000
Something Old, Something New

After just over a century of free public education, where does Arkansas stand at the beginnings of the twenty-first century? For all the educational gains and triumphs of the twentieth century, there are indeed still hurdles to be overcome. The 1990 census, for example, still showed that nearly four out of ten Arkansas residents did not have a high school diploma. In addition, the Rural School and Community Trust found that nearly one out of four Arkansans still live in poverty. A recent government report found that Arkansas teacher salaries rank sixteenth out of the 16 states that comprise the southern region of the U.S.

Although the problems that confront Arkansas and the Delta must be attended to before lasting reform can take place in the new millennium, there are countless examples of a renewed pride in education. Introduction of new digital technological teaching tools, along with the construction of new, state-of-the-art facilities, are but two examples of the renewed emphasis Delta residents are placing on the role of education. While certain aspects of Arkansas Delta education are new and innovative, others remain the same. For example, the Rural School and Community Trust recently reported that Arkansas leads the nation in the percentage of students (17 percent) who attend "small, rural schools." Although the twentieth century witnessed the demise of one-room schoolhouses in the Delta, the small, community schools have remained. The values, hopes, and aspirations of countless Delta residents remain tied to their local schools. Therefore, while the national social, economic, and educational pendulum continues to swing from one decade to the next, for Arkansas Delta residents, time, in some ways, will always remain the same. Perhaps the aspirations of the 800,000 residents of the Arkansas Delta, which accounts for 61 percent of the state's total population, are those of all Americans. In a recent speech, President Bill Clinton best summarized the support and hope of the entire nation for the Arkansas Delta in this century:

From the banks of the Potomac to the banks of the mighty Mississippi, we are listening to the true and powerful voices of the Delta, and we are committed to working together to make our vision of prosperity and opportunity a reality for the people of the Delta at the dawn of the new millennium.

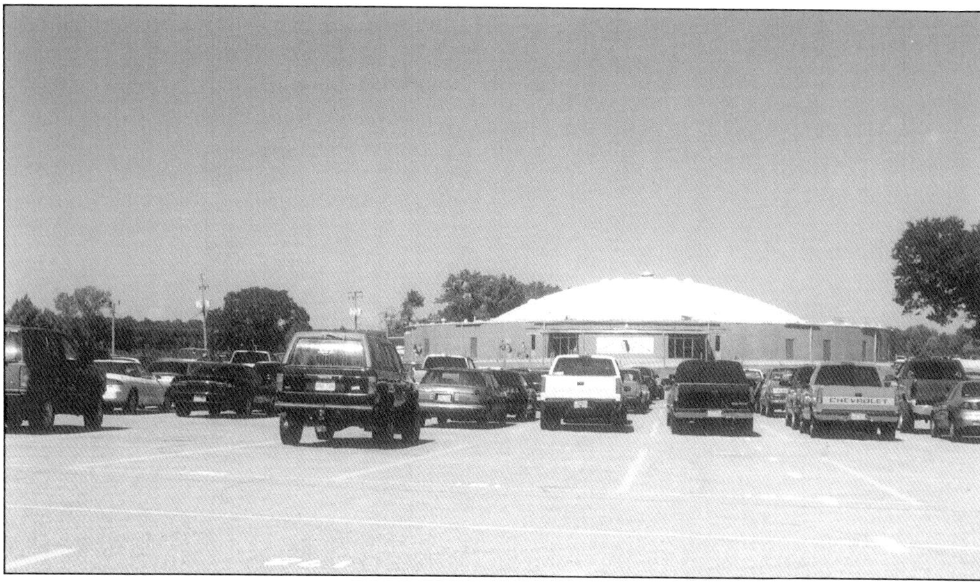

Perhaps one of the most tragic events to befall Delta residents occurred in March of 1998, when two students went on a shooting spree at their school, Westside Middle School, pictured above, in Jonesboro. Five people were killed and eleven injured as a result of the senseless, violent act. Those four students who lost their lives that day, Natalie, Brittany, Paige, and Stephanie, along with their teacher, Mrs. Wright, were remembered in a number of ceremonies and memorials that took place in schools across the Delta, including the one pictured below at Nettleton. (Courtesy of Nettleton Public Schools.)

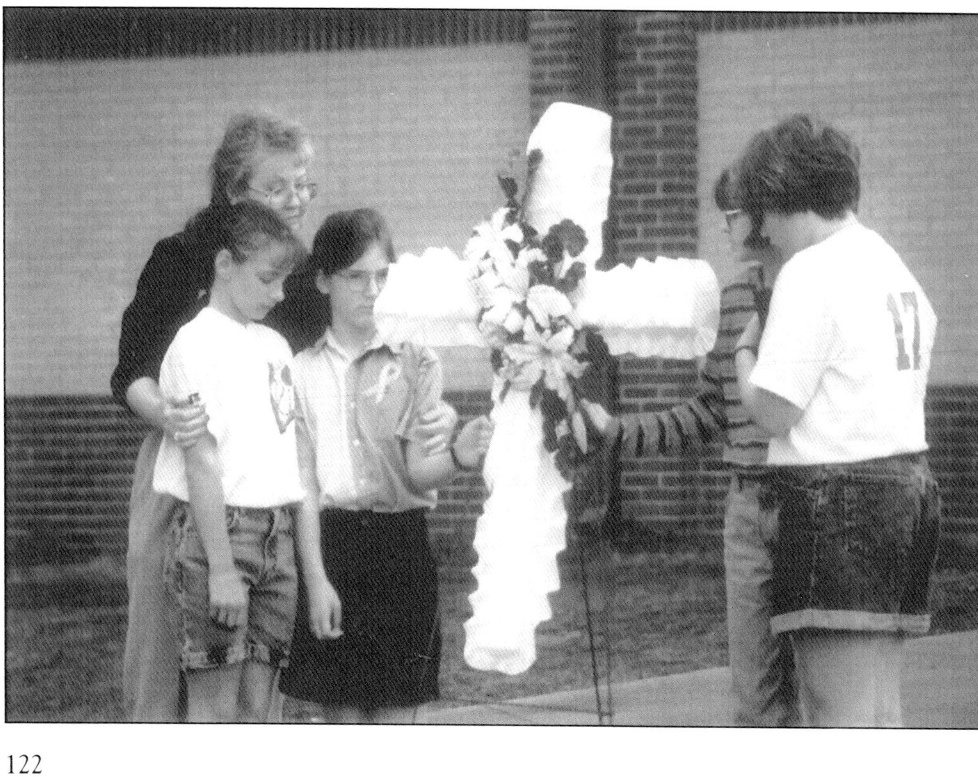

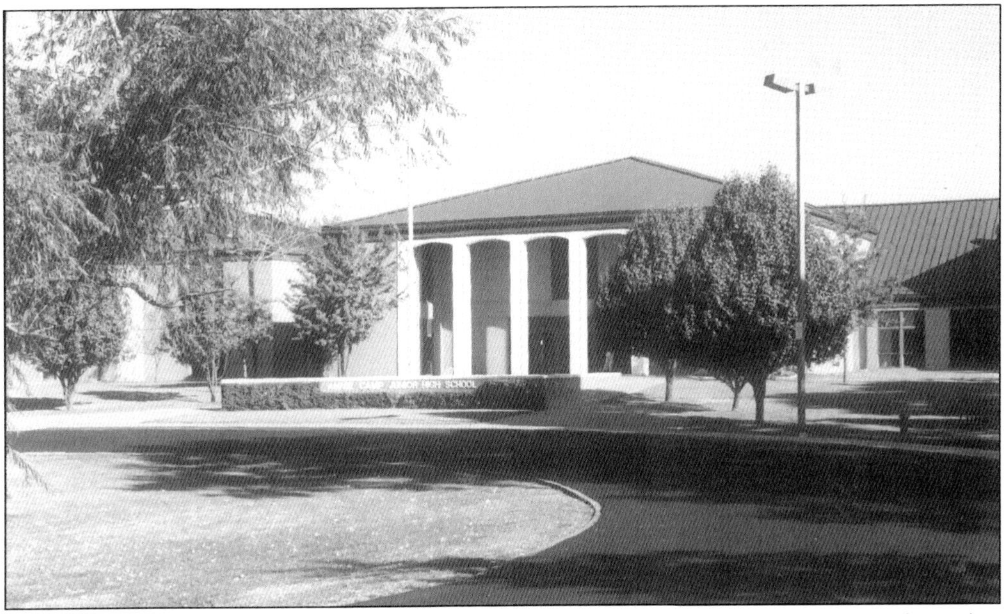

"Continuity and Change" has been a recurring theme in the history of education in the Delta. Jonesboro's Annie Camp Junior High School is a perfect case in point. For years, it was located in the older residential area of the city. Just over a decade ago, the old school was converted into an administration building and a new school, pictured above, was constructed in the fastest growing section of the city.

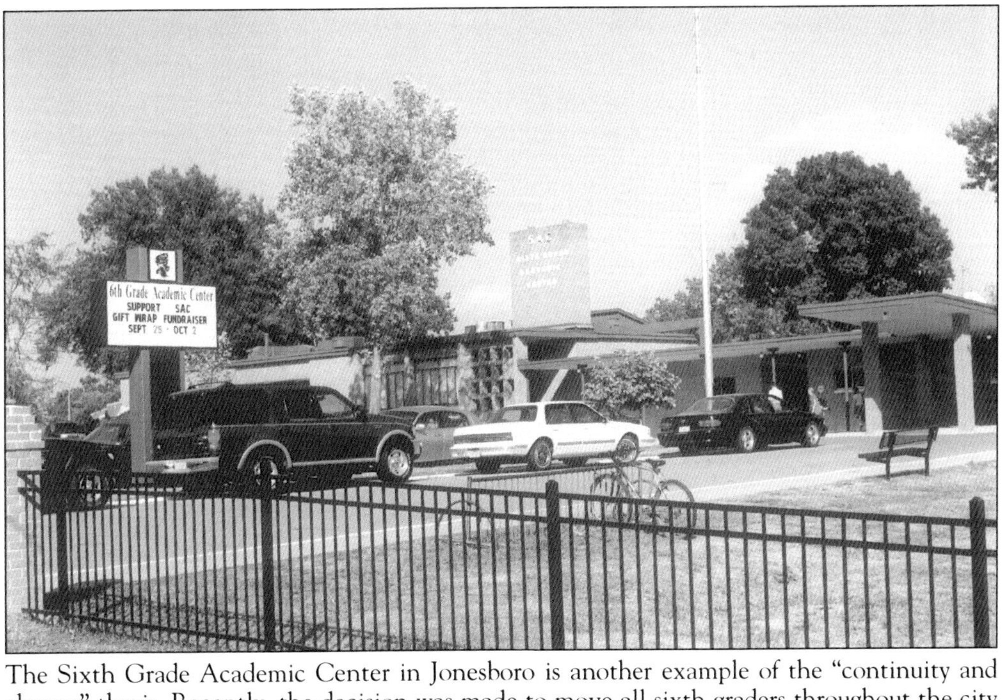

The Sixth Grade Academic Center in Jonesboro is another example of the "continuity and change" thesis. Recently, the decision was made to move all sixth graders throughout the city to this location, in part because of the growing enrollment and overcrowding at the various district elementary schools.

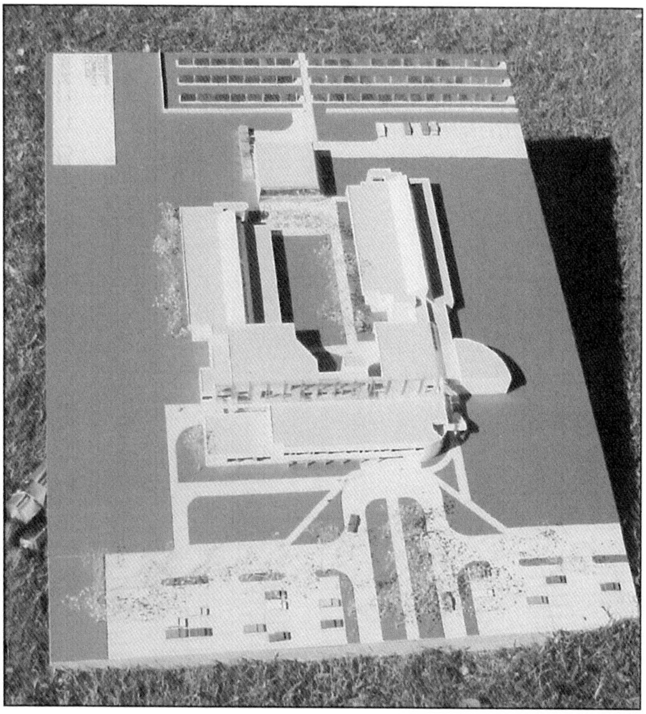

During the last quarter-century, Arkansas has been one of the leading states in the nation in establishing community and technical colleges. One of the premier community colleges in the state is Mississippi Community College located in Blytheville. Not only was the college one of the first of its type of institution in the Delta, it is one of the first in the nation to transfer to solar energy. The model displayed above, in this 1977 photograph, depicts where the solar panels were eventually installed on campus. (Courtesy of Arkansas History Commission.)

As this photograph demonstrates, some of the traditions passed down from one generation of Delta students to the next are not necessarily intellectually stimulating. These traditions do, however, demonstrate the bond of community and history that students in this region continue to share, as is evident in this 1993 car bashing festivity at Nettleton High School, a common fundraising activity. (Courtesy of Nettleton Public Schools.)

While some aspects of education in the Arkansas Delta have undergone great change, others have remained the same, such as commencement speeches, graduation regalia, and the pride that students and family members share on such occasions. This particular student, Mary Anna Bieber, pictured here speaking at her 1992 Jonesboro High School graduation, represents thousands of other Delta students who would go on to receive Ivy League higher educations, in Ms. Bieber's case at the University of Pennsylvania. (Courtesy of Arkansas State University Archives.)

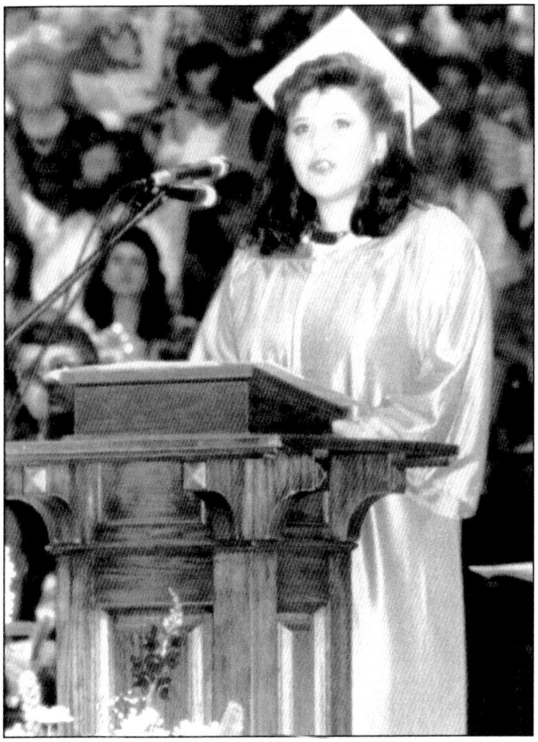

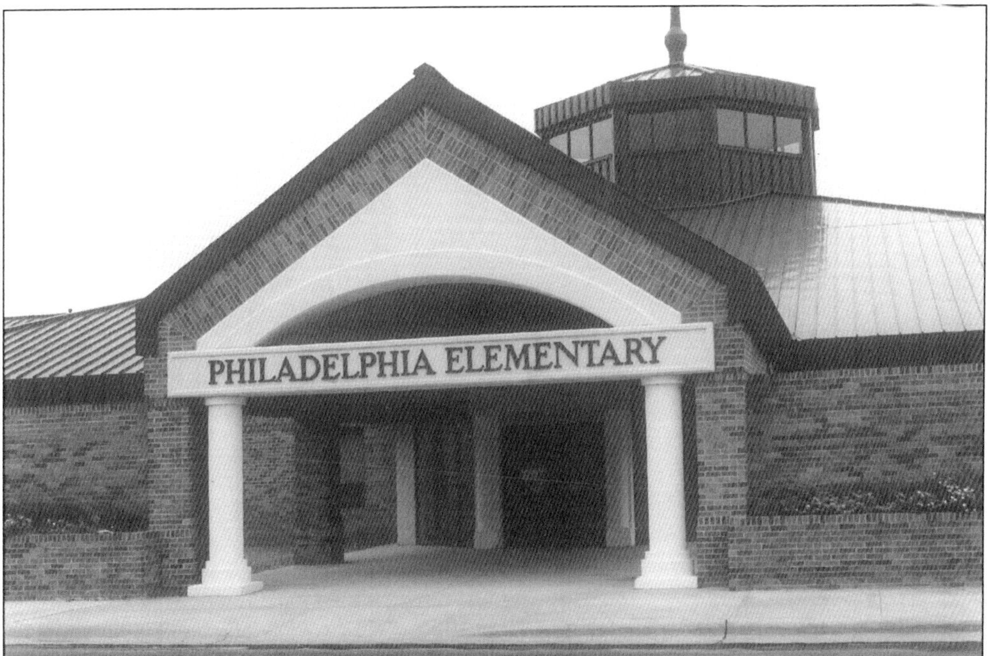

Philadelphia Elementary School in Jonesboro represents the newest school in Craighead County, if not the entire Delta. It serves as a reminder of the continued growth in enrollment throughout the region and the continued support residents provide to public education. It also illustrates how far the Delta has come since the days of the one-room schoolhouse.

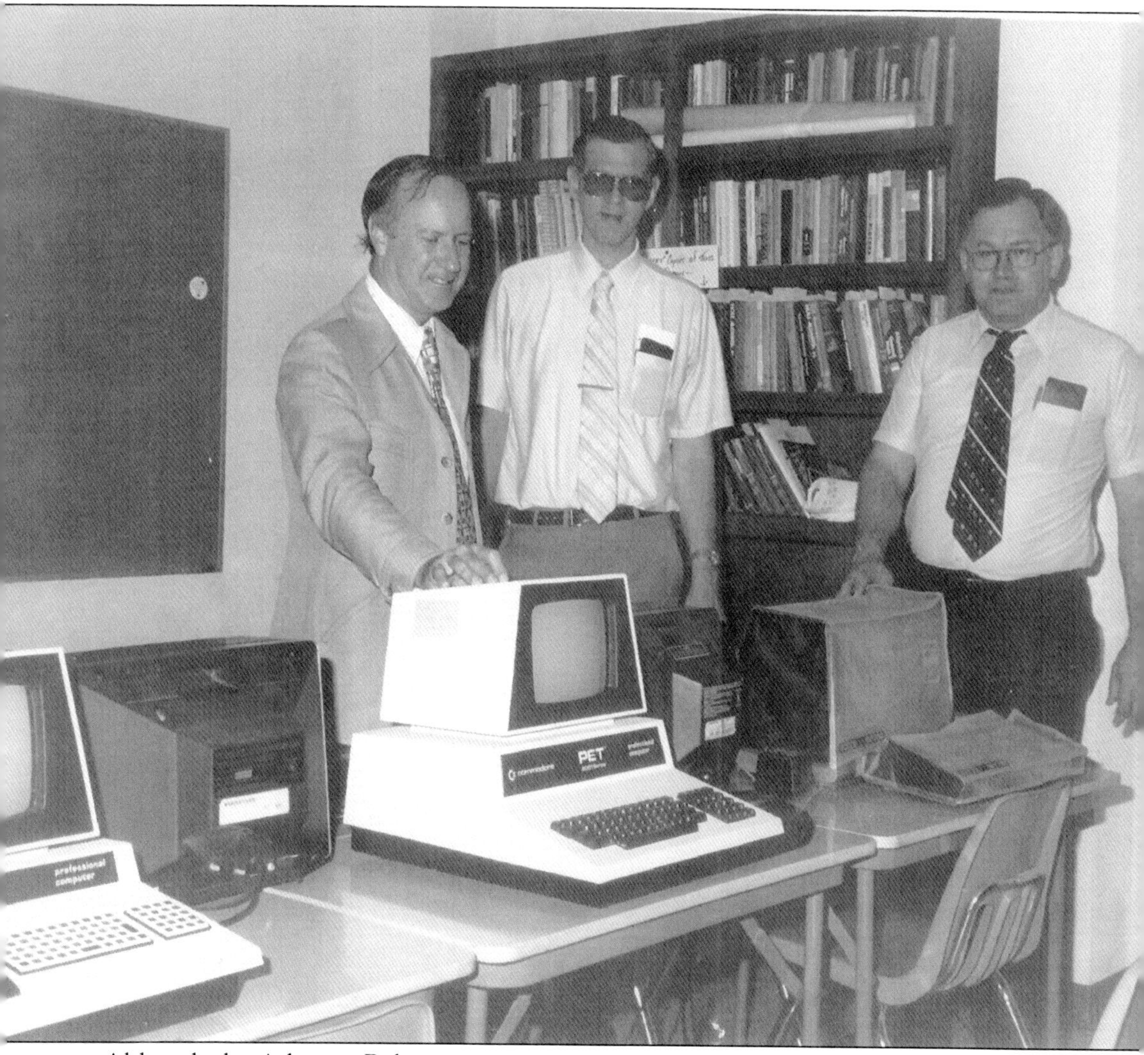

Although the Arkansas Delta, in part, missed out on the benefits of the early stages of the industrial revolution, the same cannot be said of the information technology or digital revolution. As far back as the late 1970s, pre-service teachers at Arkansas State University were trained in computer technology. In this 1980 photo, University President Ray Thornton, on the left, and two faculty members showcase the newly arrived equipment. (Arkansas State University—Communications Office.)

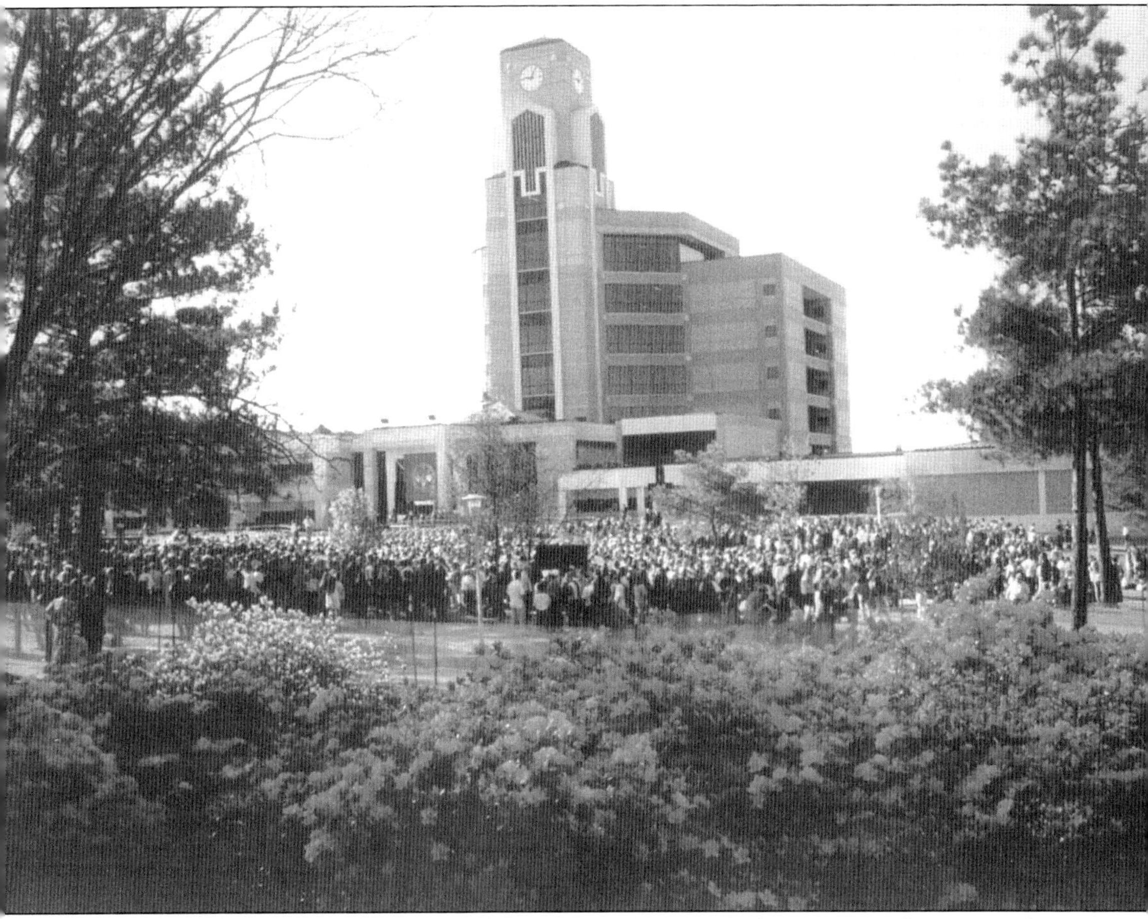

Throughout the twentieth century, Arkansas State University has continued its quest for academic excellence within the state. Today, it ranks as the second largest university in the state and the largest institution of higher learning in the Delta. This photograph captured the pride and enthusiasm exhibited by thousands of residents that day in 1995, when fellow Arkansan President Bill Clinton dedicated the new library on campus. (Courtesy of Arkansas State University—Communications Office.)

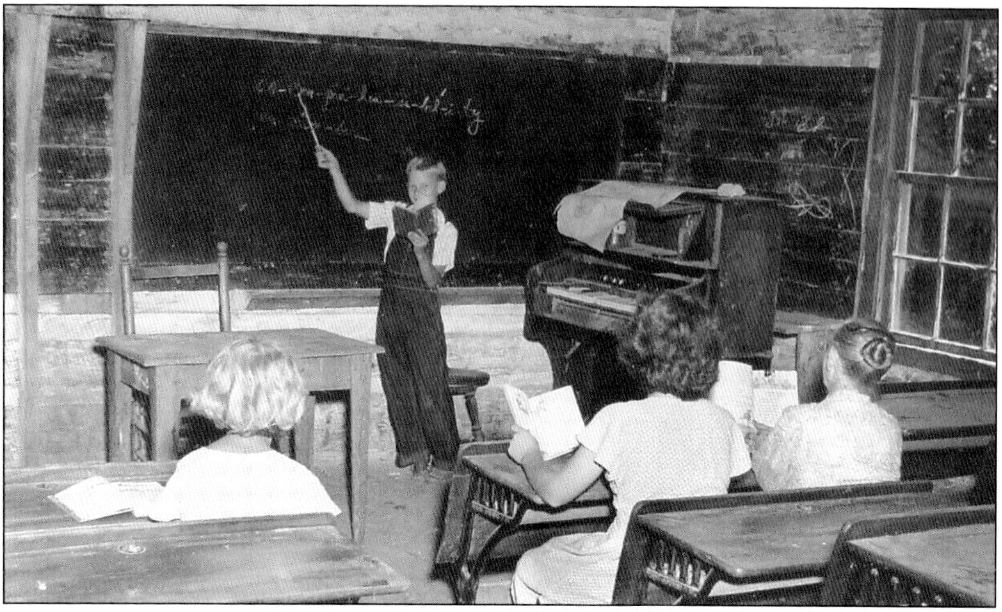

Over the past century, the Arkansas Delta has witnessed dramatic changes in the way it educates its youth. Regardless of the level of schooling, from elementary to college, Delta students have demonstrated a tremendous desire to better themselves through a quest for knowledge that has taken them from the one-room schoolhouse of the nineteenth century, to the modern, digitally equipped classroom of the twenty-first century. Although Delta students today find themselves much better suited to take on the challenges they encounter in life and accomplish those future goals they have outlined, they do so only because they stand on the shoulders of those who have come before them. This is the true legacy of the early education in the Arkansas Delta. (Courtesy of Arkansas History Commission.)

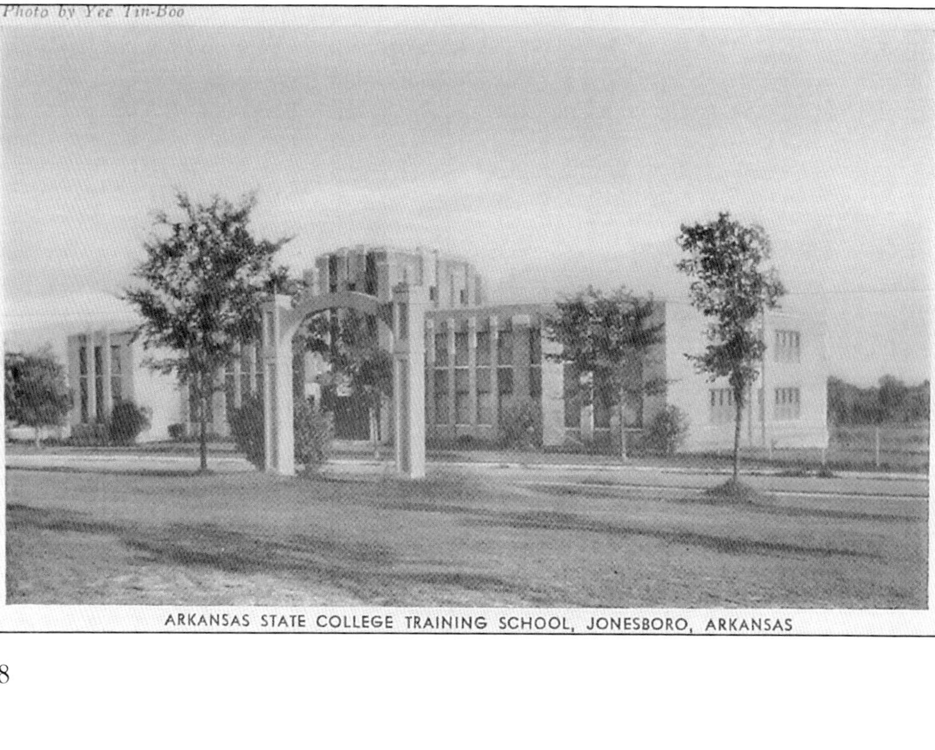

ARKANSAS STATE COLLEGE TRAINING SCHOOL, JONESBORO, ARKANSAS